THE LOST SHEEP

True Fiction Stories
DEBORAH A. ATZORI

Contents

The Lost Sheep

Introduction

Yehoshua said...

"I was not sent except to the lost sheep of the house of Israel. **Mattithyahu/Matthew 15:24**

And when He had called his twelve disciples to Him, He gave them power over unclean spirits, to cast them out, and to heal all kinds of sickness and all kinds of disease. 5 These twelve Yeshua sent out and commanded them, saying, "Do not go into the way of the Gentiles, and do not enter a city of the Samaritans. But go rather to the lost sheep of the house of Israel. And as you go, preach, saying, 'The kingdom of Heaven is at hand.' Heal the sick, cleanse the lepers, raise the dead, cast out demons. Freely you have received, freely give. Provide neither gold nor silver nor copper in your money belts, nor bag for your journey, nor two tunics, nor sandals, nor staffs; for a worker is worthy of his food." **Mattithyahu/Matthew 10:1, 5-10**

"For the Son of Man has come to save that which was lost." **Mattithyahu/Matthew 18:11**

Who is a lost sheep? The answer is obvious; one sheep that is lost. Yehoshua compares us to sheep, and He declares to be the Good Shepherd. *"I am the Good Shepherd."* **Yochanan/John 10:11**

I was finishing revising my two books when Yehovah spoke to me saying to write a novel. I was in a state of shock. I could not believe He would say that to me, because out of my own mouth I had said to a friend that I would never write fiction. *"Fictions are lies,"* I said. However the Spirit of Elohim was speaking to my inner being and giving me ideas. I would be writing true stories, but the messages would always be Biblical Truth. However I would hide the true names and places, and even circumstances. It did not seem to be too difficult writing about someone or something I was familiar with. Various names would come to my mind, until it settled specifically on one single person, Katrina.

Then one night I had a dream. Katrina appeared to me in my dream urging me to write her story. She said that there was little time, and that she could only come three times. In that strange dream she also indicated that she would be helping me. I suppose she would help me to remember the facts. I never expected to get such strong leading. I dream a lot, but I never had such dream before. Indeed that was her third, and last time, I saw her in my dreams during that period. This dream convinced me that I was supposed to write her story, and others. Eventually I saw her briefly again in another dream but I do not recall the details. Yehovah had asked me to write from the beginning of my new life in the Spirit, but my flesh has had difficulty obeying Him. I have always taken notes of the things He has spoken to me personally, but to write them in a book, that seemed to be too much for me. However, I notice that He gives us tasks which in the natural are bigger than our abilities. Certainly He has done this with me. Why does He do that? He does this to enlarge our faith. And once we obey Him our whole attitude about ourselves and Him, completely changes. This is a true fact in my own life. Once I have obeyed Him, I have discovered that I actually like to do what He told me to do. I desired to be a writer as a child, but eventually that desire disappeared in thin air, no more to be found. Or so I thought! I remember reading novels and I appreciated the authors so much. I wondered how they had such wonderful ideas! Certainly I never thought that some day, I would attempt to write a novel myself! However, this novel is based on true stories.

What Yehovah has done in my life is that He has exposed the gifts He had already placed in me before I was created. He wrote a book about me, and in that book He wrote everything He wanted me to do during my short life on this earth. (See Tehillim/Psalm 139:16). But He never forced it on me. However, when He spoke and led me, I obeyed and tried to do the best I could to fulfill His desire for my life.

He has equipped each of us to do specific things, but we may not do them because we think they are something out of our reach for us to accomplish. But He wants us to trust Him to help us to achieve what He knows that we can do through His Grace.

He has placed in each of us gifts that He wants to expose to ourselves. We may not be aware of the abilities He has already gifted us with, and we feel inadequate. I certainly felt inadequate to write this book and the others. But when He speaks and we obey miracles happens. He lifts us up to another spiritual dimension, and it is wonderful.

Gideon was born to fight the Midianites. Yehovah had placed in him the ingredients of courage that he would need, but when he was called to do it, he felt inadequate. Yehovah encouraged Him (Shophetim/Judges 6:36-40; 7:13-15). With the army that Yehovah had trimmed down to 300 men he decided to go to battle (Shophetim/Judges 7:2-7). He wanted to make sure Gideon would never think that He defeated the Midianites by his own strength or cleverness. He would always know it was Yehovah who gave him the victory. I can say the same thing, I am not the one to take credit for any writing I do, for I know very well that without Him, I am incapable of writing anything whatsoever! However, He promises to be there to help me. In my case He sent the first main character of this book to speak to me. This is amazing. I know my limitation, but I know that I serve the Creator of the Universe. He can use anyone, even a donkey, to fulfill His purpose. He is the Writer, and I try to do my best in letting Him lead me. Please do not blame Yehovah or the Ruach haQodesh (Holy Spirit) for my less than excellent writing. Do not blame Him for any mistake you may find, for I am still learning to be led by Him.

As I have said, I began to write this book with Katrina's story, but it continued to evolve into to other characters. Other names came to my mind as I commenced writing. Yehovah has continued to lead me and I am very grateful. While beginning writing this book, my very good friend Hanna called me from Vancouver, Washington. In the middle of the conversation she dropped the following sentence, *"The veil between heaven and earth is getting very thin!"* When I heard that word, I told her my dream with Katrina. She was silent. I still do not understand this whole thing, but I know the dream was from Yehovah to help me writing her story. I also heard one Pastor-Evangelist saying in one of his meeting that Ruth Heflin came to him in a dream and she prophesied to him. His ministry exploded after that dream. Please understand that we do not call on the dead, it is forbidden, but Yehovah can, it seems, use some of the cloud of witness to encourage the living Body of Mashiach. ***"Therefore we also, since we are surrounded by so great a cloud of witness, let us lay aside every weight, and the sin which so easily ensnares us, and let us run with endurance the race that is set before us. Looking unto Yehoshua , the author and finisher of our faith who for the joy that was set before Him endured the cross, despising the shame, and has sat down at the right hand of the throne of Elohim. Ivrim / Hebrews 12:1-2***

The cloud of witness is those who while on this earth served Yehovah. We know that only our body dies and decays, but our soul and spirit leaves forever either in Heaven or in Hell. We spend this life living for our Creator, and some day we will also join the Cloud of Witness in Heaven. Yehovah can use anyone to encourage us to obey Him. I dream every night a few dreams. Yehovah has given me many prophetic dreams. I do not claim to be anyone special, I am a very simple person, but Yehovah speaks to me when I am awake and when I sleep. If you will have the opportunity to buy my autobiography you will understand what I am talking about it, and I know you will be blessed.

The Lost Sheep in the Bible is speaking about Israel, however, I conclude that all of us were lost until the Good Shepherd found us. Many of you reading this book will find yourself in it. If you do, you may need to repent and surrender your life wholly, completely, and entirely to Yehovah, your Heavenly Father. There is no middle ground. Each of us is clothed in rags until Yehovah clothes us with His garment of righteousness. Without the Perfect Precious Redeeming Blood of Yeshua ha'Mashiach we are all lost and doomed to destruction. Each one of us needs to be rescued. Yehoshua paid the full price for our Redemption, therefore please trust Him to secure to you a place in eternity with Him forever. He is the Only Way, the Only Truth, the Only Life. *"For the Son of Man has come to seek and to save that which was lost"* **(Luqas/Luke 19:10)**

If you are still lost in your sin, today you can come to the True Shepherd of Your soul. He says to you now,

"Come to Me, all you who labor and are heavy laden, and I will give you rest. Take My yoke upon you and learn from Me, for I am gentle and lowly in heart, and you will find rest for your souls. For My yoke is easy and My burden is light." **Mattithyahu/Matthew 11:28:30**

Let us listen to the Word.

Then Yeshua went out from there and departed to the region of Tyre and Sidon. And behold, a woman of Canaan came from

that region and cried out to Him, saying, "Have mercy on me, O Adonai, Son of David! My daughter is severely demon possessed." But He answered her not a word. And His disciples came and urged Him, saying, "Send her away, for she cries out after us." But He answered and said, "I was not sent except to the lost sheep of the house of Israel." Then she came and worshiped Him, saying, "Adonai, Help me!" But He answered and said, "It is not good to take the children's bread and throw it to the little dogs." And she said, "Yes, Adonai, yet even the little dogs eat the crumbs which fall from their masters' table." Then Yeshua answered and said to her, "O woman, great is your faith! Let it be to you as you desire." And her daughter was healed from that very hour. **Mattithyahu/Matthew 15:21-28**

Her daughter was a lost sheep!

"So He spoke this parable to them saying: "What man of You having a hundred sheep, if he loses one of them, does not leave the ninety-nine in the wilderness, and go after the one which is lost until he finds it? And when He has found it, he lays it on his shoulders, rejoicing." And when He comes home, he calls together his friends and neighbors, saying to them, 'Rejoice with me, for I have found my sheep which was lost!' I say to you that likewise there will be more joy in heaven over one sinner who repents than over ninety-nine just persons who need no repentance." **Luqas/Luke 15:4-7**

In the same chapter we hear Yeshua telling another parable. A man had two sons. One decides to get His inheritance from his Father while he is still alive! Then he leaves the security of his home, he misuses all his money, and ends up literally in the pig-pan feeding unclean animals: The pigs. He is hungry, but no one give him food to eat. His boss does not allow him to eat the food he is feeding the pigs with!

This guy is hopeless. All his friends are gone. There is no one who can help him. He is desperate. He no longer has the means to survive, and decides to return to his Father, repent, and choose to work as a servant. He quickly makes his way home, and the Father who was waiting for him sees him coming. He runs toward him, and embraces him. The father loves him so much and He does not waste any time rebuking him, instead he gives him new clothes, puts a ring on his finger and sandals on his feet, and tell the servants to kill the fatted calf. He celebrated the return of his son who was lost. They began eat and be merry.

When the other son came home he was angry at his father for forgiving his brother. But his father answered him, ***"It was right that we should make merry and be glad, for your brother was dead and is alive again, and was lost and is found."*** **Luqas/Luke 15:32**

This parable describes the heart of our Heavenly Father. He is waiting for each one of us to come home to him. He has many blessings prepared for us, but we must choose to go to Him. Although this parable seems to be speaking to us specifically about the lost sheep of the Northern Tribes of Israel, it relates to all of us. Yahudah/Judah came back home first, but not all the ten tribes have returned yet. Many of them have mixed blood, and they do not know who they are. Yehovah is now calling them back home, to Israel, and to Himself. He is revealing their true identity. All lost sheep (all spiritually dead sheep) will be saved. Please read and consider the message in this parable in the scroll (book) of Luqas/Luke, chapter 15:11-32.

This parable applies to all believers in Mashiach that have gone astray, and have ended up in the pig pan of the filth of the world. And everyone who never knew Yehovah or His only Ben/Son needs to come home to the Father in Heaven. Everyone needs to yield his life to Yehoshua and receive redemption through the Anointed One, who is the Mashiach Yehoshua. If you are one who needs redemption and a new start in life, now is the time. Your heavenly Father is waiting on you to come home. The time is very short; the door may be close very soon. Remember the ten virgins, some made it, but some did not because they lost the opportunity to get ready for their Bridegroom. At the last minute they finally went to get ready, but sadly it was too late. The door was shut. That parable ends with these words... *"Watch therefore, for you know neither the day nor the hour in which the Son of Man is coming."* **Mattithyahu/Matthew 25:13.**

Do not delay, today, now is the day of Salvation. Now is the time!

"For the Son of Man has come to seek and to save that which was lost."Luqas/ Luke 19:10 Listen to the call today, and respond quickly. In Yehovah's House there is room for you.

The scroll of Luqas records the life of several lost sheep. The stories I have written are real. This book is written for the glory of Yehovah, and not for personal agenda. I hope it will help you, the reader, to make some adjustments in your life, if it needs to be. This book is not to entertain anyone. But it has been written with the hope to help bring an awareness of the need each of us has of Yehoshua, our Savior.

Please note that I prefer using the correct Hebrew Name of our Creator, which is Yehovah. The Savior's Name, and Yehovah's Ben/ Son's Name is Yehoshua, which the correct contracted form is Yeshua. The Name Yehovah is correctly written in various Manuscripts, which include the Biblia Hebraica Stuttgartensia, the Israel Bible, the Leningrad Codex, and over 1200 more manuscripts, and in my Hebrew New Testament. The Holy Spirit is called Ruach haQodesh in the original Hebrew Language. I prefer using the title Adonai instead of Lord. I do not use the title God because it is used to identify all false gods. I use instead the title Elohim, which is the correct Hebrew title for Yehovah. I want to give honor to my Creator, Yehovah, and His only Ben Yehoshua by calling both with their original Names, and I hope you do too. I also use the names of the books in the bible in Hebrew and in English. I may also use the correct name for the Hebrew Apostles and others. I hope you will find this interesting.

Yehovah (the LORD); Yehoshua (Jesus); Ben (Son); Elohim (God); Ruach haQodesh (Holy Spirit); Miryam- (Mary); Mashiach-(Messiah Yehoshua); B'rit Chadashah — (New Testament);

You may want to read my blogs for more information on the correct Name of our Creator at: <u>www.flameoffireministries.blogspot.com</u>

CHAPTER 1

A Lost Sheep

Clemens did not get into the kingdom of Yehovah, until she became almost 40 years old. She grew up Catholic and had very little interest in knowing her Savior personally. She lived a normal life, but also tested some of the dark side of the world. However, after being married several years with a man who chose to get involved in things he should not have, she began to search for the supernatural. She became interested in New Age and other cults for a short season. Eventually she denied the very existence of her Creator. She was a lost sheep! But one day she discovered the reality of Elohim, and after a dramatic encounter with Her Creator and Savior, she surrendered her life completely to Him, and received Yehoshua as her Savior. The Ruach haQodesh came into her heart, and she was born again.

But her marriage was not doing well. About one year after her salvation experience, her husband left her for drugs, and for another woman. It was after this experience that she decided she needed her mother's love and took a trip to France to see her. She arrived to Nice to get refreshed. The trauma of the divorce was affecting her spirit, and she knew that her mother would be very helpful to her. Clemens had no other relatives in America, Except for a son. But he was away serving the Nation. This trip would be beneficial to both, mother and daughter.

Clemens had been concerned about her mother because she was still worshiping the idol Ashtoreth, which is usually called Miryam the mother of Jesus, as she also had previously done. Nevertheless now she knew the truth, and she had to share the gospel with her mother Eloise. She took this trip in winter, just around Chanukkah. The trip seemed to take forever, but finally she arrived to Nice. When she reached her home, her mother welcomed her as only a loving mother can. She loved on Clemens, kissed her on both chicks and embraced her with so much love. Both of them cried and rejoiced to see each other again after a very long time. Soon Clemens noticed the fire place in the living room, and drew near to warm herself. She saw that her mother was roasting a leg of lamb, Clemens favored meat! She was so happy to see that, and thanked her profusely. But her great joy would come shortly after, when her mother would believe the gospel.

Clemens did not waste any time. She began to share her testimony and her mother listened attentively. Finally Clemens told her mother, that the church she attended could not save her. The baptism she received as an infant was not valid in Elohim eyes. She had to believe in Yehoshua and receive Him in her heart as an adult. All those long prayers she had been praying to Miryam and the saints had no value to Elohim.

"Nor is there salvation in any other, for there is no other name under heaven given among men by which we must be saved." Ma'aseh/Acts 4:12

She explained to her mother that she needed to be born again by the Ruach haQodesh/Holy Spirit, who is the Spirit of Yehovah and Yehoshua, One Elohim. When she would be born again, Elohim would be living in her, helping and leading her. She shared with her the Word that Yehoshua has said to Nicodemus,

"Most assuredly, I say to you, Unless one is born again, he cannot see the kingdom of Elohim." 5 "Most assuredly, I say to you,

unless one is born of water and the Spirit, he cannot enter the kingdom of Elohim. 6 That which is born of the flesh is flesh, and that which is born of the Spirit is spirit." **Yochanan/John 3:3; 5-6**

The church could not save her. She had to repent to Yehovah our Father in Heaven, for He alone could forgive her sins. The priest could not forgive her sins. She also needed to believe in Yehoshua, the Savior of the world, who had died to save all of us.

"For Elohim so loved the world that He gave His only begotten Son, that whoever believes in Him should not perish but have everlasting life. For Elohim did not send His Son into the world to condemn the world, but that the world through Him might be saved." **Yochanan 3:16, 17**

Her mother believed the gospel; she already knew that Yehoshua had risen from the dead, which is very important to know. She repented of her sin, and believed in Yehoshua to save her. Eloise had entered into the Kingdom of Heaven! Clemens prayed for her mom in her spiritual prayer language and Yehovah gave her a vision of her mother having *the crown of life*. Now that confirmed to her that her mother was on her way to Heaven. Both rejoiced and eventually sat down to eat and enjoyed the leg of lamb! Yehovah had blessed her so much by saving her mother. However, the true final deliverance for her mother would come later on. But this was the beginning of her journey with the Savior. The Shepherd had found his lost sheep, and rejoiced together with the angels in Heaven.

CHAPTER 2

Clemens The Missionary

Clemens was called by Elohim to be a missionary very early in her new walk of faith. She did the studies to be become a minister of the gospel, and Yehovah used her as a teacher, and a preacher of the Word. She was used greatly in evangelism. Yehovah led Clemens to join a Spirit Filled Pentecostal local Assembly, and the pastor asked her to go to the island of Molokai to establish a new Assembly. After much prayer, she sensed that she should take the offer, packed all her belongings, and left Maui, to settle in Molokai.

However, she never felt feel very comfortable to be there. She had a world vision, and Molokai was too small for her vision. Nevertheless, Yehovah had sent her, and she had to adjust to the change. Since her arrival to the Hawaiian Islands, her home had been Maui, and she would not live in any other island but Maui. Although the other islands were also beautiful, she preferred and loved Maui above all other islands. The Molokai residents seemed to have very little interest of anything new. The Island was still steeped in witchcraft and idolatry. However, she went there to help her Maui pastor Thomas Marrubiu to establish another assembly in that Island. Her mission was to meet as many people as possible, to pass out fliers, and to invite them to the Sunday Services, and Bible Studies. A pastor would be coming to do the services every Sunday. Personally she held her Bible studies in a rented home. One particular day, as she was doing her routine house visitations, would be remembered and cherished for the many years after.

That day the sun was very hot, and the atmosphere humid as usual. In Hawaii, the sun is always shining, and especially during the summer months it can be very uncomfortable. Clemens was hoping to be able to take a break soon in order to get some cold water to drink in a cool place. She thought, *"I need to rest a little, I am a little bit too tired, and I am very thirsty!"* Suddenly as she was walking on that particular street, she noticed a big old gray house. She came close to it, and she saw that the main entrance door was open. She heard several voices and she called… *"Halloooo!"* To her surprise a young woman cane quickly to the door and invited her to come in the house. All the noise she heard was actually the vacuum cleaner and a woman talking with her children. Clemens introduced herself, *"Hello, my name is Clemens. I came to give you this flier. Maui Church is opening a new ministry in this Island very soon, and I want to invite you visit this assembly when it will open up very soon."* *"Sure, but please come in and sit down. I hope you do not mind, I am cleaning house today."* Clemens reply, *"I do not mind at all, actually it will be nice to take a little break. Today is a very hot day, and I am so tired already!"* *"Please, please, come in and sit down. My name is Katrina, and these are my two sons, Mitz and Clayton."* *"Would you like to have a glass of cold water?"* Clemens thanked her, *"Oh, yes, thank you Katrina. I really need to be refreshed!"* After taking her shoes off, she entered the living room and sat down on the sofa.

"Thank you for the water. There is nothing like a glass of cold water on hot day. I really appreciate it. Thank you so much." *"No problem."*

Clemens began to ask Katrina some questions. *"Katrina, you do not look local, are you from the mainland?"* *"Yes, I lived in Oklahoma for a many years. But I was born in Ireland!"* *"WOW! "Where is your husband?"* *"Oh, I am single now. I am divorced."* *"Oh! I am sorry, I am sorry to hear that."* *But… are you doing well financially"* *"Yes I am. Thank you."* Katrina was very talkative. She needed fellowship, and Clemens loved to hear her sharing about her life.

Clemens handed her the flier and asked her if she was a born again believer in Yeshua. She answered with a big smile, *"Yes, I am. I am also filled with the Holy Spirit and I speak in tongues. I also went to Bible School in the mainland."*

Katrina took the flier and read it. She was very happy to find out of the new fellowship coming to town, and she promised that she would check it out. Both began to share of their experiences in the Spirit. Both had experienced personal visitation from Yehoshua. They had a beautiful visit.

Finally Clemens got up to leave. She had many more people to visit that day. But before she left she made sure she got all the information she needed from her new friend. They also exchanged phone numbers and Clemens left with a pleasant and peaceful feeling. She knew Katrina would become her very good friend.

Eventually Katrina joined the new fellowship and was a blessing to the ministry. Her knowledge of the Scriptures was useful to teach the new believers. She was also a very powerful prayer intercessor which was and is a very important ministry of any assembly. She found favor with the fellowship because she volunteered for every ministry that they open up. When the new fellowship formed the choir they invited her to join, and she did. Indeed, she had a beautiful voice and the presence of Yehovah was evident in her life. Katrina was an effective soul winner. She loved to share her testimony with people she met, and invited them to the services at her new home fellowship.

After about two months Clemens went back to her home on Maui, and lost contact with Katrina for a season.

Clemens knew her calling was not just the island of Maui, but to the world. However while on Maui, Clemens always evangelized the lost, even on the beach. Some of the homeless people believed in Yehoshua, and committed their lives to Him. Some were born again, but of course, many were not. So many people refuse the free gift of salvation because they do not want to acknowledge their need to repent of their sins to Yehovah. Others think they can save themselves by doing good works, and refuse to believe the gospel. The Word of Elohim declares that we are sinners, (Romiyim/Romans 3:23), and salvation is a gift from Yehovah. The Word declares that the penalty for our sin is death, (Romiyim 6:23) therefore someone had to die on our behalf to save us. It is impossible for us to save ourselves by doing good deeds. But Blood needs to be shed, and Yehoshua shed His own blood for us. *"But Elohim demonstrates his own love toward us, in what while we were still sinners, Messiah died for us."* **Romiyim 5:8**

He paid the full price for our redemption by giving His own life. He shed all His blood on the stake to save humanity. However, we need to believe in Him in order to be redeemed. Each of us can receive His free gift of salvation. But we must also be willing to let Him change us, and guide us into all truth. If a person is not willing to let go of their sin, they are not ready to be saved. We must pray for them and wait for the work of the Ruach haQodesh to help them. Clemens had to learn this truth, as she witnessed to many lost sheep. Yet, Clemens learned that many do not want to receive Him because of the many lies they have received from family and friends. However, she never stopped ministering to the lost, knowing the fact that if they would not be saved, they would be lost for eternity. She kept pursuing them, even when she did not receive immediate response. She knew what Yehovah said in His Word.

"For as the rain comes down, and the snow from heaven, and do not return there, but water the earth, and make it bring forth and bud, that it may give seed to the sower and bread to the eater, So shall My word be that goes forth from My mouth; it shall not return to Me void, but it shall accomplish what I please, and it shall prosper in the thing for which I sent it." **Yeshayahu/Isaiah 55:10-11**

Her faith was in Him alone, and not in her own abilities. She did what she could in the natural, and expected Yehovah to do the super-natural. In everything she gave all the glory to Yehovah alone.

CHAPTER 3

The Fruit Tree

Clemens missed her mother so much that she let go of all her projects for just a while in order to spend some time with her. No matter how old she was, her mom was in her heart and she was very much concerned of her wellbeing. Nice has been her home during her youth years. Nice was the place of her birth, and she lived there until her eighteen year of life. Therefore, she had many relatives and friends she would love to visit. But her mother was her main reason for the trips she periodically took.

While at home, sleeping in her own old bed was very special to her. While in Nice Clemens spent also a great deal of time praying and talking with her family and friends about Yehoshua. Some believed the gospel, but many did not. they had their own traditions. But several of her family members believed in Yehoshua. Most of her friends did not listen to her; however, she did not feel discouraged. She believed the Word of Yehoshua. In the Scriptures we read the following,

"If you abide in Me, and My words abide in you, you will ask what you desire, and it shall be done for you." Buy this My Father is glorified, that you bear much fruit; so you will be My disciples. **Yochanan/John 15:7**

Clemens knew from experience that she could save no one. It was the Ruach haQodesh in her life that did the work. All she knew about herself was that she was a plain robber hose. She was not a Savior, but a simple instrument used in the hands of her Master. When the hose was connected to the faucet it was used to give life to plants. And as long as she was connected to Yehoshua He would satisfy the thirst of anyone who was thirsty. She trusted in the True Vine, Yehoshua, and in the Vinedresser, the Father, to help her in the fruit production.

"I Am the true vine, and My Father is the vinedresser. Yochanan/John 15:1

Yehoshua did only what He saw His Father doing. He was one with the Father, therefore it was impossible for Him to act apart from His Father's will. He also said,

"I am the vine, you are the branches. He who abides in Me, and I in him, bears much fruit; for without Me you can do nothing." 9 "As the Father loved Me, I also have loved you; abide in My love. If you keep My commandments, You will abide in My love, just as I have kept My Father's Commandments and abide in His love." Yochanan 15:5,10

Clemens duty, in order to bear much fruit, was to obey Him and keep His Commandments, in order to abide in Him. Yehovah never changed His plan. Obedience is a fruit of our love to Him. Obedience may not be very popular in these last days, but Yehovah never changes!

While visiting with her mom, Clemens had a dream. In that dream she saw a large orange tree. The tree was full of ripe oranges. She extended her right hand to pick one fruit and the fruit fell into her hand without her touching it. She just reached out for it, and it simply fell into her hand. The following day her brother and sister in law invited her mother and Clemens to go to their home a few miles away and spend the night there. He came to pick them up with his car at the appointed time.

While at home sitting by the fire place her sister in law Amelie asked Clemens a question. *"How can I be saved? The magazine you have ordered for me speaks about salvation, but does not teach me how I can be saved."* Clemens dream flashed in her mind, and quickly she explained how she could be saved. She led Amelie in a simple prayer, and she immediately felt the Presence of Yehoshua. He came and removed all her sins forever. Now she was born again and she began to cry for joy. Salvation had come into her house.

Clemens also cries, as most people do, when the Ruach haQodesh comes upon them. Crying is a very normal thing. His love is so wonderful and causes a person to melt in His presence. When His presence comes, we feel so blessed and so little in our own eyes. Our flesh melts. We realize that we do not deserve his perfect love. When His Spirit touches us, we feel completely loved and accepted. We know we do not deserve Him, but He still loves us so much.

Once again Clemens prophetic dream came to pass. Her sister in law was the fruit that fell into her hand! Yehovah had answered her prayer! Clemens never stopped praying for her family since her salvation experience. But now she had the privilege to witness another answers to her prayers. She was so blessed to see a lost sheep, once again, being found by the Good Shepherd! Amelie had not been a murderer or a thief, yet she needed to be saved because all of us are sinners. Each of us needs to be washed in the Blood of the Lamb, Yehoshua, in order to receive eternal life.

Chapter 4

Mom Goes Home

Clemens had been busy ministering in California for while, and she came back to Maui. She was there only a few days, when her old pastor offered her to take over one of his chapels. But he would not pay her. He wanted her instead to be a care giver for one of his parishioners who had cancer. Supposedly that would provide her with a free place to live and some money to spend. When she first heard him saying this, she reluctantly agreed. However, middle in the night Yehovah woke her up and let her know that He had not called her to do such work. He had other plans for her life. He did not inspire that pastor to place her in that position. He wanted free labor. She felt offended. Early in the morning she called the office, and told the pastor that she would not take that job. Instead she called her friend Silvana in California and explained to her the situation. She quickly invited her to come up and stay with her and her husband. Silvana had always been ready to help her friend. Such friends are rare in these last days. But Silvana was not a common person. She loved her Savior and loved her Father in Heaven. She had a very special relationship with Yehovah. She was an amazing woman full of love for Yehovah, her heavenly Father. Clemens was very blessed to have such faithful friend. Soon after talking with Silvana she called the air lines and bought a ticket back to California.

An unusual miracle took place that morning. Lidia, a friend of Clemens, heard that she was going to leave again, and she talked with

Tom, who happened to be at the same bank that she went that morning. Somehow she felt impressed to ask him for an offering for Clemens. She told Him that Clemens did not have money, and if he could help her. Graciously Yehovah opened his heart, and he gave Lidia over 300 dollars cash for Clemens trip, plus he gave her some money too. What a miracle!

Clemens left Maui the same day, and arrived to California late at night. Her friend Silvana and her husband came to pick her up from the airport, and they drove home. This trip was so sudden, and Clemens did not have a clue what she would be doing next. A few days later, Silvana told her to pray and ask Yehovah what she should be doing. Yehovah spoke to her heart to go back to Nice and care for her mother. Immediately she called her mother and she asked her one question: *"Are you going to stay this time? "Yes, mom, I am."* She would not come back to America until her mom would have gone to Heaven. This was a big commitment. But she knew she had to do it. Usually Clemens and her brother would take turns caring for their mother, but now she had committed to stay in France as long as her mother would be alive. She was willing to trust Yehovah with her ministry. Her mother was now more important than anything else. She packed her suitcase and left California again. She arrived to Nice during Passover. Her mother was so happy to see her. This time with her mother was indeed the most wonderful time for her. They talked about many things. Clemens was able to learn about the life of her own mother as a child, and of her grandmother. She also ministered to her uncle salvation, and he went to be with Yehoshua soon after.

She was in Nice until December. But in November her mother got terminally ill. She could not longer eat, or even drink. Her brother came to stay at the house, but that was not a good thing. Soon she realized that his plan was to cause problems. He was a different man than the one she grew up with. It was a very challenging time for Clemens. Satan had taken control of her brother. She continually prayed and stayed very close to her mother for the next eighteen days. Satan's plan was to cause her mother to get angry and have unforgiveness in her heart. He wanted Eloise to die and go to hell to be with him, so that he could torment her. However, Clemens prayers and faith in the precious Blood of Yehoshua, caused the devil's defeat.

Two nights before her mother departure to Heaven, Yehoshua came to visit her. Clemens was present, but she did not see Him. However she saw her mother looking at her and at the person in front of her. She was sure it was Him, because she spoke in other tongues and became very calm after that experience. Clemens believes that was the moment her mother had been completely freed from the false teachings she received from her church. The sin of idolatry had to be forgiven and she needed to be spiritually cleansed. She had accepted Yehoshua, but she still hang on to Miryam's worship. However, Clemens knew for sure that when her mother saw Yehoshua she was completely set free. Then she remembered the crown of life that she saw on her mother's head many years ago. Her salvation was now assured. All glory to Yehovah! He is so patient with us. He knows the end from the beginning, and He reveals His people glimpses of the future. He does this to help them trusting in Him, no matter what circumstances they will find themselves in. He is faithful.

Yehoshua came in answer to our prayers. Clemens had been praying in America that Yehoshua would appear to her mother, in France, before she would die. And later on, on one of her visits to Nice, she shared with her mother what she had been praying. To her surprise her mother had been praying the same prayer in Nice! Indeed that prayer had been inspired by Yehovah Himself! Amazing!

Two mornings after that encounter Eloise went to be with her Savior. Her passing was very easy. She simply breathed three times and left. Yehoshua had gathered her lost sheep to be with Him forever!

CHAPTER 5

The Barren Are Healed

Yehovah gave Clemens the opportunity to preach in the Hawaiian Islands, and occasionally in other nations. She loved ministering to the lost sheep to be saved, and immediately to receive the prayer language. Speaking in unknown tongues is the most powerful weapon that the Ruach haQodesh/Holy Spirit has given us to disarm the devil. Speaking in unknown tongues is when the Ruach haQodesh and our own spirit unite in prayer. This prayer has no equals, for it is the

Prayer prayed according to the perfect will of Elohim

For He who speaks in a tongue does not speak to men but to Elohim. for no one understands; however, in the spirit he speaks mysteries. **Qorin'tiyim 1/1 Corinthians 14: 2**

The reason He has given us this gift is because we do not know how to pray effectively. *Likewise the Spirit also helps in our weaknesses. For we do not know what we should pray for as we ought, but the Spirit Himself makes intercession for us with groaning which cannot be uttered. Now He who searches the hearts knows what the mind of the Spirit is, because He makes intercession for the saints according to the will of Elohim.* **Romiyim/Romans 8:26-27** Therefore what we pray in tongues it is always the perfect prayer, and it is always answered by Yehovah.

Clemens also learned to pray in tongues for a while, then pause for a moment, and pray in her native language. When praying that way the Ruach haQodesh, intercedes in English an inspired prayer, which at times is a prophetic prayer. When praying that way she is praying with the understanding of what the Spirit had prayed in tongues. And she receives understanding of the mind of Yehovah in that particular situation. This prayer is very important when praying for direction, deliverance and, and beyond any doubt, in every circumstance. She also has learned to go to the Courts of Heaven when she may have been praying a long time for a specific situation, but there is not answer. She knows then, that the enemy has a legal issue against her, and she repents of any known or unknown sin, and repents of sins in her blood line. Finally with the testimony of Yehoshua, the blood of Yehoshua and of the testimony of the cloud of witnesses, she receives the answer she needs. The legal right of Satan has been dealt with, and his power is revoked. This particular form of prayer is done when a person is usually in communion with the Father and Yehoshua. Anyone can go to the Courts of Heaven, but their lives must be lived in communion with the Father and the Son. Consecration is very important. However, we are called to be kings and priest in the Kingdom of Yehovah, and He has granted us, through the shedding of the Blood of Yehoshua, to be able to function in the spirit at the Courts of Heaven. Clemens has received many answers to prayer since she has adopted this form of prayer. Once she has gone to the Courts she has the power to rebuke Satan because he has been defeated. He cannot attack anyone unless he has a legal right to do so. Sin gives him legal right. Once the sin is dealt with he is legally defeated. Deliverance is sure to come.

Yehovah has given her great boldness and great faith in many situations. Also, because Clemens became barren after giving birth to her son, Yehovah blessed her with the gift of healing the barren women.

From the beginning of her ministry she discovered Yehovah had given her special faith and favor in that area. Every time she prayed for the barren women they conceived.

Once she volunteered to pray for Miranda because she has lost two babies through miscarriages. After praying in tongues for few minutes, Yehovah led her to have Miranda pray the prayer of Hanna (See 1 Samuel 1:8-11). Basically Hanna dedicated the life of the unborn child to Yehovah if she would get pregnant. Yehovah answered Hanna. She not only got the one child that she wanted, whom she called Samuel, but she also bore three more sons and two daughters, (Shemu'el 1/1 Samuel 1:20; 2:21). Clemens led Miranda and her husband in prayer dedicating the future child to Yehovah to be used by Him according to His perfect will. Miranda's hope began to rise in her heart, and she believed for the miracle. Shortly after that prayer she conceived and gave birth to twins boys. Remember that she had lost two babies through miscarriages, and now Yehovah gave her back what she had lost in one single pregnancy! And after that she gave birth to a baby girl. I think they stopped there. But she was healed, and in spite some difficulties, she was able to give life to three children. Yehovah is no respecter of person, what He did for Hanna and for Miranda and her husband He will do for anyone who trusts Him. Miranda and her whole family are very happy and thankful to Yehovah for answering their prayers. These things are written for you, beloved reader, to encourage you, and to let you know that Yehovah loves you. He will answer your prayer when you choose to come to him in humility believing. No matter what the situation you may be facing, He will listen and answer you.

CHAPTER 6

The Nazirite

Yehovah has placed on Clemens a call for intercession. Therefore many times He would wake her up during the night to pray. One of those times after praying for a while in tongues and in English, He clearly spoke to her to take the Nazirite vow. The Hebrew word is Nazir, which means to be consecrated or to be set apart unto Him. We can read about this vow in Sefer /Scroll Bemidbar/Numbers 6.

She knelt down to consecrate herself to Yehovah, and He spoke to her saying, **"Peace in the midst of the storm."** *That peace stayed with her. No matter what happened in her life or in the world she has had complete peace.* At the end of one year she had to shave her long hair. Of course, most people thought that she had taken chemo therapy and had lost all her hair **(Bemidbar 6:18).**

A few years later she was asked to take the vow again. Although there was no Temple on Maui, or Jerusalem, and there were no priests to do the ceremony, she obeyed her Elohim. Presently we, believers are the living temple.

"Do you not know that your body is the temple of the Ruach haQodesh (Holy Spirit) who is in you, whom you have from Elohim, and you are not your own?" Qorin'tiyim 1/1 Corinthians 6:19.

Not only is the believer the temple of the Holy Spirit, but is also the priest in the temple. Yes, each believer is now a priest unto Yehovah!

"You also, as living stones, are being built up a spiritual house, a holy priesthood, to offer up spiritual sacrifices acceptable to Yehovah through Yehoshua haMashiach." **Kepha 1/1 Peter 2:5**

Yehovah instructed her to cut her hair and to save them in a plastic bag. She did as instructed. Those times of consecration were very special to Clemens. The Presence of Yehovah and Yehoshua increased during those special times. Blessings seemed to be multiplied. She felt so special and so humble at the same time. Let us remember that the prophet Shemu'el was a Nazir from birth. Also Samson and Yochanan the Immerser were both Nazir from birth. But many Yahudim took this vow in the past, and possibly there may be some Nazir today. Yehovah knows His own people who are consecrated unto Him. Clemens obedience in taking this vow has been the result of many blessings in her life.

CHAPTER 7

The Deceived

While on the island of Maui, Clemens was always involved in ministry at the same Assembly. That was the place Yehovah led her when she first left the idolatrous church. This time she noticed that Sally, the worship leader, was no longer there. She missed her because she had been taking piano lessons with her, and now she could not continue her practice. Well, she thought, *"I still have the books, and can learn on my own."* She had no choice but to try learning on her own, because she was determined to continue to learn, even without a teacher. The next time she attended the service on Wednesday, she noticed that a young man, and a complete stranger to her, seemed to be in control of the worship. She found out that the other worship leader had been replaced with Ronald. During the service she heard him singing, and she was amazed at the sound of his beautiful voice. *"He is a really good singer,"* she thought. Clemens and the whole fellowship loved his voice very much! He had also a very unique way to entertain the fellowship. Undoubtedly he was a professional singer. He was also very friendly and many people loved him. Almost no one discerned who he really was, or better yet, what kind life style he was living.

Eventually he began to date Theresa, a young lady, and they were married soon after. They seemed to be happy. Very soon Theresa conceived and gave birth to a lovely baby girl. Not too long after she gave birth to a boy. Now they were a complete family. They seemed to be always excited and express so much joy. No one suspected that there was anything wrong with this family. His wife was not as friendly as he was, but she did get along with people. She also had gotten her ministerial credentials from some organization in the Mainland and now she was supposed to be called Reverend. No one realized there was a big problem in his life. He was on Maui several years when everyone was taken aback of what they found out.

One day, Clemens went to visit her friend Juliana. When she arrived she was surprised to find two other visitors there. One was her friend Claudia and the other was Ronald, the young worship leader. This situation seemed strange to Clemens, but she joined the group. Soon Ronald asked for prayer. All three girls prayed for him. Then suddenly Claudia left saying, "*I am going to tell the pastor.*"She practically ran out of that place. Clemens was perplexed. *What happen to her? Why is she running downtown to talk to the pastor?*" "*What is the big news?*"-*Claudia is usually so well behaved and very nice.What is she going to report to the pastor?*"Soon after Ronald also left, Clemens was left alone with Juliana. Now was her chance to ask questions. "*Juliana, what happened, why Claudia left running saying that she would tell the pastor something… but what is the news? Telling him what? Is anything wrong?*"Clemens could not fathom what was going on.

Juliana had difficulty telling Clemens what happen. Ronald was her friend. She loved him and his wife and children. When he first came to Maui he stayed at her house, and so did the family later on. Finally she decided to speak up and informed her that Ronald was a homosexual. He had gotten saved at a Baptist church in the Philadelphia, before he came to Maui. The only reason he married a woman was to be able to minister at churches, it seems. Otherwise the pastors, rightly so, would not hire him knowing what he did. Of course a person who is in Covenant with the Almighty Elohim of the Universe cannot disobey Him and live habitually in sin.

"Little children, let no one deceive you. He who practices righteousness is righteous, just as He is righteous. He who sins is of the devil, for the devil has sinned from the beginning." **Yochanan 1 / 1 John 3:7-8**

Clemens was in shock! But she knew the Word. Our part of the Covenant is obedience to His Kingdom Rules. A habitual sinner cannot serve on the altar. The pastor told Ronald that he was lost in sin. He was a **lost sheep.** He needed to renounce that sin, and obey Yehovah. However he chose not to repent, because he believed he was not sinning. Therefore He left Maui with his wife and children. Eventually He got a divorce, and began openly dating men. As soon as the same sex marriage law was passed he married his present boy friend. Years later Clemens had opportunity to talk with him, but he still believed that he was not sinning. He was and still is deceived, unless at the writing of this book he has repented.

How sad! He had such great ministry but chose to live in the wilderness of sin. He is not aware of his blindness. Of course all those who became aware of the reason of Ronald's departure, felt very sad for him and his family. They loved him and missed him for a very long time. Prayer continued to be lifted up to Yehovah's Throne of Grace for his deliverance and salvation. Some day he will come back home as the prodigal son spoken of in Luke 15. Yehoshua's Blood is powerful enough to forgive every sin. Yehovah's love and forgiveness will reach down to him and make him whole. Yehoshua invites us to pray in His Name.

"And whatever you ask in My Name, that I will do, that the Father may be glorified in the Son. If you ask anything in My Name, I will do it." **Yochanan / John 14:13-14**

We have asked our Father Yehovah in the Name of Yehoshua, and we believe that He will eventually come home to Him. Yehovah alone will be glorified. Our love for the brother has not diminished; therefore we pray and believe for complete victory.

After this heartbreaking incident, Clemens left Maui again and returned to the Island of her temporary home. She was used by Yehovah as Assistant pastor of a little congregation that she helped pioneering. During that time Jacks, a young man, began to occasionally attending the fellowship. Clemens discovered that Jacks was Sabina's brother and that he loved to sing at churches. Sabina was a faithful servant of Yehovah and attended the service every week from its inception. She lived a holy life and had a pleasant personality. Clemens loved Sabina and the whole family.

One day when Jacks came to the service Clemens invited him to sing a solo. He sounded alright, not as Ronald had been, but she decided to let him sing each time he would visit. He actually attended regularly the local Baptist Church, however because his whole family attended this fellowship, he also visited when he could.

Sabina, Jacks' sister, suddenly, being deeply convicted of her silence, approached Clemens. She told her that her brother Jacks was a homosexual. She could no long endure the silence, she said. *"I have to let you know about this. Did you not know that he is a homosexual?"* Clemens answer was negative. He seemed kind of an introvert, but never in a million years had she thought of such think. She could have never let him sing if she had known it. Clemens asked Sabina how did that happened. She answered saying, *"When he was a little boy, his older sisters dressed him as a girl. They bought him all girl dresses, and girls toys. He played with dolls instead of trucks. They made him believe that he was a girl."* Eventually, while still a child, he was continually sexually abused by his uncle. No one stopped this situation.

Although he dressed as a man, he was only interested in man. He seldom read the Word of Yehovah to receive its instructions. It is possible to believe that he never read the whole book. If he did he would have know the will of Yehovah on this subject. He may have read, as many people do, only what was pleasant to him. We do not know for sure if or how much he read the Word, however, he did not have a deep relationship with His Savior although he claimed to be "Saved." He was indeed a *lost sheep all the days of his life.*

Clemens was shocked to hear this sad story from Sabina. But why she had waited so long to inform her pastor about this horrible situation? Clemens at that time was not yet a veteran in ministry. This position as a pastor was her first assignment, and she lacked experience. She had a lot to learn yet. She felt very bad about this situation, and asked Yehovah to help her in the future, and to give her discernment. She felt so much compassion for Jacks, and she tried to convince him to repent. But he resisted her words, and of course he never came back to the fellowship. Clemens could not help thinking how cruel his sisters and mother and father had been toward him. They had ruined his whole life. How could they do such thing to their family member? From His birth they deceived him and raised him up as a little girl, but he was a boy. He did not seem to be very intelligent, and believed his sisters. However, they ruined his whole life. He grew up believing he was not supposed to be a man, but a girl. Eventually he became a sex slave to his uncle, and later on to many others. He died of Aids. Did he repent before his death? Clemens never found out for she no longer ministered at that Island. No one knows if he may have repented before his death. However he is remembered as a **lost sheep.**

The Word of Yehovah instructs us very clearly. If we are in Covenant with Him, we have to obey His Commandments. There will be no excuse on judgment day. He has told us what He expects of us, His children. And He has given us His Ruach haQodesh/Holy Spirit so that we can obey Him. We have been given Divine Help, therefore we have no excuse. Yehoshua has also given us His Helper to be with us. The Holy Spirit helps us to do the will of the Father in Heaven.

"But now I go away to Him who sent Me, and none of You asks Me, "Where are You going? But because I have said these things to you, sorrow has filled your heart. Nevertheless I tell you the truth. It is to your advantage that I go away; for if I do not go away, the Helper will not come to you; but if I depart, I will send Him to you. And when He has come, He will convict the world of sin, and of righteousness, and of judgment: of sin, because they do not believe in Me; of righteousness, because I go to My Father and you see Me no more, of judgment, because the ruler of this world is judged." Yochanan/John 16:5-11

Yehovah has also given us His Word to obey.

"You shall not lie with a male as with a woman. It is an abomination." Wayyiqra/Leviticus18:22

"If a man lies with a male as he lies with a woman, both of them have committed abomination. They shall surely be put to death." Wayyiqra/Leviticus 20:23

"For the wrath of Elohim is revealed from heaven against all ungodliness and unrighteousness of men, who suppress the truth in unrighteousness, because what may be known of Elohim is manifest in them, for Elohim has shown it to them. For since the creation of the world His invisible attributes are clearly seen, being understood by the things that are made, even His eternal power and Godhead, so that they are without excuse, because, although they knew Elohim, they did not glorify Him as Elohim, nor were thankful, but became futile in their thoughts, and their foolish hearts were darkened. Professing to be wise, they became tools, and changed the glory of the incorruptible Elohim into an image made like corruptible man-and birds and four-footed animals and creeping things. Therefore Elohim also gave them up to uncleanness, in the lusts of their hearts, to dishonor their bodies among

themselves, who exchanged the truth of Elohim for the lie, and worshiped and served the creature rather than the Creator, who is blessed forever. Amen. For this reason Elohim gave them up to vile passions. For even their women exchanged the natural use for what is against nature. Likewise also the men, leaving the natural use of the woman, burned in their lust to one another, men with men committing what is shameful, and receiving in themselves the penalty of their error which was due." **Romiyim/Romans 1:18:27**

We are called to be holy unto Him.

"For I am Yehovah who brings you up out of the land of Egypt, to be your Elohim. You shall therefore be holy, for I am holy ." **Wayyiqra/Leviticus 11:44**

"Hear, O Israel: Yehovah our Elohim, Yehovah is one! You shall love Yehovah with all your heart, with all your soul, and with all yours strength" **Devarim/Deuteronomy 6:4**

If we sincerely love Yehovah, who is our Creator, and we are His children, we cannot continue to sin against Him. We should live our lives having a holy fear of Yehovah.

The fear of Yehovah is to hate evil; Pride and arrogance and the evil way and the perverse mouth I hate." **Mishley/Proverbs 8:13**

The Fear of Yehovah is a fountain of life, to turn one away from the snares of death." **Mishley/Proverbs 14:27**

We are commanded to fear Elohim.

For in the multitude of dreams and many words there is also vanity. But Fear Elohim." **Qohelet/Ecclesiastes 5:7**

Jack's sisters did not fear Yehovah; they sinned against their Elohim when they caused their brother to **pervert** his ways with their deceptive lies. They sinned against their brother. They did not realize that all sin has a consequence. They practically cursed him with their words and their actions. Obviously they did not fear Yehovah. May Yehovah be merciful to them, and to all of us!

"Like a madman who throws firebrands, arrows, and death, is the man who deceives his neighbor, and says, "I was only joking!" **Mishley/Proverbs 26:18-19**

They did it as a joke. They had their fun, but destroyed their own brother's life for eternity. Unless he repented just before he died he is in hell now. Presently we do not know that for sure. But I hope they have repented for their own sin. Obviously Jacks sisters although they said they knew Yehovah did not honor Him, because they did not know Him intimately. They only had a superficial religious relationship with Him.

If the fear of Yehovah would be taught in the churches, many believers would not break His Commandments. Usually the modern churches refuse to speak against sin because they are connected to the government through their licenses. Their mouths are stopped. They prefer a bowl of soup of red lentils instead of the blessings!

Clemens, as result of the Jacks' experience, became very concerned about the little children and the teachings they receive in their own homes, in their churches, and in their schools. Yehovah now seems to be removed so far away from society. He is no longer the center of everyone's life. Families and churches need reformation. The whole world is in spiritual chaos.

Clemens read the Word of Yehovah, and she knew He will be judging the whole world very soon. Mankind needed to repent, but will they repent? She began to pray for every person who like Jacks had been deceived. The minimum each person can do for the **lost sheep** is to pray.

After finding out about Jacks, she needed to hear some good news. And she prayed.

Chapter 8

Without Spot or Wrinkle

Clemens was resting and drinking a cup of hot coco that she enriched with a generous amount of whip cream, and sprinkled with some nutmeg and cinnamon. While sipping her favored drink she was reading the one passage in her Bible that spoke of healing. Yehoshua healed all who came to Him. She noticed that He did not look for the sick to be healed, but the sick came to Him to be healed. The sick people had to want to be healed and make the effort to come to Him from all parts of Israel, and He always healed them. He did not look for demons but the demonized came to him to be set free. While she considered this Word, she heard one knock on her front door. Quickly she rose and run to open the door. Clemens loved running, and she ran even in her own home depending on the space available!

She opened the door and exclaimed, *"Gladiola! What a surprise, come in. I am so glad to see you again. It has been a long time since I saw you. Sit down; I fix you a hot cup of coco." "Oh, yes, thank you, I love your coco when you add the whip cream." "Oh, you remember! Great, I get you one. Sit in the recliner, and I bring you the coco in a few minutes."* While she was preparing the coco for her friend, she wondered what could be the reason for her visit. She usually came to speak with Clemens only when she needed to clear something in her own mind. Yehovah had blessed Clemens with a lot of wisdom, and she was always ready to help anyone who came to her for prayer. She relied only on the Ruach haQodesh to give her the correct guidance for those Yehovah sent to her. She did not use psychology; in fact she hated that aspect of counseling.

Clemens waited on Gladiola to speak. Finally she began to tell her what she experienced that very morning. *"Clemens, as I was praying this morning, I asked the Ruach haQodesh to help me to pray for those things that are on the Heart of the Father. And I began to cry thinking on the day I cut my long blond hair for the first time."When my father came home from work he looked at me, and said, 'Why did you cut your hair, you look like a prostitute!'"* She continued to tell her friend that she ran away from home and went to stay with her aunt Rosen. She was there for about a week, when her mom came to take her back home. She was also upset with her mom because Gladiola had asked her mom to give her the money to cut her hair. The mother, without thinking on the consequences, happily gave her the money. She liked to cut her hair because she had to do three braided tails every day, and maybe she was tired of doing it. And I suppose that she loved short hair, since she gave the money without questioning. After all she was a modern woman, and braided hair in those days was old fashion. Gladiola was a teen ager now and she wanted to look good like her best friend who also had cut her braided hair. But she had no clue that her father would be so much against it.

Eventually when she grew up, she tried to find a good job, but she did not have enough training and she had to work on jobs she was not tailor for it. She tried to be a seamstress, a tailor, a sales girls, and office secretary. Then the family in desperation sent her to the big city to work as a maid. However, after one month she came back home. In the process of time her father was told he would not be alive for a long time, for he had angina pectoris and the doctors gave him a death sentence.

The unforgettable day that she left home to go to the new job, her father when she was already on the bus, looked intently at her and said, *"Do not come back, for the door will be closed."* This sentence made her feel unwanted and rejected. She did not know why her father had said it. She did not know how close to death her father really was. After that day, she knew she had to do whatever to survive. When she found a man who showed love to her, she went out with him, without thinking that he had plans to have sex with her. He enticed her and she lost her virginity. From that day a spirit took over her. She did not care anymore about her life. Gladiola did not know Yehoshua and His Word. She had been raised Catholic, and all she knew was that some day she would go purgatory a long time to pay for her sins. But that would be later on, certainly not now. Therefore she did what she wanted to do.

Then the enemy really came into her life to destroy her. She did not know at that time, but her uncoffessed, and unrepented sin, gave Satan authority over her life. She continued to date men, and she became pregnant. When she told the young man that she was pregnant and he needed to marry her, he told her that he would marry her on one condition. She would have to prostitute herself for him. She felt shame, and was upset, but she feared telling her father and mother that she was expecting a child unmarried. She believed the lies that that boy had promised her, and eventually she agreed and said yes. She figured, *"After I do this he will marry me."* She told Clemens, *"I only did this for about one year. He ended up in prison, and that freed me.""I did not want to marry a criminal. I was doing this because I wanted to give a name to my child. I wanted him to have a father."*

As she spoke she was relieving the shame and humiliation that she went through. At this point Clemens tried to comfort her. *"Gladiola, prostitution is not the unpardonable sin, as you know. In reality is not much different than worshiping another god, or the worship of idols. Please do not let this be a hindrance in your life anymore. You are now over seventy years old, and Yehovah has forgiven you. You are serving Him for so many years. That situ-*

ation happened so many years ago. Let Yehovah, your heavenly Father, heal your soul completely. The blood of Yehoshua was shed for you and me. All of us have sinned, each of us deserved going to hell." "Yes, Clemens, I know." "Yehoshua has completely removed this shame and rejection I have felt for so many years. He has completely healed my soul this morning. He reminded me of this Scripture, **"For Elohim did not send His Son into the world to condemn the world, but that the world through Him might be saved." Yochanan/John 3:17.** *"However, He has led me to share the secret of my life with you. I needed to talk about it with you, because you are my best friend and I know you will not consider me less worthy after I shared my secret with you. His grace is sufficient for me. But it has been something that I never could share with anyone outside my own husband. Now I had to share this with you, in order for me to begin to accept me, who I am and who I have been. His blood has cleansed me forever. Yehoshua is my sin offering, and my guilt offering, my asham. Now I am free. Thank you for being my friend. I love you very much. Thank you for listening to me. Yehoshua has come to remove my spots and wrinkles, so that if He should come today I am clean inside and out." Amen."*

After that intense time of remembering Gladiola was finally completely at peace. They decided to spend some time thanking Yehovah and Yehoshua for the release and for His goodness to them, and to all of us.

Gladiola had been a sick little sheep, but now had received Yehovah's and Yehoshua's healing with His peace. To Elohim be all the glory and all the praise forever and ever. Amen.

Many girls have gone into perdition because of lack of love. Gladiola also felt lack of love from her father, and even from her mother, as she was growing up. Maybe that was the wrong perception; however, to her it was real. When the father told her that the door would be closed, she did not understand that he was saying he would not be there to great her. In fact he had died shortly after she became pregnant. Yehovah's love is the only true love any human being needs to feel complete. Without His love we are lost and engage in things we would normally never consider doing. Gladiola gave her life to Yehovah about twenty years later while married. Her life was dramatically changed, and Yehovah called her by name, and gave her a ministry. Yehovah used her to change many lives even when she still needed healing in her own soul. He used her pains and difficulties to help others. Her love for Him is manifested in her personal life.

CHAPTER 9

Rotten Bones

Clemens needed to go to the bank to do a deposit. Since she loved walking, she decided not to take the bus. It was a marvelous sunny day, and there was still a little breeze which benefited her a great deal as she began to walk down the road. When she reached the next corner, she saw a woman on a wheelchair that made her way ahead of her. As she watched that woman wheeling herself down the road, she noticed that she used only one leg. She was wheeling herself using the single right leg and her two hands. But she was energetically trying to reach her destination.

Clemens practically ran to catch her! When the woman saw her she stopped to look at Clemens. She immediately introduced herself, and the lady also gave her name, Miryam. Clemens started a conversation and asked her if she ever asked Yeshua to be her Savior. The lady with a big smile answered emphatically, *"Yes."* Clemens rejoiced with her, and then she asked the reason why she had her leg amputated. Miryam did not mind the question. She quickly informed Clemens that she lost her leg a very long time ago. *"I drank al lot of whiskey and my bones became like cotton. They had rotten, and they cut my leg."* Clemens was surprised, for she did not know that alcohol would rot the bones.

She continued talking with Miryam, and commented on the fact that she noticed how much joy she had. She was so excited to share her testimony. She did not feel sorry for losing her left leg at all. She loved her Savior so much and was very thankful that she was still alive. Suddenly one of her friends came near them, and Clemens politely left Miryam, and continued her walk.

After Clemens returned to her apartment, she decided to find out more about the damage that alcohol does to the body. She checked on Google, and this is what she found:

"High level of Cortisol seen in people with alcoholism can decrease bone formation and increase bone break-down. Chronic alcohol consumption increases parathyroid hormone, which leaches calcium from the bone, she said. Also, excess alcohol kills osteoblasts, the bone making cells, Kaur adds"

She became very concerned because she knew many people who drank more than they should. However, as a believer in Mashiach, she also read the Scriptures and found several verses that may also have contributed Miryam's loss of her left leg.

A sound heart is life to the body, but envy is rottenness to the bones. **Mishley/Proverbs 14:30**

A merry heart does good, like medicine, but a broken spirit dries the bones. **Mishley/Proverbs 17:22**

Envy is sin, and all sin has a consequence. We do not know for sure, what was the real cause of Miryam's loss of her leg, but these verses will help us to guard our emotions. We should love our neighbor as ourselves, and we should never be envious of their prosperity or well being.

Joy, peace, and a good report will make our bones healthy. If we speak pleasant words, we will also have peace in our soul, and our bones will be healthy.

The light of the eyes rejoices the heart, and a good report makes the bones healthy. **Mishley/Proverbs 15:30**

Pleasant words are like a honeycomb, sweetness to the soul and health to the bones. **Mishley/Proverbs 16:24**

Our good health depends on our good attitude, besides the food we eat. We must live a holy life. Sin, which includes being a drunkard, will not allow us to enter the kingdom of Heaven.

Do you not know that the unrighteous will not inherit the kingdom of Elohim? Do not be deceived. Neither fornicators, nor idolaters, nor adulterers, nor homosexuals, nor sodomites, nor thieves, nor covetous, nor drunkards, nor revilers, nor extortioners will inherit the kingdom of Elohim. And such were some of You. But you were washed, but you were sanctified, but you were justified in the name of the Lord Yehoshua and by the Spirit of our Elohim. **Qorin'tiyim 1/1 Corinthians 6: 9-11**

Miryam is now sanctified, for she has called on the Name of Yehovah and was saved. She has ben found of the Good Shepherd. She has believed in Mashiach Yeshua and is now free from any addiction. She has the joy of Yehovah, which is a miracle. She does not complain for the loss of her leg at all, and is ready to testify of the goodness of Yehovah. She was a lost sheep but the Shepherd has found her! She will be in Heaven with many ex-lost sheep enjoying the blessings of Yehovah.

CHAPTER 10

Forgiven!

Although Clemens' mother had told her to forgive her brother Francois, it did not happen immediately. She did it with all her heart, but inside of her soul she still carried some hurt. She had very difficult time forgiving him for what he did to their mother. Clemens prayed for him all the time, but he was far away from his Savior and from her. He still lived in Nice. She did not know how he did spiritually. The first think she did after she left Nice was to send him a letter of rebuke. She rebuked him for what he did to their mother, and then she assured him that she had forgiven him. She wrote twice about the fact that he needed to be forgiven by Yehovah, and believe the Gospel. Yehoshua had carried His sins on the Cross. But he had to do his part. Yehovah gave her complete peace and after that time, she believed that he had indeed repented of his sin, and made peace with Elohim.

A few years before he went to be with Yehovah, Clemens called him as usual, and the conversation was as special as when they were young again. He sounded different. She felt in her heart the same brotherly love she had for him in the past. Before she hanged up the phone she told him, *"Francoise, I love you."* And he answered her, *"I love you too."* Now she knew he was saved. Yehovah had done the work in his life too. She had a chance to talk with him a few more times before he passed on.

He was no longer a lost sheep, she knew that now the Good Shepherd had found Him and she would see him in Heaven. He went to Heaven twenty years to the day their mother had passed on. That was a sign to Clemens that he also has given His life to his Savior before He came to take him home to be with Him forever. Yehoshua must have visited him as He had also come to visit their mother.

Now she firmly believes that Francoise is in Heaven with his Savior and his mother, sister, and other sibling who went to heaven long ago. He was eighty nine years old when he passed on to eternal life. What a blessing it will be when Clemens is also united with her mother, brother and other siblings, worshiping Yehovah in Heaven.

CHAPTER 11

Refreshed

Clemens sat in her living rooms relaxing and sipping a cup of warm lemon water when the telephone rang. She had a house line, for the cell phones were not that popular at that time yet, and the loud ring shook her. She had gotten up to answer and to her surprise she heard a very familiar voice saying to her, *"Hello Clemens, how are you?"* Clemens was in shock, and said, *"Tamara, how did you get my new phone number?" "Oh, I called the fellowship and the secretary gave me your phone number. I want to come and see you. Give me your address please."* Clemens was very happy to give Tamara her new address. *"Tamara, I give you the address, but let me know the time you come because I have to go out today. I need to do some shopping. When can you come?" "Oh, I am available now, can I come now?" "Yes, of course, I want to see you. I love you my good friend." "OK, I will be there at 3:00 pm." "Fine, Yehovah be with you and bless you."*

Clemens hanged up the phone and her mind began to race. *"I won-der what happen to her. Has she changed? She sounded happy? I hope she is doing well now."*

Meanwhile she changed her clothes, for she was still in pajama when the phone rang. Then she prepared some snacks for her friend, and prayed that she would have some good news. She had been a little melancholic after she was told the truth about Jacks life. Hopefully Tamara would give her some good news. She had known Tamara for long time. Her life had been disastrous. Tamara had gotten pregnant as a young girl, and gave birth to a child. But when she discovered that she was going to become a mother, she talked to Shaul, the man she thought was the father of her son. He did not deny that he was the father, but he forced her to change her life style. He deceived her telling her that he would marry her. Her story was very similar to Gladiola. She was scare to death, but because she feared her parents finding out about the baby, she eventually said yes to him, and did what he told her to do believing that he was going to marry her. She also found a job and was working at a spa. She was living a double life. Many young girls fall into this trap. He would take all the money. She never had a penny for herself.

During this very trying time she received a telegram informing her of the death of her father. She looked in the suitcase for the money she had hidden from her boyfriend. But she did not found it. He had stolen it. That money could have bought the train ticked to go bury her father. Now she had no money, and she could not go home. When her boyfriend came home she tried to kill him with a butter knife! That was the only weapon she had. However, he was much stronger than Tamara, and he stopped her very quickly. All she could do was cry. She also naively had tried to get a loan from the Bank, but they laughed at her. She did not know what to do. In fact later on she found out from her mother that she had waited one extra day to bury her father, hoping she would come, but she never did. All she could do was to write a letter to her mother telling her that she had not money. Those days were very difficult for Tamara. She thought that her life would never change. She was completely hopeless.

The day arrived for her to give birth to her son. When they placed her son for the first time in her arms close to her heart, she was so happy. Tamara experienced motherly love for the first time. It was a wonderful feeling. She loved that boy so much. Now she had a child to care for. What a blessing! But things would change quickly.

When she came out of the Hospital Shaul convinced her to take the child to the orphanage for the nuns to take care of him. She had no clothes for the baby, or a crib. She had no money to buy anything. She was forced to leave the baby at that orphanage. Tamara was allowed to go there to nurse her son once a day. The rest of the time she would take her milk in a bottle for him. The baby was there only a very short time for her mother came to help caring for her son. She became his nurse while Tamara went to work. But the living conditions were very bad. They were living in a single room, all three of them! The mother and the child lay on the floor to sleep. This situation went on for several months. Her mother did not rebuke her for her life style, or told her to leave that guy who was abusing her. I suppose she felt that her daughter was old enough to know what was right and what was wrong. She did not want to interfere. This was sad, because if the mother would have told her to let him go, she would have done it immediately. The only reason she submitted to her boy friend was because she feared her parents. But if her mother would have counsel her to let him go, she would have jumped for joy. However that did not happen. She still would be going through some other drama.

One day Shaul slept her in front of her mother, and she left the following day. But she still did not tell Tamara to leave him. Eventually Shaul left her because he got into trouble. At the same time she met Naval, a friend of her ex-boyfriend who tried to help her. Meanwhile the Child Protective Services came to take away her child because she was out for a few hours every night and the child was left alone. She did not surrender her child but threaten them to jump out of her fourth floor window if they would take the child. They came twice, finally they stopped.

Now Naval, this new friend, took her to see Abner, the bar manager and asked him to hire her. She was hired immediately and now she was earning more than enough money without having to break the law. She was happy. Her mother continued to come periodically to help with her son and that was a true blessing. But eventually she had to place him in a Children Hotel. That place was expensive but now she was earning enough to be able to pay for her own living expenses and for the son.

One day Naval, told her that he had divorced his wife and she had remarried. In fact, he also said that his wife gave birth to another child with her second husband, and she had moved to another town. Tamara believed everything he said because she had fallen in love with him. When he told her that he would marry her, she believed him. However, he told her she needed to give him a certain amount of money to put in the bank to buy a house. Only after they would get the house they would be married. No problem, she still believed him. Tamara completely believed him because she loved and trusted him. After it all, he worked for the Government; therefore he was not a liar! Or so she thought!

Clemens realized it was almost three o'clock and Tamara would be arriving very soon. She finished dusting the furniture and got ready for her good friend. She sat by the window admiring the wonderful blue sky. Her mind was focused on the Creator of the Universe who has fashioned this earth and the heavens just for her! She was one of the many believers that were part of the Body of the Jewish Mashiach, the Anointed One. She felt at peace and ready to meet Tamar.

The door bell rang. Clemens ran to the door and opened it. The smell of frankincense enveloped her as she hugged Tamara. Words were not necessary. They simply hugged each other. Finally Tamara exploded with, *"Clemens I am born again and spirit filled! I have been visited by the Ruach haQodesh and my life belongs to Yehovah and Yehoshua now!"* Clemens was in shock! *"What did you say? You are born again?" "Yes, I am!"* Now Clemens almost fainted for the joy! She had difficulty taking it all in. This was the good news she needed to hear.

Both sat down, and Tamara began to share how she finally became free from Naval. She learned the truth about him. Naval had lied to her all along. He did not divorce his wife, he was still married. He also lied to her about his job. He was not working for the government. He lied all along in order for Tamara to trust him and give him the money. He was actually some kind of spy. Tamara had completely cut off her relationship with him.

Now Tamara was living a clean life and had her son living with her. After she stopped seeing him, she began to think on the supernatural. *"Is there an Elohim in the Universe?* She began to read about new age and other cults, but did not fully get involved in them. However, she was older now and began to contemplate the possibility of eternity. Was there an Elohim in this Universe? However, she was not looking in the right places and soon she completely lost sight of reality and stopped believing on the possibility that Yehovah existed. She completely denied the existence of Yehovah, the Creator of the Universe. And for sure she did not believe in Yehoshua. Tamara according to the Scriptures became a fool!

"The fool has said in his heart, 'There is no God." They are corrupt, they have done abominable works, there is none who does good." Tehillim / Psalm 14:1

However, she would not die in that horrible condition. Yehovah had another plan for her life. But for several months she continued to be a fool *"lost sheep."* Without Elohim in her life, Tamara was not happy. Actually she felt empty and often she drank alcohol more than she should. She could not speak about the condition of her soul to anyone. She had no friends around her who could lead her the right way. Her mother was far away and she was also a *lost sheep.* Who could help her? There was no one who could. She was all alone, or so she thought.

Finally one amazing day she picked up a book to read. As she flipped the pages, her eyes caught a phrase. To her surprise she read that Yehovah loved her. Tamara also read that Yehovah's Son died for her sins and He also loved her. She could hardly believe that there was an Elohim in Heaven that loved her. She decided quickly to call up to Heaven and ask Elohim to reveal Himself if He was indeed real. Many people do this with a surprised response. Yehovah always answers them. Clemens knew of other unbelievers who had done the same thing. But now Tamara was telling her that she too had had the courage to personally talk to our Creator to find out if He was indeed real. After crying out to Heaven asking for Yehovah to reveal Himself to her if was up there, He did reveal Himself to her. After crying out to Him a few times with great intensity, she "knew" deeply in her heart that He was indeed real. Then she remembered the teaching of her Sunday school. There was a Heaven for the good people, and there was a Hell for the bad people. She had learned as a child to confess her sins in repentance. Immediately she asked to be forgiven for everything she ever did. Her time being promiscuous, the lies she spoke, the cigarettes she stole from her father when she began to smoke…and on and on… She spent a long time repenting and crying out for Yehovah's mercy. Then she sensed the presence of the Holy Spirit on her left side, and from inside her heart she heard Yehovah saying, **"This is the Holy Spirit."** And immediately she literally felt the Ruach haQodesh/Holy Spirit entering into her. This was her born again experience, as she found out later on. Yehovah came to reside in her. He had forgiven all her sins. She felt so light, so clean, and at peace. She stopped crying.

All her past sins were gone forever. And now she wanted to learn more about the Holy Spirit. A few months later she received the baptism in the Holy Spirit and spoke in unknown tongues. Her life of miracle began. After that experience all she wanted to do was to get everyone she knew to be filled with the Holy Spirit and for them to speak in the heavenly languages! After that experience Yehovah had been using her to minister to many people. She wanted everyone to know Him, and to be filled with the Ruach haQodesh.

Clemens was so happy to hear her testimony. Now Tamara was part of the Universal Bride of Messiah! Both rejoiced and worshiped Yehovah together thanking Him for their own salvation. That day was a day that Clemens would never forget. Now the two friends were united in their faith, and were serving the same King. Both dedicated to honor Him in their lives and to make His wonderful Name known to the world. Eventually Tamara got up to leave, but promised to keep in touch and to visit again soon.

Clemens rejoiced knowing that her friend, a *"lost sheep,"* had been found by the Savior!

Chapter 12

The Unloved Wife

Clemens was sitting in the living room facing the back porch land-scape. The mountains were covered with dark clouds, and soon the rain violently came pouring down. Clemens loved watching the rain. Since she was a little girl she would sit by the door on a little chair made just for her, and watched the falling rain. This habit never left her, and she always loved stop doing whatever she was doing in order to see the rain falling. Somehow the rain brought calmness to the soul. This day was not different that the others. As she watched the rain her mind went back to the time she was in France and met a very unusual young lady. Leah was a single mother, a young woman who had experienced great humiliation and great sorrow, and much pain. She had been abused and misused by men.

One day a young soldier introduced himself to her, and invited her to have some drinks with him. His name was Solomon. He was young and not very talkative. He always seemed to be aloof, remote an unapproachable. He was different that anyone she ever met. Yet he invited her and seemed very much interested in her life. But although he was there with her, he seemed to be thinking on something not related to her. Surely, he had something on his mind that was keeping him quiet. Maybe he had only a short time to make a decision, and that caused an avalanche of thoughts pressing on his mind and soul. He did not know what to do, but soon he would find out. Leah was perplexed to say the least, but continued to see him when he came around. Finally six days later he came to her and told her to keep a set of gold rings, and one of them had a diamond. He asked her to keep them for him. She felt almost offended at his words, and told him, *"I cannot keep them; you keep them, or put them in the bank. I do not want them."* Solomon answered her, *"Please put them on, I want to marry you."* Leah was taken by surprise and finally she accepted the rings. He asked her to help him write a letter to her mother and brother to ask them for the privilege of allowing him to marry her. She was so happy to hear him saying this, and immediately Solomon wrote those letters to her family. The mother and brother answered immediately, Leah and Solomon began to prepare the documents to be married. It took about a year, and they finally were married in France. But even before the marriage Leah noticed something about Solomon that bothered her, but she shook it off. She did not want to be jealous. He seemed to love women's adulation al lot, and he loved dancing with other women. Solomon, before the wedding, one day had told her that he married her because she loved her son, but of course that he loved her too. He had been exposed to radiation and became sterile. He said that it happened while in the military service. But he wanted to have a son, and he really liked Leah's son. Therefore it would be a great blessing in marrying her who already had a child, although she herself had become sterile. Finally the day came for them to leave France and fly to America.

While in America Solomon one day took her to meet her old girl-friend and her family. The rings he had given her were the same rings he had given to this girl. She had been committed to him in marriage, but she changed her mind and went to California to meet with her true lover. Gianna, the ex girl friend was there when they visited. Needless to say that Leah felt some jealousy. Solomon continued to visit that family without his Leah, his own wife. Leah discovered that

Solomon's family and Gianna's were good friends, and probably they encouraged the marriage of their children, however, it was not Yehovah's plan for them.

This situation went on for a while, until Solomon became addicted to drugs, and pornography. He met many women, but one of them, Naomi, was very bold and would come to their home to talk with Solomon outside their house in the yard. She would never come inside the house to talk with Leah. She did not consider her at all. Naomi would come to talk only with Solomon. She would be out in the yard talking with him for hours, while he was fixing his car. Naomi was heavily involved in the hippy movement, and taking a lot of drugs. She, and others, got Solomon involved in that life style. She flirted with Solomon in front of Leah, without any apparent consciousness of being doing anything wrong. During that period Solomon would stay out for days at the time. He did not care of the son he adopted, or his wife Leah. He seemed to be in another world. He was also selling drugs. Leah was unloved. She drank more than she should at evening when her husband was out doing what he loved to do without her. Alcohol helped her to forget her misery. This situation went on for about three years. Husband and wife, Solomon and Leah, and his friend Naomi were all *lost sheep,* until one glorious day Leah's life was changed forever. She came to America with her son and her husband, and no one else. No other family member came with her. All her family was in France. She could not run to her mother for comfort, for she was so far away. She needed to be loved by her husband, but that love had vanished into smoke, it was gone forever. The little love he felt for her had been replaced with drugs and promiscuous living. She felt trapped living so far away from her home, married, but alone. She cried out in desperation to Yehovah to reveal Himself to her. And He did. She repented of her sins, and Yehovah was now living His life in her. She was no longer lonely and miserable. She forgave her husband,

and his lovers, and sought to know her Elohim with all her heart. She bought a study Bible and read avidly from the beginning to the end. During those trying times He spoke to her from the book of Isaiah.

But now," thus says Yehovah, who created you, O Ya'aqov, and He who formed you, o Israel: "Fear not, for I have redeemed you; I have called you by your name; You are Mine. When you pass through the waters, I will be with you; and through the rivers, they shall not overflow you. When you walk through the fire, you shall not be burned, nor shall the flame scorch you. For I am Yehovah your Elohim, the Holy One of Israel, your Savior;" **Yeshayahu/Isaiah 43:1-4**

These verses and the following verses were very comforting to Leah.

"Sing, O barren, you who have not born! Break forth into singing, and cry aloud, you who have not labored with child! For more are the children of the desolate than the children of the married woman," says Yehovah. Enlarge the place of Your tent, and let them stretch out the curtains of Your dwellings; do not spare; lengthen your cords, and strengthen your stakes. For you shall expand to the right and to the left, and your descendants will inherit the nations, and make the desolate cities inhabited. Do not fear, for you will not be ashamed; neither be disgraced, for you will not be put to shame." **Yeshayahu 54:1-4**

Leah read the whole chapter of Yeshayahu 54 over and over again. She received her strength from Yehovah through His written Word. She sensed Him speaking to her during her trials. Indeed she was in good company now. The Creator of the Universe became her Friend, and her Companion. And Yehoshua now was her heavenly Husband! He was with her, even when the divorce became inevitable she had the strength to overcome sadness and depression. She found strength in Him alone. She read over and over Yeshayahu 53 which describes in detail the sacrificial death of Yehoshua, and she also read Tehillim/ Psalm 22. All these verse were too much to take in. Leah could hardly understand why Yehoshua suffered all that pain for her. How could He do that? Why did He do it? Love is the answer. The supernatural complete love of Elohim is the reason of Yehoshua dying on the cross for her. He did it to rescue her from the hand of the enemy and bring her to the Father in Heaven, Yehovah. If Yehoshua would have not died, she would have never being able to go to Heaven. Yet, she felt was so unworthy! But He made her clean. He was pure, and when she believed in Him and repented from her sin she became pure again. Yehoshua, her true atonement, the perfect Sacrifice offered Himself to save her. His blood cleansed her and made her whole. This is the love of the Father and of the Son. Yehovah loves the sinners, and make them new again. No wonder Yehoshua said that we must be born again! (Yochanan/John 3:3)

Her life now became completely dedicated to her Savior. She learned to pray and seek His presence daily. She felt a need to share her testimony to everyone who asked her. Leah was not longer a lost sheep, and the fact that her husband was cheating on her and left her, did not matter anymore. Leah interceded for her husband, and Yehovah assured her that Solomon also would be saved. His salvation was her main concern. Now that she knew someday he would also come to the knowledge of Yehovah and of her Mashiach, Yehoshua, gave her the peace that she needed. She no longer needed to drink, worrying about her husband, because Yehovah had completely set her free.

Clemens was very happy to hear Leah's testimony, but she heard bad news about their common friend Devina. Although she had received a supernatural healing and kept her healing only for one whole year, now she was experiencing the same sickness again. Satan attacked her again because her house had been cleansed, but left empty, and a worse thing happened to her.

"When an unclean spirit goes out of a man, he goes through dry places, seeking rest, and finds none. Then he says, 'I will return to my house from which I came.' And when he comes, he finds it empty, swept, and put in order. Then he goes and takes with him seven other spirits more wicked than himself, and they enter and dwell there; and the last state of that man is worse than the first. So shall it also be with this wicked generation." **Mattithyahu/ Matthew 12:43-45**

Leah had not stopped praying to her friend Devina. However, Devina could not let go of the religion she grew up with, and that kept her in bondage. Satan knows the Word and he has legal rights to anyone who disobeys the Commandments. Sadly many new believers if they stay at the same church they were before being born again, they cannot break loose. Yehovah had given her grace for one full year to repent, but she did not repent. However, eventually Leah ministered to her before she went to be with Yehovah, and she renounced idolatry and went to heaven in peace.

Leah was divorced, just about fifteen months after she was born again and about six months later her ex-husband Solomon married Naomi. Their marriage lasted only 12 years, and Naomi, sadly, died of an overdose of drugs.

At that time Solomon asked Leah to re-marry him. He gave her only a few days to make up her mind. When she got the letter, Leah was visiting with her evangelist friend in Kentucky. She asked her friend Diane to please pray with Solomon over the phone. She talked with him, and after she hanged up the phone she told Leah that Solomon had no love in him. He could not give her any love, for he had none. He was spiritually dead. Leah wanted more confirmation, for she was willing to go back to Solomon, and she asked a pastor what she should do. He simply asked Leah a question: *"Is he changed?"* Her answer was, *"NO."* Leah could not see any change in him, he was worse than before. Therefore she could not go back to him. She knew that her future did not include marriage, however, at times, she still hoped to remarry. But this was not the perfect will of her Father in Heaven. He remarried shortly after, and the marriage also ended up in divorce and much pain. He will not find peace and joy until he also will recognize that he needs help. He needs to find the perfect love of Yehovah and Yehoshua. That day will be coming soon.

Leah found the perfect love of her Father in Heaven to be sufficient for all her needs. His love is unconditional. He does not commit adultery and we humans have a tendency doing. He is always faithful. He forgave all her many sins, as He forgives everyone who comes to Him in true repentance. Yehoshua is her Bridegroom, and she is complete in Him. She has learned that this life is only temporary, and we are just pilgrims on the way to eternity. Soon each of us, those of us who have chosen to love our Creator, and to serve Him, will be together with Him for eternity.

Leah ministers the Word anywhere Yehovah sends her. She is satisfied and has no fear of her future. Her sufferings and the feeling of been unloved has been replaced with the full complete wonderful Love of Yehovah and Mashiach who gave His life for her. She kept contact with Solomon, and is still waiting for the day he too will find that complete and perfect love in the Mashiach Yehoshua. Yehovah's Word cannot fail. What He has declared will come to pass. Leah will see Solomon in Heaven one day soon. This is the rewarding gift she can expect from her Redeemer, Yehovah, for He is faithful to do what He promises. All glory and praise to Yehovah and to His wonderful Name forever and ever.

CHAPTER 13

Reconnected

Clemens came back to Maui to be settled. When she went back to her fellowship she saw her old friend Katrina. She was surprised to see her. *"Katrina, how are you? I am so glad to see you. Are you going to live on Maui now?" "I came here a while ago."* Katrina asked Clemens the question," *Where were you?"* Clemens replied, *"I went to the Philippines, Canada and Washington for a while. But I am back now."* Katrina answered, *"You travel a lot!" "Yes, I do."* Katrina informed Clemens that she moved back to Maui to be close to her mother. Her two sons were still young and attending a Christian School. She had become a helper at that School in order to pay for the tuition of her two sons. She seemed to be happy.

Katrina was also involved in worship and outreach ministries. She was a great help to everyone around her. She had a very friendly attitude and people were drawn to her. She knew the Word and shared it with those around her. She wanted everyone to serve her Savior as she did. Katrina did not compromise her faith. She would not drink alcohol, or smoke cigarettes. However, Katrina still followed the teachings of the church, and did not yet have the revelation of keeping the Sabbath day holy. Nevertheless, she did her best to obey Yehovah in every other way. She always prayed for Yehovah to give her a clean heart. She also expressed great faith in many situations concerning herself and others. Katrina had been a lost sheep as all of us, but after Yehoshua came into her life, she was completely transformed by the power of Yehovah. She became a very strong disciple of Yehoshua, our Jewish Mashiach. She loved to intercede in prayer for the lost and for all mankind. Katrina herself needed continuous prayer for her back pain. She always asked for prayer. Many people knew about her problem and prayed with her and for her. She had many friends in Hawaii and other states. During this period Clemens and Katrina did not see each other a lot. Katrina was working, and Clemens was always coming or going somewhere. Soon she would be leaving again. But while on Maui she was always ministering with the same fellowship as Katrina.

Clemens was used greatly by Yehovah at that fellowship; however she always sensed that she needed to do more in the Kingdom of Yehovah. She felt that that Fellowship was not allowing her to fulfill her calling, and she was right. Although she was always very busy in ministry, it did not fulfill her spiritual need. She knew her message had to go to the world, not only to little fellowships in the Islands of Hawaii. Yehovah had another plan for her life, but He did not yet revealed to her exactly what it would be. She kept on seeking Him and serving Him the best way she knew how, and kept on waiting for an answer. Meanwhile, in just a few weeks she would be going to another Island.

CHAPTER 14

Humbling Days

Clemens felt that she needed to do something else in the King-dom of Elohim. She told the pastor that she was considering moving to another island. However, her pastor suggested that she contact the pastor of the extension church in another Island. She did, and that pastor was very happy to have her as an assistant. Quickly she packed her few bags and left Maui again. While there she helped the pastor doing all house visitations, for that pastor did not like to do that aspect of ministry. He loved to play golf! But he was a great pastor and the people loved him. He was a California person, and did not receive the training on how to pastor the sheep. He was very spontaneous, and did also other things to help the community. For instance he was involved in helping the police stop the drug crime in the Islands. He traveled many times to other states and Clemens did all his duties while he was away. Those times were great times for Clemens, and she felt that she was indeed fulfilling one of her callings. Clemens taught the bible studies, and besides preaching twice a month at the little fellowship, she also flew to other islands to minister the Word. Although in the past she never felt really com-fortable there because that Island was very small, however now she had found some joy and contentment ministering to the locals. Yeho-vah used her mightily while living there. She was able to stay there one full year, fulfilling the commitment made to her senior pastor.

While there, on her spare time, she worked on her second book that she eventually published.

Clemens lived a healthy life style. Three times every week she jogged with two other friends. Every morning, at five AM she went to the new church building to lead the prayer meeting. Not many people attended the prayer meeting, but there was always a Japanese elderly man who would come to pray. He was very faithful to Yehovah, and prayed for revival all the time. He was the most faithful person in that fellowship. He was also very kind and generous. He always shared his vegetables with the town people. Some other believers also came, but only occasionally. Not many people loved to pray publically. However, Yehovah always has a remnant. Clemens believed in personal prayer, but also the prayer of agreement. Yehoshua said:

"Assuredly, I say to you, whatever you bind on earth will be bound in Heaven, and whatever you loose on earth will be loosed in heaven. Again I say to you that if two of You agree on earth concerning anything that they ask, it will be done for them by My Father in Heaven. For where two or three are gathered together in My name, I am there in the midst of them." **Mattithyahu / Matthew 18:18-20**

Many days at prayer were literally only two persons present, Clemens and the Japanese man! But it was enough for Yehovah to give ear to their prayer. He was faithful, and He answered many of their intense heartfelt prayers. The church building was eventually finished with the joy of all parishioners.

After that experience Clemens flew to Houston, Texas with the intention of opening up a rehab home for women. Rosina, a new friend that she met at the fellowship, offered her the use of her five bedroom house in Houston for the women's ministry. Clemens felt this was the answer to her prayers and she accepted the offer because she always wanted to set abused women free. She also had first-hand knowledge on how to minister to women who were under the bondage of drugs and alcohol. For a very long time she yearned to have the opportunity to set up such ministry. Preaching was her main calling, but she also wanted to do a rehab house because the need for such ministry was so great everywhere.

Before Clemens left Maui she introduced Rosina to her own son Caleb. When she met him she asked him if she could leave her car in his house, while in Santa Fe, New Mexico, and he agreed. Then Clemens and Rosina flew on the plane together to Texas. Eventually Rosina continued her trip to Santa Fe to visit with her mother who was very hill. She wanted to be near her in case she would need her help. The main reason she left the Hawaiian Islands, was to be near her mother.

While Rosina was in New Mexico, Clemens was working hard to get to know people who may want to support her ministry. She visited many fellowships in the area, and formed several valuable relationships. Everything seemed to be going very well. While in Huston she received a visit from Maui. Her very close friend Georgina came from Maui to visit her for one week. During that time they visited special areas of the city, and had a wonderful time. Clemens also invited her new friends for a special dinner and ministry time. It was wonderful indeed. The presence of the Ruach haQodesh was awesome! Everyone was blessed.

After Georgina left the storm came unexpected. Suddenly when everything seemed to be going the right direction, the bomb exploded. It was only about three months after Clemens arrived to Houston when Rosina came back from New Mexico and prepared to fly back to Maui to care for some business.

She would of course see Caleb, Clemens son, because she had to pick up her car. She was so excited to go and prepared herself with the best clothes to go to the airport. She noticed the great excitement in Rosina as she dressed preparing to fly out. She was speaking about Caleb and she mentioned that she bought him a brand new Bible. Clemens did not feel at easy about this trip. She sensed in her spirit that trouble was around the corner. Of course she was beginning to be concerned about Rosina meeting Caleb. She noticed that Rosina spoke too much about Caleb. Rosina liked her son, and Clemens was very concerned about their coming meeting. She did not have peace about Rosina meeting with her son without her bein present. However, there was nothing she could do to prevent anything that may be happening. She began to pray, and the Holy Spirit instructed her to call her son. She needed to warn Caleb about Rosina's visit, and told him plainly what was on her heart. *"Caleb, Rosina is going to Maui, please do not have intimate relationship with her. She is a Christian. Please do not entice her."* Caleb answered her, *"Mom, if she would do that she would be a hypocrite. Do not worry. Do not think that way." "OK, Caleb, but please do not touch her."*

Clemens kept praying about this situation. She did not have peace. After a few days she could not resist the thought of calling her good friend Dalia who lived next door to her son.

"Hello Dalia, how are you?" "I am fine, what about you?" "I am OK, but have you seen Rosina? She is on Maui now." "Yes, I saw her. The car is no longer parked on the street, but inside your son's yard." "What are you saying?" "Yes, she has been sleeping there." "What?" "Are you sure?" "Yes, I am."

Clemens heart fell almost still. She suspected something would happen, but now the suspicious became a reality. She felt betrayed and deeply hurt. Clemens whole world fell apart, it seemed. In a moment's time the ministry that was beginning to start ended. She could no longer be involved with such a person. Rosina was one of the leaders in the ministry, and the house was hers. And now Rosina herself was living in sin and needed deliverance! The ministry could not go on. That was it. Clemens cried a lot, and prayed a long time. Finally she called Rosina and asked her if she had slept with Caleb. She cried. Clemens rebuked her at first.

"How can you sleep with my son? He said that when a Christian sleeps around is a hypocrite. So you sleep with him. My son! He is coming close to Yehoshua, but you ruin it all." She answered Clemens, *"You are judging me."* The conversation went on for a while, but Rosina did not take responsibility of her sin. Clemens felt betrayed. She had to let go. Rosina was not in condition to help anyone because she needed deliverance. At this point in her life, although she was a believer in Yehoshua, she was also a lost sheep, and needed to repent and change her ways. She needed to learn to be in the world, but not to be part of it. Yehoshua instructs us to walk in the narrow way.

"Enter by the narrow gate; for wide is the gate and broad is the way that leads to destruction, and there are many who go in by it. Because narrow is the gate and difficult is the way which leads to life, and there are few who find it." Mattithyahu / Matthew 7:13-14

"A good tree cannot bear bad fruit, nor can a bad tree bear good fruit. Every tree that does not bear good fruit is cut down and thrown into the fire. Therefore by their fruits you will know them." Mattithyahu 7:18-20

"Not everyone who says to Me, 'Lord, Lord,' shall enter the kingdom of Heaven, but he who does the will of My Father in Heaven. Many will say to Me in that day, 'Lord, Lord, have we not prophesied in Your Name, and done many wonders in Your Name? And then I will declare to them, "I never knew you; depart from Me, you who practice lawlessness!" Mattithyahu 21-23

Clemens was also guilty because she blindly trusted her friend who seemed very faithful to her Savior. She should have prayed about it to know the mind of Yehovah before accepting the offer. However, now she knew that although it was a very difficult and painful situation, she had to separate from her. The ministry was aborted.

Clemens asked Rosina where she could leave the keys and Rosina told her where. As Clemens was preparing to leave Houston, a new Christian with her husband, loaned her a little cottage to do the ministry. Her husband blocked a check that was written to Clemens ministry because he wanted to be in charge of the ministry finances. He was a pilot and very shrewd with money matters. The little cottage would not be free. He would take over the whole ministry! Once again Clemens trusted man, instead praying and trusting Yehovah alone to provide for her.

That situation once again revealed the true nature of immature Christians. Those two new "friends," were also *lost sheep*, and she needed to intercede for them. Clemens had difficulty understanding how Christians would do such things. Christians are called to be holy unto Yehovah. They supposed to be salt and light, in order to change the world, not to be as the world. A Christian is called to be separated to Yehovah. But those three friends were not yet surrendered to Yehovah's will and had not really experienced His presence in their lives. They did not know Him in an intimate manner. They were still walking in the flesh, instead of trusting Yehovah and lovingly serving Him.

The prophet Yirmeyahu cried out to all of us to ear.

"Return, your backsliding children, and I will heal your backslidings." **Yirmeyahu / Jeremiah 3:22**

"Break up your fallow ground, and do not sow among thorn. Circumcise yourselves to Yehovah, and take away the foreskins of Your hearts, you men of Yahudah and Yerushalayim, lest My fury come forth like fire, and burn so that no one can quench it, because of the evil of Your doings." **Yirmeyahu 4:4**

Yehovah used these circumstances to help Clemens redirect her life. She knew that she should not have gone to Texas. She went because she thought that she needed to do more in the Kingdom of Yehovah. She felt her ministry in that little Island was not enough, and it was not fulfilling her vision. However, it was not what Yehovah had called her to do. She went thinking that now she could be in the position of serving as a pastor again. However, Yehovah had something else on His mind for her life. She would be doing something that would be much more fulfilling for her.

She had been the first resident pastor at that extension assembly in that Island. But now she was only used as a visiting missionary. It was a very humble experience for her. She should have waited on Yehovah to provide the right opportunity to serve Him as He had been doing from the beginning of her life in the Kingdom. However, impatience caused her to leave that Island, and go through those problems. But, Yehovah would turn the situation around for her very soon. He is merciful and uses even our mistakes for our own good.

She learned two important lessons; one is to be patient and wait upon Yehovah to open the correct door, and the second, is to never place her trust in humans. The Word teaches us that when we trust in men it brings a snare. *"It is better to trust in Yehovah than to put confidence in man. It is better to trust in Yehovah than to put confidence in princes."* **Tehillim/Psalm 118:8-9**

CHAPTER 15

The Key to Success

Yehovah had other plans for Clemens, and eventually she would know about them. However she learned her lesson. And next time she would be wiser and would commit her ways to Yehovah alone and wait upon Him until He would speak to her.

Commit your way to Yehovah, Trust also in Him, and He shall bring it to pass." **Tehillim/Psalm 37:5**

"Wait on Yehovah; be of good courage, and He shall strengthen your heart; Wait, I say on Yehovah! **Tehillim 27:14**

She should have remembered the Scriptures and avoided this whole mess. Humans need to learn from Yehoshua. He could do nothing on His own. He only did the will of the Father because He and the Father are one.

Then Yehoshua said to them, "When you lift up the Son of Man, then you will know that I am He, and that I do nothing of Myself; but as My Father taught Me, I speak these things. And He who sent Me is with Me. The Father has not left Me alone, for I always do those things that please Him." **Yochanan/John 8:28-29**

We need help! Without Yehovah's Ruach haQodesh we are helpless! But Yehoshua sent His Spirit to help us.

"But now I go away to Him who sent Me, and none of You asks Me, 'Where are You going? But because I have said these

things to you, sorrow has filled your heart. Nevertheless I tell you the truth. It is to your advantage that I go away; for if I do not go away the Helper will not come to you; but if I depart, I will send Him to you. And when He has come, He will convict the world of sin, and of righteousness, and of judgment: of sin, because they do not believe in Me; of righteousness, because I go to My Father and you see Me no more; of judgment, because the ruler of this world is judged." **Yochanan/John 16:5-11 (See Yochanan/John 15:4-5)**

Clemens did not seek Yehovah about this trip. She did not ask Him to find out if it was His will or not. She needed a place to live and do her ministry, and she thought it was a perfect plan for her. She had been gullible, and that seemed to have been the history of her life before her salvation experience. Now Yehovah was letting her see with new eyes. She also was required to forgive them quickly in order for her to be forgiven. Forgiveness is a necessity if we want to be forgiven.

"And forgive us our us our sins, as we forgive those who sin against us" **Mattithyahu/Matthew 6:12**

For all of us sin one time or another. Sin is universal. The Scriptures declares all of us guilty. But, as I mentioned, Yehovah uses even our mistakes for our own good. He wastes nothing. In this situation once again Clemens learned to love those who hurt her. And from then on she learned to wait upon Yehovah. She learned to submit completely to Yehovah everything she did. And she learned to trust Him to lead her as He had done so many times in the past. She could not make her ministry happen. Yehovah alone would lead her to do what He had pre-ordained for her to do in this world. She discovered that He had a book written in Heaven concerning her life, and that knowledge made her feel secure in Him.

"Your eyes saw my substance, being yet unformed. And in Your book they all were written, the days fashioned for me, when as yet there were none of them." **Tehillim/Psalm 139:16**

Clemens began to pray for revelation concerning her life. After this experiences first and foremost she sought Yehovah's will. She learned to wait on Him to direct her path. She wanted to do nothing apart from what was written in her book in Heaven. Her life became much more peaceful for her, and the stress to want to succeed was lifted up. She realized that Yehovah had other plans for her, and she let go of the idea of having a rehab home for women. However, Clemens continued to minister to such women personally when Yehovah gave her the opportunity. Yehovah blessed her in the process, for He is the Healer of the broken hearts, and He receives all the glory.

However, the leaders of her home church branded her as rebellious. Yes, they did, because they could not convince her anymore to be doing the kind of ministry they planned for her. Yehovah eventually removed her from that ministry and opened the correct ministry for her life. Her pastor never understood her calling. She was declared unfit to receive the promotion that she needed. She was used by the pastor to do only certain things, because of her traveling ministry. He never fully understood who she really was; he did not know her heart. This fact caused a lot of pain in her life.

CHAPTER 16

The Assemblies

Many assemblies want their congregation do whatever they need to have done in order for their ministry to flourish. Regardless of what the callings of that person may be; they are supposed to help the pastor do what he has purposed in his heart to do. As long as the pastor needs a ministry to be done; that is what the person is supposed to do. They expect their plans to be accomplished by the congregation. And they teach the persons will be blessed if they do what there are told to do. They expect obedience. This may sound good, but it is not for everyone.

Many pastors act this way. In fact it may depend on what denomination they ascribe to. The pastors do not teach the new born again believers to pray and wait on Yehovah for guidance concerning their specific calling. They feel because that person has entered their door, they belong to them. This is a false assumption and causes a person to make many mistakes in their lives. The new believers must be taught to pray and to find out for themselves what their specific call is. Each new born believer in the Mashiach has a personal calling. Yehovah will reveal to them what they supposed to be doing in His Kingdom. But if they are told to do "this and that" in a church, they will never know what Yehovah has planned for them to do. Yehoshua is the One who has saved them, and they belong to Him, not to the pastor. Yehoshua is their Head **(Qorin'tiyim 1/1 Corinthians 11:3),** not the pastor. He will lead them in the work of the kingdom.

Just as not everyone supposed to be a pastor; judge; doctor or nurse, neither is a believer created to fill the gaps in a ministry. For instance some ministers charge the believers to do cell groups. They are still drinking milk, they do not know the Word, and are immature. Yet, the pastors want to use them to have as many cells as possible. They think the leaders will help keeping the other people in the church. The motto is *"Church growth at all costs."* Many times it is all about becoming the greatest largest church in town or even in the world. But numbers without spiritual personal growth do not help the individual. If the pastors would pray and teach the parishioners to hear the Word of Yehovah for themselves, the whole congregation would benefit. If he would wait on Yehovah, He would bring the right persons to do whatever he needs help with. The result of pressing people to do things they are not called for it, it is disastrous. Those people get burned out and eventually many of them leave the assembly. No wonder so many new believers end up back in the world! They become frustrate it, and leave. This is not Yehovah's way. Others stay at the church, and become pastors, but they become the carbon copy of the senior pastor, and continue to do the same mistakes he has done with their congregation.

Clemens was thinking on these issues when Aliza called her. *"Hello Aliza, how are you""Thank you Clemens I am well, and you?""I am fine, where are you?"" I am outside your door!"What?* *"Come in."* Clemens opened the door and gave a big hug to Aliza. Both rejoiced to see each other again since both had left the same assembly years ago. Aliza began to tell her old friend what she had been doing since she left the assembly doing the bus ministry and children choir. She told Clemens that she never felt free to serve Yehovah. Now the cords that pulled her into ministries that she was not called to be in, were broken. She experienced *new zeal to serve her Savior. "Aliza how is your new book doing? Have you finished writing it?" "Yes, I did publish it one year ago. I am writing another one now." "WOW! I am so excited for you." "Thank you." And what have you been doing lately for your Bridegroom and King Yehoshua?" "I am praying a lot and He has been giving me many insights on the End Times."*

Clemens enjoyed the visit with Aliza, and she was so thankful that Aliza left the assembly she had been for many years, to finally listen to the call Yehovah had placed upon her life. Her life is a success story. But still many pastors have not understood her ways. Even after she has been successfully writing several books; doing her own radio program; traveling as He leads her, and teaching Torah, she is still considered to be a rebellious person. Aliza was obedient to Yehovah and left when He called her to leave. She never regretted her decision. She knows who she is in Him, and she has much joy, as her own name implies.

However, the result of getting the new believers quickly involved in ministry before Yehovah specifically calls them, teaches them to do things in the flesh, get frustrated, and never learn to hear the voice of Yehovah in their own lives. They just become as hired workers for their pastor, which is a terrible mistake. Other members simply leave that congregation and they are called rebellious, just as Aliza had done.

But, once they leave, they will be in a position to listen to Yehovah and fulfill His will for their lives. This situation happens many times, and it should not happen. Probably the fault lies in immature pastors. They want to have mega churches and copy from other pastors' methods. They are thought to do things one way and they keep on doing that way at the cost of many disappointed lives.

The pastors' preeminent duties are first and foremost to equip the saints. What that means is they are responsible to be good shepherds. They have to teach individuals to hear and obey the voice of Yehovah.

Themselves they must be an example and show and tell how to enter into the Most Holy place. If they only have head knowledge, but lack experience, they will fail in their ministry, and cause many parishioners also to fail.

They also need to allow the congregation to function in the gifts of the Ruach haQodesh/Holy Spirit that Yehovah has graced them with, for there are diversities of gifts in the Body of Messiah.

"There are diversities of gifts, but the same Spirit. There are differences of ministries, but the same Lord. And there are diversities of activities, but it is the same Elohim who works all in all. But the manifestation of the Spirit is given to each one for the profit of all: for to one is given the word of wisdom through the Spirit, to another the word of knowledge through the same Spirit, to another faith by the same Spirit, to another gifts of healings by the same Spirit, to another the working of miracles, to another prophecy, to another discerning of spirits, to another different kinds of tongues, to another the interpretation of tongues. But one and the same Spirit works all these things, distributing to each one individually as He wills." **Qorin'tiyim 1/1 Corinthians 12:4-12**

This chapter in the book of Qorin'tiyim is neglected. Many assemblies teach about this book, but the parishioners are not permitted to function in the congregation service according to its teachings.

If we continue to read this Book we learn that we, the Body of Mashiach, are indeed One Body with many members. However, not all the members have the same function. The reason we have lost many sheep in the assemblies is because lack of teaching on the gifts of the Ruach haQodesh. We have muzzled them, just like we muzzle dogs and horses. We have forbidden the congregation to function in the areas of ministry the Ruach haQodesh has gifted them to bless the whole assembly.

I have experienced these phenomena personally. When the congregation allowed the gifts of words of knowledge, prophecy, and testimonies to operate in the meetings, they were blessed and flourished. People were healed and brought many into the fellowship. But when pastors stopped the congregation, they literally muzzled them, then the Spirit left and flesh began to manifest. They called the flesh Spirit, but it was only flesh. Entertainment came in to substitute for the true move of the Spirit.

Most pastors do not trust Yehovah to use any of their members in the prophetic gift in their congregation. They want to be in control. Therefore they do not allow the congregation to be blessed during their services on Wednesdays, Sunday morning, and Sundays evening.

Some pastors allow the parishioners to move in the gifts at the "one hour bible study" during the week. However there is minimum worship time because of the time limit, and the Ruach ha'Qodesh has no time to effectively minister to individuals according to their personal need. Besides this fact, the gifts are for the whole Body, not only for the few who attend the Bible Study.

Many pastors need to repent of the spirit of control and must allow the Ruach ha'Qodesh to be free to use the congregation according to His will. People need to hear a fresh Word of encouragement that will change their lives. The Services are to honor Yehovah not the pastor or the choir.

The Spirit of Yehovah knows what to do. If we trust Him, no one will speak anything sinful or out of order during His Worship Service. He is more than capable to watch over His sheep. But fear and control is not allowing Him to manifest Himself in the meetings. He is forbidden to speak. The pastor wants to keep the time straight and wants to be the only connection to Yehovah. This in many cases is idolatry.

The gifts are to be exercised for the congregation's benefit, and the congregation should not be muzzled. Yehovah has a special fresh Word for each of us. And we cannot muzzle Him. He cannot be silenced. If this continues to be done, He will leave the services, and the people will never reach their maturity. This is sin, and the pastors will have to give an account on Judgment Day.

However, not all churches are that controlling. Some pastors are open to the working of the Ruach haQodesh and allow the members to speak when He leads them. I have been in a congregation Oklahoma where the pastor allowed prophecy to come forth in every service. Everyone was blessed. That pastor loved and respected the Ruach haQodesh and the sheep! He trusted Yehovah in every area of ministry. I also know that other pastors who are open to the move of the Ruach haQodesh, but mostly are not. Yes, most assemblies will not allow anyone to use their Holy Spirit given gifts during the gathering services.

In each gathering there is special time the Ruach haQodesh wants to minister prophetically. However, as mentioned above, the congregation is forbidden to speak when the congregation meets. Instead of allowing the Ruach to Minister to us, He is silenced. We no longer are blessed by listening to heartfelt testimonies, prophecies, and other gifts that function according to the will of the Father. This is very sad indeed, and places the few leaders way above the other brethren in the Body of Mashiach. This is the Nicolaitans spirit, which Yehoshua hates. **(Chazon/Revelation 2:6)**

Yehovah can use anyone who obeys Him, and serves Him with holy fear, not just the elect ministers. He seldom uses the pastor to give a prophetic word. Not all pastors are used by Yehovah to prophesy. Their main gift is teaching.

The assembly is the one to bring out the needed prophetic Word from the Throne of Yehovah that will set free the discouraged sheep.

The assembly does not have to wait on the "prophetic confer- ences" to receive a "prophetic word." Those prophetic pastors are not able to meet the needs of the congregation. Not everyone will attend because they have to pay large amounts to get a Word. Many people refuse to pay for that. It is like going to a witch, they say. Frankly Yehoshua said,

"Heal the sick, cleanse the lepers, raise the dead, cast out demons. Freely you have received, freely give." Mattithyahu/ Matthew 10:8.

The prophets are highly paid, which the congregation is charged to pay for the word they receive. Most times the word they receive is a simple word of knowledge. They could receive that word every time they go to the service, if the pastor would allow the Holy Spirit to speak through the congregation.

When the pastors freely give, they will freely also receive. Yehovah would always provide for their needs if they would trust Him. People would freely give without been forced to pay for a word from the prophets. This control has to be removed from the congregation. The Ruach haQodesh does not offend anyone, He ministers freedom and encouragement. The pastors should never stop the Ruach haQodesh from speaking in His Meetings.

Yehovah has to reign or He is no King at all! Now is the time for reformation. The Body of Messiah has to be free to operate in all the gifts in the meetings as it was in the beginning when the apostle Paul wrote the letter to the Qorin'tiyim. If this does not happen Yehovah will remove the shepherds and the doors of the churches may end up to be shot down. It is time for Yehovah to rule in the assemblies. He will use whatever means to accomplish His will.

I know of friends of mine who were anointed to prophesy during the special time in the services. The pastor allowed it for a season, then he forbade anyone from using the gifts of the Ruach haQodesh during the service. My friend left and went to another congregation.

But she was not the only one that left, others have also left in order to be free to serve Yehovah. They were disappointed with the church and started their home groups as Yehovah led them to do. No wonder we have so many house fellowships. It could be that Yehovah is preparing us for when the congregations will go underground because of persecution.

Yehovah will be dealing with much secret sin through the gifts of the Ruach haQodesh/Holy Spirit. And pastors must allow Him to do so, or they will be removed.

Clemens discovered sin in the choir. When the choir director needed a choir he enlisted anyone in the church to be in it. That proved to be very bad choice. Clemens was leading a healing ministry and one lady who was in the choir came to confess her sin of incest. She actually had sex with her own children! Clemens was aghast! That woman prayed and she repented. She continued to be singing in the choir. However later on she confessed to Clemens that she had been given the children for the weekend and she molested them again. When Clemens informed the choir director of this situation he did nothing about it. She was not removed from singing. This should not have happen. The worship team needs to be holy. How can a person who is addicted to such horrible sin be in the worship team?

Some church leaders teach that the parishioners will grow up spiritually when they are kept busy in some ministry. But that never happens because they do not have the necessary time to minister intimately to Yehovah. They are always rushing to go church to do what the pastor wants them to do. But they have no personal time to minister to Yehovah, they Father in Heaven. This is very sad indeed!

Ministry needs to be holy and should express the maturity of the minister. There is such thing as transference of spirits that takes places when ministering, and many times the spirit is not the Ruach haQodesh, but an evil spirit. Sin has to be eradicated before a person ministers on the altars or in any other ministry. Clemens is praying for this and other problems in the Body of Mashiach.

Being busy in ministry does not make a person holy, but can literally destroy them. For they still continue sinning and no one knows what they do in secret. And even if they know, they disregard the sin, and simply let them continue ministering thinking they will be healed. If the gift of word of knowledge was active in the congregation this woman may have been set free. The choir director neglected to minister correctly to this woman. His duty was to temporarily remove her from singing, and minister to her in order for her soul to be cleansed. She needed to go to the Courts Rooms of Heaven, and to personally repent of all sin. Her blood line needed to be cleansed from all iniquity through her repentance. She needed to consecrate her life to Yehovah and choose to serve Him alone. For at that time, she was serving Satan, not Yehovah. he had legal right to her life. But the Choir Pastor completely ignored Clemens information. Why? Whatever the reason, there is no excuse. Could it be that he was also involved in secret sin? We do not know, and we hope he was pure.

Once again, let us remember that each of us has a specific calling, and we are responsible to find out what it is. Yehovah has a book written in Heaven about our life. We should aim to accomplish His will, not the leader's will.

Sadly, generally speaking, the congregation is only allowed to come to worship and pay the tithes. And the pastor uses them according to his will, and not necessarily according to the will of Yehovah.

The widows and orphans are neglected. The strangers are also not helped in their transition.

The followers of Mashiach have forfeited their duties toward the poor, and have allowed the government to care of them. But the tithes and offerings are there to be used not only to support the pastor, but also to help those in need. We learn in the Book of Acts that the congregation shared everything with those who had need. As result of them sharing their own things with those who did not have, miracles took place. We miss this aspect of ministry therefore Yehovah is not moving in the miraculous as in the book of Acts because we are not taking care of the sheep.

We would avoid many problems if we would wait on Yehovah before getting involved in any ministry. If we venture in a ministry that Yehovah has not called us to do, we will fall miserably. We will get into stress, and bear no fruit. Yehovah desires to let us know His will for our lives, for He knows that we are but dust. He created us from dust and to dust we shall return. We need His supernatural guidance to avoid pitfalls. He is willing to help us anytime we need. He longs to have a continuing close relationship with each of us. He longs to reveal His will to us, but we must spend time in His Presence daily. He is the most caring Father we could ever desire. Our earthly fathers may not have been very carrying toward us, because they too were nothing but dust! But our Father in Heaven is perfect and loves us perfectly. He will always be available to us when we need Him.

Each of us, as human beings, sometimes need a long time to learn, but Yehovah is patient. He loves us and He is very merciful and gracious to us. He gives us time to grow up. He continues to lovingly teach us until we learn the lesson. When we miss the mark He forgives us. His ways are wonderful, not to be compared to anyone here on earth. There is no one else like Him. He is not caught by surprise by our mistakes, for He knows the end from the beginning. Yeshua said,

"I am the Aleph and the Tav, the Beginning and the End," *says Adonai, "Who is and who was and who is to come, the Almighty."* **Chazon/Revelation 1:8**

"I am the Aleph and the Tav, the First and the Last." **Chazon/Revelation 1:11**

CHAPTER 17

Changes

After Clemens went through so many disappointments, she was led by the Ruach haQodesh to call her good friend Annabel in Vancouver, Washington. She needed to be among friends who loved her and did not judge her in any way. Actually they had been always very supportive and encouraging. Never the less, while on the airplane she was wondering, *"When am I going to fulfill my calling?"* But those thoughts vanished as soon as she landed on the Portland Airport. Annabel came to pick her up with her husband and she was as joyful as always. Clemens would be having a very pleasant time of restoration while in Vancouver.

Annabel was always very uplifting and encouraging. She was also a gardener and raised most of the vegetables she prepared for her family. She was an excellent cook and a prayer warrior. It was an excellent time of refreshing for Clemens to be there at that particular time of her life. Both enjoyed great times of fellowship together. They shared the Word and prayed together most mornings if Annabel would be not going to work. She would fix breakfast and then they would read the Scriptures and pray together. Having both a close relationship with Yehoshua is what made their relationship so special. They would wait upon Him and He would be always blessing them with His Presence. Yehoshua and the presence of Yehovah's Ruach haQodesh is the most important element in any relationship among believers. He is the only One who can unite His Body that is us, His children.

When men try to bring unity in the Body of Mashiach is like mixing oranges and apples and make them one fruit, this is almost like syncretism. We cannot unite with those religious groups that do not believe in the essentials of the gospel. Yet, this is what a religious leader is now doing. However, that religion has done it since its inception. We must unite with those of like faith. Not all gods are the One True Elohim with different names as he is now teaching the public.

The Word of Elohim and His Ruach haQodesh is the reason we can have great fellowship among believers. We love one another even in our diversities.

While at Annabel's home Clemens was able to have the privacy she needed to seek Her Saviour as long and as often as she desired. She enjoyed His presence in a peaceful and holy atmosphere. Both Annabel and her husband were assistant pastors at a congregation in Portland, Oregon. Therefore they were spiritually, very compatible and could talk and act their faith without hindrances or argumentation.

Clemens was so thankful to Yehovah for giving her such good friends. She would have been homeless at that point of her life. However Yehovah had given her this family to help her in times of need. They knew each other many years. Actually they met after Clemens mother went to be with her Savior. She went to Vancouver, Washington, to visit with her friend Rachel during this very difficult time in her life. Annabel and Rachel were friends therefore she also became friends with Annabel. Rachel was another one of her Divine Connections. Annabel and Clemens continued their relationship all the days of their lives. In fact they also went to Canada together. Annabel was Canadian and most of her relatives lived there.

When Clemens came back from the Philippines for a few months of evangelism, Yehovah led her to go to Canada for ministry, but she had no money. Yehovah provided her the means for the full trip. When Clemens called her friend Annabel to inform her that she would be going to Canada, she offered Clemens to drive to Canada with her for free! Annabel had to return the Van that her Canadian brother had left with her in Vancouver when he visited.

Meanwhile Clemens had not money to fly to Vancouver, Washington, for she had only 32 dollars left when she came back from the Philippines! However Yehovah had prepared another very good friend, Ariel, in California to help her reach Annabel in Vancouver. She invited Clemens to come and spend a few days with her on the way to Vancouver. When she realizes that Clemens had no money for the airfare, from Maui to California, she sent the money for the airfare, and then she also provided her with a ticket for the bus to go to Vancouver. Indeed this trip was organized by her Savior. Clemens reached Washington, and after a few days Clemens and Annabel began the long trip to Winnipeg, Canada. It was a long, but pleasant trip.

They drove through some beautiful landscape. Clemens was amazed of the different colors of the land as they drove through the states. Finally after three days they arrived at their destination. Annabel introduced Clemens to some of her friends in Canada, and when she left, one week later, Clemens was asked to stay with Annabel friends. Clemens had not money to go anywhere, until a week later when she met a Christian who had a room for rent. She needed the freedom to be able to do her ministry. And his room was perfect, for the owner of the house worked every day, and she was alone. She could pray and seek Yehovah. Now Clemens had to completely trust Yehovah to open up doors for her ministry.

Clemens met other new friends who opened doors for her ministry. Yehovah's grace was upon her, and she had opportunity to preach nine times while in Winnipeg, Canada. The Ruach haQodesh visited the youth, and restored some lost sheep, with His Presence and power. It was an awesome time of visitation for everyone present.

Yehovah blessed Clemens tremendously during that trip. She was there two and half months. When she left Canada, she carried with her great memories, that she cherished the remainder of her earthly life.

While visiting Annabel in Vancouver, she had enough time to continue writing her women's devotional, and also her autobiography. Everything was wonderful, but she began to feel unrestful and somewhat anxious not knowing how she could fulfill her calling. She began to worry about her future. She was always at home, and she needed to be busy ministering to the lost. Annabel house was in the outskirts of Vancouver, therefore she needed to get an apartment somewhere around there. However the rentals in that area were too high for her income.

One day she felt led to call Marge, one of Katrina's old friends. She let her know about her finances and her housing situation, and Marge suggested she call Katrina in Oklahoma, and she gave Clemens Katrina's phone number. She was very thankful to Marge and did not waste any time. Immediately she called Katrina who was now in Oklahoma City. Katrina was very happy to help and in just a few days she found an apartment for Clemens.

When Clemens got the phone call informing her of the apartment, she immediately told Annabel who was a little sad to see her leaving, but she understood. While preparing to leave Clemens knew in her heart that Yehovah would open doors in Oklahoma for her to minister. She bought an airline ticked and flew to Oklahoma.

Chapter 18

New Adventure

Katrina picked up Clemens from the airport and took her to her home. Then both went to see the apartment. Clemens signed the contract for one year. Now she needed furniture, and everything else to survive. Katrina helped her by driving her around the stores to buy what she needed. She was very happy that Clemens came.

Clemens was not very impressed with the city. Her heart was always in Hawaii, but now she would have to enjoy living there at least for one year. However, she missed the flowers and the sunshine of the Hawaiian Islands. Oklahoma City was another world, much different than what she was familiar with. But now, at least for one year, she had to be there, and thanked Yehovah for her friends who helped her to get the apartment. She prayed for open doors for her ministry, and Yehovah certainly answered!

However, now she had to learn to take the city bus to go anywhere. While on Maui, she would walk to wherever she needed to go in the city she usually lived in. But in this city she was forced to take the bus to go almost anywhere.

However, there were some nice things that she could not have in Hawaii. She loved when winter came and the snow began to fall. She saw black ice for the first time in her life. She loved the snow. It was so beautiful when it snowed! Of course she did not have to drive on it; therefore she could enjoy the beauty without any concern!

Yehovah used Clemens to minister at a Four Square Assembly during her special time in Oklahoma. The pastor of that Assembly invited her to preach a few times, which encouraged her very much. Yehovah used her prophetic gift almost in every service. She also did a two days Women's Encounter at the Congregation, which was very successful. The Encounter consisted of preaching several specific teachings, with personal prayer ministry. Most women repented of some sin in their lives. It was a very refreshing time for every woman that attended.

The ministry is called an Encounter because each woman should experience a personal encounter with Yehovah, and Yehoshua during this shot in. They were away from their homes and slept at the Congregation ministry hall for one night. Some women took sleeping bags, others only blankets and pillows. But the fellowship time was indeed great and uplifting for everyone.

Clemens met some new sisters during her time in Oklahoma, who became her friends for life. While there she also finished writing her autobiography, which was immediately published. Meanwhile Katrina and Clemens became very good friends. However, Clemens began to notice something disturbing about Katrina. She could not imagine what the problem would be.

Katrina was mostly very nice, but other times she snapped at Clemens for no apparent reason. She also could be very demanding toward her son because he spent most of the day in his bedroom. He was a recluse. He avoided people as much as he could. His mother was concerned about him, who could be watching pornography secretly. Both of us had no idea what he did, but we surely prayed for him.

One day Clemens asked Katrina about her family. She told her that her father was born in Ireland, as she was. She believed he had Jewish blood. He had been divorced once, but now he was married with a woman who was a witch, according to Katrina. This second wife did not get along with Katrina at all. She took all her father's finances which left Katrina without inheritance. She felt alienated from her father and even from her mother at that time. Her father was also very sick with cancer.

At that time, Katrina did not have a good relationship with her father or mother. She said that her father had changed so much since he married his second wife. He was not the same father that she knew. She missed her father's affection, especially since Katrina did not get along with her own mother. She felt unloved and rejected, and probably that was the root of her temper at times. That lack of love may have been why she had so much anxiety in her heart. Yehovah does not want us to have any form of fear, or anxiety, which causes many sicknesses and diseases. His Word instructs us to not be anxious.

Be anxious for nothing, but in everything by prayer and supplication, with thanksgiving, let your requests be made known to Elohim; and the peace of Elohim, which surpasses all understanding, will guard your hearts and minds through Messiah Yeshua. **Pilippiyim/Philippians 4:6 -7**

Yehoshua invites us to come to Him, and He will give us His rest.

"Come to Me, all you who labor and are heavy laden, and I will give you rest. Take My yoke upon you and learn from Me, for I am gentle and lowly in heart, and you will find rest for your souls. For My yoke is easy and My burden is light." Mattithyahu/ Matthew 11:28-30

But during those days she continually fought with her mother. Although I know that she loved her mother, however she seemed to have deep roots of unforgiveness. Maybe we will discover the root of the unforgiveness later on.

Katrina's two boys gave her some problems. She allowed the older son Mitz to go to Arabia to be with his father. He worked there for a while. Katrina was concerned that he may have left his faith in Yehoshua. She prayed a lot and called him often on the phone as any mother would. She loved her two boys. Eventually he did accept the Muslim faith, which, probably was the cause of her anguish that caused her to be moody. Katrina had been married with a Saudi Arabian man for several years. He loved to live in Saudi Arabia with his concubine, and never wanted to convert to Christianity. That of course was a problem in her life, because he would have wanted his children to be with him. But she always prayed to Yehovah, and He kept her children close to her wherever she lived, except now that she allowed her older son to spend some time with his father in Arabia.

CHAPTER 19

Preparation

While in Oklahoma, Rick, the apartment manager on Maui called Clemens offering her one apartment immediately. But she could not accept at that time because of the contract she had signed when she moved into the apartment in Oklahoma.

The manager was disappointed but he understood, and kept her name on the list for the next apartment that would be available. She was very happy about the offer, however she had to wait another two months before she could leave. If she would leave ahead of time, she would have to pay 1000 dollars penalty to the landlord! She had no choice but to wait and hope that he would give her the apartment when she would come back to Maui. Finally the time came for her to be able to leave. But before leaving, she needed to stay a few days with Katrina until she could fly out. Katrina was still preoccupied about Clayton her younger son. She feared for his mental and spiritual health. Clemens and Katrina continued to pray for him, and also for her other son in Arabia. Yehovah gives us rest as we trust in Him to be in control of our lives. But we must have a deep relationship with Him. We must seek His presence and worship Him. Worship is the key for our wellbeing. When we worship Him, we lay aside our problems and simply yield our whole lives in to His care. Worship is the best cure against fears and anxiety. When we enter into His Presence we simply trust Him, and he comes to us giving us His shalom, and His rest.

Clemens and Katrina strengthened their relationship at that time because of their times of prayer together. Katrina was much younger than Clemens and she loved her like a mother.

Before Clemens left, Katrina began to speak a little more about her personal life. Clemens discovered that Katrina had joined an assembly that also had a School of Ministry. She took a class to be able to go to mission field. Her desire was to go to Muslim countries to teach the Word of Yehovah. She also went to another Bible School to get more training. Her desire was always missions especially to the Arab nations.

Then one day she had an appointment with her doctor. The reason for this appointment was because she had been having big problems with her back. When she came back home she was concerned about something. I asked her what the problem was. She let me know that the doctor told her to see an oncology specialist. But she did not want to accept the fact that she had cancer. She said, *"I will not go. I will be fine." Yehovah will take care of me."* She did not want to believe the doctor, and refused to mention the word cancer. She was now a Christian, a Spirit filled believer in Yehoshua, and she believed that she would be healed. Clemens tried to convince her to go to the specialist, but she refused. Katrina was very adamant about it. She knew better. It is very possible that Katrina was afraid to find out the real truth, and avoided going to the specialist. Clemens felt sorry for her, but she could do nothing to help her, except pray and encourage her. Destiny had to take its course.

Katrina's back pain continued to increase. A few days later Katrina took Clemens to the airport.

C H A P T E R 20

Clemens Back Home

Clemens arrived to Maui, and after a short while she was able to be settled in her new apartment in Kahului. Just a few months after she arrived back to Maui, Yehovah instructed her to leave the assembly she had been ministering with for a very long time. One main reason He wanted her to leave was that that assembly taught Replacement Theology NAR (New Apostolic Reformation), Kingdom Now, and the Seven Mountains. Replacement Theology is the false teaching that the church has now replaced Israel. This teaching had become a movement in the world. That particular assembly had accepted that teaching and all the others mentioned above. Yehovah was not happy about that. They also refused to keep the fourth Commandments, which Yehovah has given us with the other nine Commandments. Yehovah Commands us to keep the Sabbath day holy. However, this Commandment has been removed in the third Century AC by the Roman Catholic Church because of anti-Semitism. They removed some Commandments in order to accommodate their own. I speak about this fact in my blogs. Sadly the churches have not gone back to their roots after the reformation with Martin Luther. However, in his 100 thesis that He placed on the Vatican door, he did not include that the Catholic Church removed the Sabbath, all the Feasts, and Dietary laws. He did not have that complete revelation. But he did a great reformation in spite of the known fact that he turned against the Jews and cursed them.

The assembly Clemens attended did also not teach on the Feasts of Yehovah as we read specifically in Leviticus 23. The reason for that may be that the Feasts include at least two extra Sabbaths or days of rest during their celebration. The Scriptures are specific about these teachings, and Yehovah calls them "My Feasts" not Jewish Feasts! They are His Feasts. He ordained for Israel to come to Yerushalayim three times in a year to celebrate.

Three times in a year all your males shall appear before Yehovah your Elohim in the place which He chooses; at the Feast of Unleavened Bread, at the Feast of weeks, and at the Feast of Tabernacles; and they shall not appear before Yehovah empty –handed. **Devarim/Deuteronomy 16:16**

If we love Yehovah we should read and obey His Word, however, the assemblies have chosen to abstain from teaching and keeping these important historic and prophetic shadow pictures of the Life and Death, and Second Coming, of our Savior Yehoshua haMashiach. They are to be celebrated only three times in the year, and are very important to Yehovah and to each believer. They are also called Moedim, or Appointed Times. During these special times Yehovah visits His People.

Each of us is required to read the Word and be convinced of the truth. In reality individually we must appear before Mashiach. Our pastors will not be there. We are personally responsible to read and obey His Word.

That assembly I had been part of for such long time also completely disregarded the Dietary Laws. They consider it irrelevant to their walk of faith. Could it be the reason why so many parishioners were dying with cancer and were afflicted with the same sickness as the heathen? The Scriptures promises we will not be affected with such diseases if we obey His Word. Besides this fact, those foods are not beneficial to our health. Those animals that He forbids us to eat were not created for consumption, and our Good Father let us know in advance in order to protect us. We will remain healthy if we obey His dietary instructions.

Please read Devarim/Deuteronomy 28:1-14; 15-68. This chapter begins to list all the blessings if we obey Him, and then lists all the sickness, and other problem we will be afflicted if we do not obey His Word. Please read the whole chapter beginning with the blessings, and continue reading all the curses that follow the disobedient. The death of Yehoshua did not change that. Satan is still your enemy and he will afflict those who do not obey the Commandments.

Most of the assemblies disregard the Feast of Yehovah and other special teachings. They say that they pertain only to the Jews as though we are not grafted in to the same tree! We are together part of the same Body of Mashiach! He is not divided. There is only One Body, Jews and Gentile converts. And the tree that the Gentiles are nourished by it is the same tree as the Hebrew people!

The problem is that most assemblies, which are called churches, are in apostasy since the beginning of the organized church, but they do not realize their error. They forget that the Nazarene obeyed all the Commandments. The Apostle Shaul/Paul was one of them who always tried his best to be in Yerushalayim/Jerusalem for the Passover and all the Feasts. He kept the Sabbath and so did all followers of Yehoshua. The Sabbath and the Feasts have not been changed by Yeshua. In fact He declared that He did not come to destroy the Torah/Law and the Prophets, but to fulfill.

"Do not think that I came to destroy the Torah/Law or the Prophets. I did not come to destroy but to fulfill. For assuredly, I say to you, till Heaven and earth pass away, one jot or one tittle will by no means pass from the Law till all is fulfilled. Whoever

therefore breaks one of the least of these Commandments, and teaches men so, shall be called least in the kingdom of Heaven; but whoever does and teaches them, he shall be called great in the kingdom of Heaven. For I say to you, that unless your righteousness exceeds the righteousness of the scribes and Pharisees, you will by no means enter the kingdom of heaven." **Mattithyahu/Matthew 5:17-20**

He fulfilled the Torah (Law) when He abolished the animal sacrifices, and became our Passover Lamb. We have no longer need to kill animals and apply their blood, for Yehovah paid the full price for our salvation. The Commandments were never meant to save us, but they are holy because they give us understanding of our short comings. The penalty for sin is death, and Yehoshua gave His life to redeem us and restore our relationship with our Father in Heaven.

Yehovah has not two kinds of children. One gets all the blessings, and the other only a few. We are all equal. If we would think that way, then we should keep none of the Commandments and we would be lawless! No one could be entering the Kingdom of Heaven. Sure, we are saved by grace. When we were born again, we repented of all our sins, which mean we had broken all the Commandments. This is what sin is all about. Therefore after the salvation experience we choose to obey His Commandments because now we love Him, and serve Him with all our hearts. He has given His Ruach haQodesh in order to be able to obey Him. He is our Helper **(Yochanan/John 14: 16-17).** We cannot choose to keep only what is convenient to us, and leave the others to the "Jews." We are all His children, and He expects all of us, His children, to love, serve, and obey Him with all our heart.

Yeshua once said,

"If you love Me keep My Commandments." And I will pray the Father and He will give you another Helper, that He may

abide with you forever- the Spirit of Truth, Whom the world cannot receive, because it neither sees Him nor knows Him; but you know Him, For He dwells with you and will be in you. I will not leave you orphans; I will come to you." **Yochanan/ John 14:15-18**

I heard a good church going friend saying that all Yehoshua said to obey is two Commandments. But she failed to realize that the two Commandments, to love Yehovah with all our hearts, mind, soul and strength, and our neighbor as ourselves include the whole Torah, what is called "Law." Actually Torah means utterance, teaching, instruction or revelation for Elohim. It derives from*"horah,"* which means direct and teach, and comes from *"yara"* meaning: to shoot or throw.

The commandments are holy, and teach us how to live a holy life. The two Commandments encompass, all the Commandments in the Word of Elohim! So when we obey them, we are indeed obeying all Commandments. When we sin, we must repent of the specific sin, not simply saying to Yehovah, "Sorry I did not love You enough, and I did not love my neighbor as myself." You and I have to repent speaking the specific sin we committed, or which Commandment we have broken. He has given us detailed Commandments, and He expects us to be specific.

He said the Holy Spirit was with them while He was with them. Here is the Mystery of the Triune Elohim. Yehoshua is in the Father, and the Father is in Him, and the Holy Spirit (Ruach haQodesh) is of the Father and the Son. He lives in us, and when the Ruach is in us, the Father and the Son is also in us spiritually.

When Yeshua was with the apostles, and He had been telling them that He would leave, but not to worry, for He would be preparing a place for them. They also would be able to go later on. Thomas had a problem with His Words. (See Yochanan 14:1-5) Yehoshua declared to them the following,

"I am the Way, the Truth, and the Life. No one comes to the Father except through Me. If you had known Me, you would have known My Father also; and from now on you know Him and have seen Him." Philip said to Him, 'Adonai, show us the Father, and it is sufficient for us.' Yeshua said to him, "Have I been with you so long, and yet you have not known Me Philip? He who has seen Me has seen the Father; so how can you say, 'Show us the Father'? Do you not believe that I am in the Father, and the Father in Me? The Words that I speak to you I do not speak on My own authority; but the Father who dwells in Me does the works. Believe Me that I am in the Father and the Father in Me, or else believe Me for the sake of the works themselves." Yochanan/John 14:6-11

Indeed when we see Yehoshua we have also seen the Father! Let us therefore obey Him, for His Word is the Word of Yehovah.

Once again, let us remember, that if we say we love Yehoshua, we must obey what He has taught us. He has not taken, or removed, anything away from the Word, for He is the Word of Elohim in the Flesh.

In the beginning was the Word, and the Word was with Elohim, and the Word was Elohim. Yochanan/John 1:1

And now let us continue to hear what Clemens did when she returned to her local assembly. While still in Oklahoma Yehovah let her know prophetically to not get involved in her old assembly. She did not know the reason why. However, she ended up helping them when asked, and later on she volunteered two days a week, but they hired her full time. She disobeyed Her Elohim and He was not happy about it. Yehovah did not bless her good will. He had other plans. He told her plainly to leave that congregation or He would leave her. When He spoke she immediately obeyed.

She was actually relieved in her heart, when He told her to leave, for she had been feeling uneasy while helping them. She did not feel that was what she was supposed to be doing. But she still did it. She did not realize that she was sinning. But now that He has spoken to her, she was very happy to receive His direction for her life.

However, at first when He spoke to her to leave that assembly she did not understand the reason. But eventually she knew and realized she should have left a long time ago!

After leaving that congregation, her life was changed. She no longer had a desire to go back as she did often in the past. Yehovah had set her completely free, and she enjoyed that freedom. He told her that if she continued to attend that assembly He would not longer be with her. He had other plans for her, and soon she would find out.

She began to do a Friday night Shabbat meeting, and the group grew to about twelve persons. She began teaching on the Sabbath and the feasts of Yehovah. The students were very eager to learn and had wonderful times of fellowship together. After they learned about the Feasts they began to study the scriptures from Bereshit/Genesis. Clemens taught the weekly Torah teachings. This portion of study is called Parashah and includes portions the first five books of the Scriptures, (Bereshit/Genesis through Devarim/Deuteronomy), and some portions of the Prophets and of the Renewed Covenant, known as the New Testament. Clemens and the students enjoyed these weekly meetings. She would prepare a light dinner, and after the dinner they would study the Word together. The weekly Parashah was only a few chapters long, but it helped to strengthen each one and brought unity in their common faith.

Although believers in the Messiah, they felt that they had been as *lost sheep,* because they never knew how the Feasts related to the gospel. But now they were learning about their Shepherd and loved

Him in a very special way. They finally felt complete in Him. Until that time, they did not know the Scriptures, but now their eyes were open to the deception they had been receiving in their individual congregations. Each one of them became very much alive as though He had opened their eyes to His Word. They were very happy to learn, and celebrate the Sabbath and all His Feasts.

One day while Clemens was worshiping in the dance to Yehovah, He spoke to her saying, "*You are Jewish.*" Clemens was in shock! But she reasoned in her mind that according to the Scriptures she was adopted and became part of the olive tree of Israel. However, He did not say, that she was adopted as a Jew, but: "*You are Jewish.*" Shortly she received two confirmations that she was indeed Jewish. At the same time, she also began to do some research concerning her roots which confirmed what she already knew.

For a while Clemens ministered exclusively to Yehovah and taught the Bible studies. In due time she began to do the radio broadcast as she did in the past, which she enjoyed doing very much. But her ministry was mostly to Him, and concentrated herself to do only what her Elohim would instruct her to do. The pressure of doing things she had been doing for years was lifted up. For the first time in years she felt free and content to serve Him. She sensed that all the struggles concerning ministry had lifted. Finally she did not have to force herself to do what was asked of her. She only did what He led her to do. That alone was a tremendous blessing in her life. Yehovah is gracious and He waits on us, but if we do not respond He let us know what He expects of us. If we love Him, we will obey Him.

CHAPTER 21

Returned

One day as Clemens was preparing her radio messages the phone rang. Katrina was on the phone. *"Can I come over and stay at your house a few days?"* *"Sure, but you only can stay a couple days, I am not allowed to have guests for more than one week."* *"OK, that will be fine."* Then Clemens said, *"You may have to sleep on the couch."* And she answered, *"I bring an air mattress."* *"OK."* *"I come over now"* *"OK, I'll see you soon."* Katrina was in a big hurry to come to see Clemens, it seemed. Clemens sensed that Katrina needed time out from her mother. She did not sound peaceful. Something was bothering her. Immediately she stopped taping the message for the radio broadcast in order to prepare for her visit. Clemens checked to see if she had enough food in the house for her friend, and she was happy to notice that there was enough to share.

Katrina arrived and immediately unloaded her trauma. *"My mother and I fought. She is so mad, I cannot stay with her, I have to get away, I can't take it anymore."* She began to share about her teen years. According to Katrina her mother had a bad temper. Katrina never felt loved by her mother or anyone else in her family. Her mother had gotten a divorce early in her marriage, and she remarried with a man who had a very bad temper who abused her younger sister consistently. No matter how Katrina tried to stop him, he would continue to beat her little sister. This was the main cause why she had run away from home, and fell into sexual relationships trying to find that love she missed in her home.

She would run out of the house for months at the time. No one missed her. Then one day she discovered that she was pregnant. Katrina did not feel shame or remorse at this time. Her mother had also been very much a free woman. Katrina may have thought that the way she was living was the way to live.

But now she needed to know what to do with a baby growing in her womb. She went home to tell her mother, but her uncle who heard her conversation immediately gave the solution to her minor problem. He told her, *"No problem, here is the money, go get an abortion."* And so she did. At this point she did not yet realize of the gravity of her action. She did not consider the "thing" growing in her was alive and that it was her own flesh and blood. After that experience she continued her free life style. She became pregnant again. At first she thought that maybe this time her mother would beat her up, or do something terrible to her. But this did not happen. She seemed to ignore the situation. Someone handed her the money and told her *"Go and take care of it."* She went and got the second abortion. Now she murdered two human beings. Guilt began to surface, but it was not enough to make her run to Elohim because she did not know Him. No one taught her the Word of Yehovah. No one in the family taught her about her need to know her Creator. They did not attend a fellowship or bibles study. She did not know Elohim. No one, in her family, seemed to have fear of Yehovah. If they did they would not let her get abortions one after another.

In mercy and truth Atonement is provided for iniquity; And by the fear of Yehovah one departs from evil. **Mishley/Proverbs 16:6**

A wise man fears and departs from evil, but a fool rages and is self-confident. **Mishley/Proverbs 14:16**

They were either heathen or backslidden, she did not know. They lived in darkness and did not discern the gravity and consequences of that darkness. Elohim did not exist for them. If they had known of Him, Katrina did not know, because they never mentioned Him. They ate and drank without a thought of eternity.

Her family was lost in sin. They did not serve Yehovah and were in bondage to Satan, but did not know, they were blind. Their blindness caused Katrina to grow up without knowledge of Elohim. She did not receive any good teaching concerning human behavior. She had no idea about been pure, or respecting her own body. What she saw in her house was actually demonic. They lived as heathen, or without knowledge of the Holy One. They were all *lost sheep*. They needed to repent, but did not recognize their need for it. They lived in the world serving self. They were oblivious of their need to repent. They did not consider one single thought that they may ended up in a place of torment if they did not stop their lifestyle. Sin desensitizes a person. "Live and let live," but do not bring Elohim into the picture. That family did not consider they were murdering their descendants. Their heart was hard as granite stone. Katrina had three more abortions. She could have had five live children, but had none. Now her soul was wounded it seemed without possible repair. She felt empty and useless. No family to turn to, and to get real love. No one cared.

"What is there about life? I lost my virginity; my self esteem, and now I killed my own children" "My mother hates me, and I am all alone." "I wonder if I had boys or girls? "What name could I have called these children?" "Is there a God that cares for me?" "Is there anyone that can help me?"

She chose to shake off those thoughts, and continued to be promiscuous as before. Now she had lost all self respect. Who would marry her? After she killed her five children, she was now a series killer. But that thought did not come to her mind because she was still a *lost sheep* who had no Shepherd. She was still wondering in the wilderness, however, the Shepherd would one day come into her life and rescue her from her sin.

Finally a young man asked her to marry him, and she accepted him. They were married in a very short time. He was a handsome Saudi Arabian young man. He seemed very polite and courteous with her family when she introduced him to them. And they did not question him. The family encouraged her, and helped her to prepare for her wedding. Maybe her generous uncle was the one who financially helped her. He had paid the money for her abortions, and it is possible that he is the one who helped paying for her marriage expenses. But Katrina did not mention who specifically paid for her marriage reception and dowry. However, she married this man and things did change for her. Now she was going to become an idolater without knowing. Her hopes of happiness vanished very quickly in thin air.

Katrina continued to tell Clemens her whole life story. She said, *"I married an Arabian man. He seemed to be very loving. I needed love, and he loved me, or so I thought. After my marriage He took me to Saudi Arabia to stay with him, I had to wear those black long clothes called niqab. I was always watched by the family. My mother in law did not like me. I was a foreigner to her. I felt lonely and trapped. When my husband had visitors I stayed in the kitchen and he only would call me to bring the drinks for him and his guests. I never heard what they talked about." "I was not allowed to visit with him and his guests. They talked a long time, and I was alone. He did not spend time with me." "I felt like a maid. I had not rights. My husband was not the same as in America. He became like a stranger to me. I wanted to leave, but I could not. While there he took me to the Mosque. I had to agree to what they said. I guess I became a Muslim. I was there for several years.We left America after we had two children." "I did not like that kind of life. Eventually I found a Christian family who helped me to get away, and I came back home to Oklahoma City with my two children and no husband or family member that cared." "Nevertheless, I kept in touch with him, and sometimes He would send me some money for his sons. But he wanted them there with him. I refused However, I refused until lately when my older son wanted to go and I let him go. He was now 18 years old, and could do what he wanted to do. However, I prayed for him to return, and eventually he came back home. Life is hard when you have two children. It is also though to rent a place to live with kids."*

Clemens asked her, *'How come you became a Muslim? Did you not read the Bible?'* *"No. When I married him, I did not know God was real. I did not believe that there was a God that could love me." 'No one witness to you?' "No. Not until I came back from Saudi Arabia." "What happened then? Did anyone invite you to church?" "Well, yes, and I also watched television and got interested in God." "When did you get saved?" "After I came back from Arabia I was in Oklahoma City several months when a girl, who also became my close friend, took me to her church." "Did you like it?" "Yes. She took me to a ministry meeting, and one woman saw a vision of me with the niqab, black Burqa, and she commanded the devil to leave me. I felt the power of God come upon me, and then I felt free." "So you believed in Yeshua that day?' "Yes, and they had me renounce the Muslim spirit. I had to renounce Allah, and then I prayed a little prayer."*

"How did you feel when that happened?' "Oh, I felt as though the heavy weight had lifted off from me. I felt so clean." Now I could call on Yehovah and He would help me." "I had no knowledge of Yehovah until that day, and I did not know that He loved me. I did not know that Yeshua, Yehovah's only Son had become man and died for my sins." I never knew that Yehovah could love me, especially after I killed my five babies!"

Katrina was overcome with emotion when she told this part of her story. She wept uncontrollably. Clemens was there to comfort her, and assure her that Yehovah had forgiven all her sins. She prayed for Yehovah to heal the pain in her heart. She had gone through so much pain and sorrow, and now Yehovah was restoring her to become the woman He had created her to be. Katrina also knew that her babies were now in heaven, and that helped her to somehow release her pain to Yehovah.

Clemens knew when to talk and when to be silent. Now she simply let Yehovah's compassion and love fill Katrina's heart.

During that visit Katrina mentioned George, a young friend she knew in Molokai. He seemed to like her and she was planning to go there to see him. Clemens did not sense in her heart that it would be a good thing to do. But Katrina said that she could live with his mother while she visited. She needed to leave her mother's house, and now she thought that would be a very good opportunity for her. She basically needed a husbands and a place to live.

Katrina stayed with Clemens a few days, and then she went back to her mother, a very changed person. The anger and hostile feeling had been removed by her Savior. His love and His blood cleansed her soul giving her peace.

Katrina after a few days went to Molokai. One day she called Clemens informing her that she was getting married to George. Not too long after this announcement she published the photos of her wedding on face book, and Clemens sensed in her spirit that this young man was not in love with Katrina. He did not show any affection to her new bride. He seemed almost embarrassed. His heart was not with Katrina. But Katrina had made her choice believing he would solve her problems. There was nothing anyone could do now. She was married and she assured Clemens that she really loved him, and that George also loved her.

CHAPTER 22

Memories

It was a very unusual day for Clemens. The weather seemed to be changing as thought a light storm was on the way. It was one of those days that a person feels like having a cup of hot coco and just lay down to rest, or take a long nap. Clemens sat in her living room recliner looking at the light blue sky. There were some clouds that seemed to be dancing around maybe getting ready to release some light showers. She felt very much at peace, and began to think back on her trip to Germany many years ago. The weather there was so different than Hawaii. The sky usually was filled with ominous dark clouds, especially during the winter months. In Germany snow never lacked either in winter or even in spring. Clemens loved the snow and she loved going out into the mountains to admire the trees covered with the fresh fallen snow. Although she did not have too much time to enjoy those escapades do to her job, at times she did go. But when she went she saw the reindeers, which was a real treat for her. The scenery was very beautiful when covered with snow. Germany had many trees everywhere. The water, the weather, and even the snow, was excellent for such trees. While in Germany she also admired some old fashion little towns. She took a little tour on the Main River to admire the landscape with its old fashion houses and little castles. During that time she did not know the cruelty of Hitler, how he had murdered and incinerated the Jewish people. Clemens was a little child at that time. Had she really known this history she probably would had never gone there. She could not have gone to that wilderness of lost sheep! It seems that all Germans had lost their faith. Hitler and the whole nation were encouraged by the very words of the monk Martin Luther, who cursed the Jewish people. Kristallnacht massacre was carried out by Hitler and his army and citizen motivated by his writings against the Jews. He had rejected much of the false teachings of the Roman Catholic Church, but kept the hate for the Jews. Sadly we have no record declaring that he repented of his hate toward the Jews. Many churches still are anti-Semitic.

Hitler became as god to the German citizens. He was able to sway their minds and to convince them that the Jews were not human, and deserve to die, and die quickly by any means. Only a demon possessed person could convince a nation to murder its citizen. He did not stop murdering the Jews in Germany, but he ordered their execution, men, women and children in other nations as well. He had no respect for anyone. He convinced Mussolini to follow him in his quest. Mussolini in Italy was just as guilty of murdering the Jews as Hitler had done, and all those who supported his doctrine and helped him. And let us not forget that even some of the clergy, especially in Italy, were in agreement with the final solution. May Yehovah be merciful to the descendants of those murderous human beings.

While Clemens visited Germany she noticed that they had no real love for Italians, since Mussolini betrayed Hitler, according to some history records. However, Clemens was completely naïve. She had no clue why they ridiculed the Italians and even the Greeks, at times. They actually used derogatory names for them. She felt they were very proud of themselves.

While still thinking on Germany she thought on some unusual friends she met while in that nation. She remembered Mina who was a young lady of about thirty five years. This young lady worked in Munich. Clemens had opportunity to get to know her and learned what kind of life style she had been living. Mina was very open to tell everything she did or did not do. She lived her life without any knowledge of Yehovah. She never spoke about Yehovah or Yehoshua as though Yehovah did not exist. She also never mentioned her mother, her father, or any other member of her family. She gave the impression that they were all dead. But her life style was very worldly. She was very promiscuous as most girls were at that time. She could date a woman or a man. When she got pregnant she would get an abortion without any apparent sense of guilt. She spoke about as if it was a normal thing to do. Many times she did the abortions to herself and explained how to her friends. She was proud to be able to instruct others to do the same. It was gruesome! Although she apparently was very loving, inside of her was a wilderness and chaos. There were no rivers or wells, or any cool fresh clean water. In her landscape there were no perfumed flowers or fruit trees, but only thorns and thistles, and other ugly weeds. She was indeed a lost sheep who needed a Savior, but did not know.

Clemens saw Mina on day, and she noticed that she was very happy. She said that she had fallen in love with a younger man who loved her and he married her. Clemens was surprised for he was at least twenty or more years younger than Mina. Not too long after their marriage she became pregnant and this time she kept the child. She gave birth to a pretty baby girl. This baby was very cute, but her right hand was not formed. It was a stump. Clemens could not yet make the connection with Mina's right which had been used to do evil, and the innocent stump of this little baby girl. Eventually she realized that there was a lesson to be learned. No one knows for sure how many babies she had killed. Mina was a series baby's killer! Sadly now her daughter would never be able to use her right hand, for she had none! Truly the sin of the fathers pass on to the third and fourth generation,

"For I Yehovah am a jealous Elohim visiting the iniquity of the fathers upon the children to the third and fourth generation to those who hate Me." Shemot/Exodus 20:5

While in Germany Clemens was also a *lost sheep*. She had no relationship with her Creator. But after coming back to the united States she had a personal encounter with her Savior and decided to get in touch with Mina. Clemens knew now that Mina was a **lost sheep** who desperately needed to be brought to the Shepherd. Clemens shared her testimony with Mina, and wrote her a passionate letter pleading her to give her life to Yehoshua. Although she was still a new believer herself, and did not yet know many Scriptures, she did her best to share her transformed life, and invited Mina to do the same. Clemens did her best to tell her old friend how happy she felt now that her sins were forgiven. She told her that she also had received the Spiritual prayer language. Yehovah had given her the gift of speaking in tongues; tongues that she never learned. Now Clemens had a personal relationship with the living Elohim. She wanted Mina to repent assuring her that Yehovah would forgive her all her sins. She was very concerned about the spiritual condition of her old friend. Clemens knew that if Mina chose not to repent of her sins she would be lost for eternity.

Of course she did not know if Mina may have been insane? However, she knew that Mina had murdered her own children which was a grave sin, and she needed to make things right with her Creator. And beside those sins, every one of us has sinned, and each of us needs to repent. She also knew that the Blood of Yehoshua would cleanse Mina, if she would call upon His Name.

But Mina's answer to her letter was curt and final. She did not want to hear the salvation message, and said that her relationship with Yehovah was her own personal business. She refused to talk about her personal life. Clemens was very sad, but this situation could only be left in Yehovah's hands, for Clemens could do nothing about it. Those thoughts were making Clemens very sad. She tried to stop thinking about Mina, and she walked toward the kitchen to make herself another cup of warm chocolate. She needed something to help her forget the thought that Mina, if she did not repent, would be going to hell. The best thing to do was to continue thinking on her family, and on other friends she had left in the old country. She got up and looked for the little box that she kept in her closet which contained her family and friends photos.

She found photos of her parents, who now were gone into eternity. She sensed a longing in her heart for her father and mother, but they were gone a long time ago.

There was a photo of her father Yochanan, mother Miryam, and older brother Alonso. Everyone was standing up in that photo, including Clemens. As she contemplated this photo she could not dismiss the fact that she, as a child was very serious. Every photo she took revealed her sadness. She never smiled, maybe because she was self-conscious and did not want to be photographed. She also noticed that her mother never smiled on any of her photos; maybe she also did not want to be photographed! Was this unusual? Maybe it was. This particular photo was taken when she was about ten years old. He older sister Rachael had already gone into eternity.

Clemens was the only daughter now, but felt unloved. Oh, yes, her parents loved her, but she needed more than that. She also grew up feeling that she was different from the other children. She could not fit in with the crowds. What was missing? Eventually she would find out the reason why. Many years later, after she had her encounter with the living Elohim, she understood. He opened her mind and healed her soul.

CHAPTER 23

Reconnect

Clemens stopped looking at the photos for a moment as she remembered a special young girl she met while in Germany. This girl was very pretty and petite. She had very long dark hair and used little makeup. She was very attractive. She knew how to attract men and dressed with very short dresses. Her name was Karin. She was married, but her husband Tommy Grant was in Vietnam. Therefore he gave Karin permission to return to Germany to be with her mother. However to stay idle at home was not what she wanted to do! She needed to be out with people, and found a job at the restaurant bar.

Karin needed to be loved, and she had a few boyfriends while her husband was away. When her husband came back on vacation he found out of his wife's loose lifestyle, but he did not react negatively. He actually saw her while working at that place, but did nothing to stop her. That seemed to be a strange thing to Clemens and all the workers. He was very enigmatic, and spoke very little.

He returned to America to serve his Country, and left his wife in Germany working at the restaurant bar. Karin continued to live her promiscuous life style and she seemed to have no concern whatsoever about her own husband. She loved to be admired, and sex was very important to her. I suppose that because her husband was away, who seemed to be a little frigid, she lacked the love that every wife should receive. It is possible to believe that her husband did not consider this fact, and was not aware of her emotional needs. Karin was very sweet and Clemens liked her, although they never became close friends. However, when Clemens left Germany they exchanged addresses. Eventually Karin also went to America and settled in Arkansas with her husband.

Approximately thirteen years later Clemens remembered Karin's old lifestyle. She knew that Karin did not have a relationship with Yehoshua, and she wanted to get in touch with her. She felt in her heart that she needed to speak with Karin face to face. She wanted to share with her about our life in this world in view of eternity.

She cared so much for Karin that when she took a trip to North Carolina on her way back to Hawaii, she took a bus to Arkansas to meet with her. Karin came to pick her up at the bus stop and drove her to her home. It was very nice to see her friend again. That evening they shared many memories. But Karin seemed changed. Clemens shared about her new faith, but Karin seemed aloof.

The following morning Karin got up and she looked like an old lady. She had no teeth! Top and bottom teeth were missing! Clemens was shocked to see this beautiful woman completely changed for the worse! What happened? Karin prepared some breakfast and some coffee. While sipping the coffee Clemens began to ask her questions. *"Karin, where is your husband?"* Karin explained that he was away on a trip. After eating the breakfast she took Clemens into his private studio and opened some drawers to show Clemens what he had been doing. Clemens had already knowledge of such cult and their paraphernalia. She learned about cults when she had done the studies to become a minister. Clemens was in shock! She had met her husband Tommy when he came to Germany and could not understand why he would do such thing. All cults are against the Creator of the Universe,

Yehovah. Did he learn about this cult while in the Army, or had he always been a Mason? Karin did not have the answer. But she said that he would bring people home and have private secret meetings. She was not allowed to attend any of those meetings in his studio.

Karin continued to share her life with Clemens. She spoke on the day she had lost all her teeth. She said that one day Tommy and Karin and their big dog were in the back yard playing and having fun. Suddenly Tommy had the dog chase his wife. She fell on the steps and the dog would not lose her until her husband made it to stop. Meanwhile all her teeth were broken. She had to get dentures. This was how Tommy avenged himself of his wife adulterous affairs. He did not want to divorce her, but continually abused her. She had to call the police many times on a private police number they had given her. Her husband did not know the number. Tommy acted as a demon possessed man, and she was a prisoner in her own home. Clemens tried to share the gospel again, but Karin was not yet ready to surrender her life to her Creator. She did not understand the reason why she had to be born again. She had been raised a Lutheran. Clemens saw the despair in her old friend, but was unable to help her. Karin was in a state of deep depression, and Yehovah could have helped her, but she refused. She was still a *lost sheep.*

Clemens left that day before Tommy would return home. She did not feel equipped spiritually to deal with such person by herself. Clemens also through her many travels lost contact with Karin, but kept praying for her salvation. She prayed for Yehovah to send someone to Karin to help her surrender her life to her Savior. Yehovah will answer our prayers, especially when we pray in faith for some one's soul. Yehoshua said,

"And whatever things you ask in prayer, believing, you will receive." Mattithyahu/Matthew 21:22

CHAPTER 24

Wonderful Victories

Clemens kept on looking at the photos and found one of her photos holding a newborn baby girl. She was beautiful, and as all babies, innocent and pure. Clemens, at that time was still in her forties, and looked still wrinkle free! This little girl was the daughter of a Filipina young mother. Clemens was serving as assistant pastor in that Island and visited everyone in town. Of course she also visited Arlene. She had come from the Philippines with her husband and a little boy. The little baby girl was born in Hawaii. He came to work for Dole Pineapple Company. Arlene was a Catholic girl, but she claimed to love her Savior. However, she did not want to come to any Bible study or to any of the services. This was a real test to Clemens who was a new pastor. She had to still learn to wait on Yehovah, and to persevere in prayer. She tried to do that, however she expected quick responses. She needed to give the attendance to her pastor every Monday and if she did not have any new person, it did not look too good! This situation was frustrating to her. She was doing all she could, but things were not moving fast enough. She feared her senior pastor would consider her incapable of being in the ministry as a pastor. She was stressed out each time he would call on the phone to ask how the ministry was going. He always wanted to know how many people were coming to church.

Although Arlene seemed very far from surrendering her life completely to Yehovah, Clemens kept visiting her. Many times, Arlene confessed years later, that she would hide and refuse to open her door when she saw Clemens approach her house. However, Clemens was persistent because she loved Arlene as her little daughter. She wanted Arlene to be ready for Heaven when she would die. She was indeed very dear to Clemens and she was very concerned of her spiritual life. Arlene had to surrender her life to Yehoshua, and attend the services and bible studies in order to be discipled. Because Clemens would be soon leaving that island, she wanted to make sure Arlene's name would be written in the Book of Life, and would be serving the Savior with all her heart.

Finally one day Arlene came to the services with her two children. Clemens was so full of joy to see her! What a blessing! She was so thankful to Yehovah for answering her prayers. She was happy to see her taking the first steps toward serving her Savior. Both rejoiced together and had a great time worshiping and thanking Yehovah. Arlene became very faithful and soon was baptized in water in the pool. She was also baptized in the Holy Spirit and spoke in tongues. But, even though Clemens ministered to her husband Rudolf, he would not respond. However although he hardly spoke, he listened attentively to everything Clemens told him about Yehovah and Yehoshua. Many years later he finally gave his life to Yehovah, and became an usher at the church. Eventually both were serving their Savior together with their children. Yehovah had given Clemens a great victory, all praise and glory to Him alone.

Once Arlene began coming to the services, she encouraged other family members also to join the fellowship. Her sister in love, Catherina and her husband Alfonso, and their son became faithful members. Clemens had been also visiting them, and they eventually became missionaries to the Philippines to minister to their relatives and friends. They would take yearly trips; come back to work in Hawaii, and save the money for the next trip. They were also very useful at that local congregation.

Clemens was very concerned about the lost sheep in that little island. She encountered lost souls every day. Not many people were born again. Many workers came to Hawaii only to make money, but did not consider eternal life. She prayed for them and did what she could in the natural to share the gospel of Salvation. Each of us has sinned. Each of us was born into this world with the propensity to sin. Each of us sins. But once we come to Yehovah and enter into Covenant with Him through Yehoshua who shed His Blood to save us, we become holy unto Him. To be holy means to be separate unto Him, and to leave our past passions behind us. It means to come out of the world, although we live in the world, but we no longer do those things of the world. Clemens taught on holiness, and some responded, but others were too concerned about making money. Clemens was so sad realizing that so many people love money above Yehovah. But she continued to pray believing things would change. Eventually that fellowship became stronger in devotion to their Elohim, and in membership.

We cannot live as the heathen and think that Yehovah is so happy to have us that He closes His eyes and let us do what we want. The contrary is true. He will chastise us when we sin. His motive is pure love. He knows the consequence of our sin in this life and in eternity. He does not want us to end up in the lake of fire with the devil and his demons to torment us. Therefore, as a Good Father, He will correct us. Some die prematurely because they reject His ways, and refuse to change. Many times their lifestyle is result of iniquity in the blood line. But unless they take the steps to serve Yehovah, they will never achieve their potential in this life. Yehoshua has defeated the enemy on the cross, but they do not know and continue to sin. They do not realize they are losing their eternal position in Heaven with their Father. How tragic for them.

Now is the time to repent. Tomorrow may be too late. We only have this breath, and we are not assured the next one..

C H A P T E R   2 5

A Debased Mind

Clemens left that Island for a season, and took a trip to France to care for her mother. While in France she received a letter from her bookkeeper informing her that she owed 800 dollars to the I.R.S. The church she had been working for it did not pay the Social Security tax for her. She did not know this, and now she was charged 800 dollars and she was not able to pay it back. She had a very limited income from her mother. Needless to say she was in shock, but she knew that she had to pay that money back very fast. Clemens would never let herself get into debt, but now she was in debt and had no finances to take care of this situation! She had to return immediately to America and find a job. In view of the fact that she did not have the money for the air fare, her sweet and generous mother gave her the money to return to America. She flew to Portland Oregon, and rented a room from a good friend. As soon as she arrived in America got busy finding a job. She had to get a job very fast because the IRS charged 8% interest. She prayed and went to the same working agency she used earlier. She was hired immediately as a live-in companion to a very sick man. She went to work there on Monday morning, and leave Friday evening. She did not want to work for a single man, but there were no other openings at that time, therefore she took the job.

Mr. Brown, the man assigned to her was dying of cancer. He was bedridden and could do nothing for himself. He was completely dependent to the nurses and companion helpers. He had stopped eating regular food already. Clemens, knowing from the head nurses that he had not long to live, tried to minister to his spirit. She sensed that Mr. Brown did not believe in Yehoshua because he was very moody and distant. He did not want any communication concerning anything, and least of all about Yehoshua. One day, Christy, his daughter, came to visit. Clemens and Christy were sitting on the couch in the same room with Mr. Brown. He had a large television in the room, and the daughter put it on without asking her father. Mr. Brown was silent. After a while his daughter got up to leave. Clemens followed her outside and asked her if her father had at some point in his life believed in Yehoshua. *"Excuse me Christy, are you a Christian'"'Yes I am.'"Can you tell me if your father ever believed in Yeshua?"She answered, 'Yes, he did.' "But now he seems opposed to the Gospel." "Yes, I know. He was a new believer and idolized his pastor. Until one day he found out that his pastor was living in adultery. And because of that, my father stopped going to church." "Oh, that is what happened!" "He got mad at the pastor and Yehovah. After that he did not want anything to do with religion."* Christy after having a long conversation with Clemens left, and she never saw her again. Clemens went back into the patient's room, and Mr. Brown with a very deep voice told her, *"Shut that thing off." "But Mr. Brown, this is the 700 Club, do you not want to listen?"* His answer was very authoritative and said," *"Shut it off!"* He sounded like another person. His voice was so deep, and very angry. That voice did not sound like him. For sure Clemens realized by now that Mr. Brown had a demon inside of him. But she was not afraid. She no longer feared Satan, for as a Spirit filled believer she had power over Satan and His demons in the Name of Yehoshua.

"You are of Elohim, little children, and have overcome them, because He who is in you is greater than he who is in the world." **Yochanan1/1 John 4:4**

Yehoshua conquered sin and death on that cross. Believers should never fear demons because He is greater than all the hoards of hell. Our confidence should be in the Victorious King Yehoshua.

Clemens had to obey Mr. Brown, and turned off the television. However, she tried to talk to Him about his need to be saved. He did not want to listen. Clemens asked Yehovah not let her be there when Mr. Brown would die. She did not want to have to care for his body alone. She also suspected demons would be in the room when he would die. He probably would have a very difficult time dying. When unbelievers die their death is not peaceful. She knew this from being around death at the nursing home.. However, she continued praying for his salvation.

Then one day she made and appointment to go to the doctor for check up. She called the office and asked the manager to have the following morning off because she had to go to the doctor. They told her to take the whole day off. At first she was a little disappointed because she needed the money to pay the bill, and did not want to lose any hours. However, she was free to go, and she had to obey the leadership. That same evening, while she was resting in her room, she heard pounding on her door. She got up and there was Mr. Brown who wanted to come in. Somehow he got out of his bed and walked to her door. I suppose that room had been his bedroom before he became so hill and he did not realize his wife was not longer there. His mind did not seem to function well. Clemens had to pick him up, for he was by now only skin and bones, and managed to put him back in his bed. But Elohim flashed in her mind the following verses...

And even as they did not like to retain Elohim in their knowledge, Elohim gave them over to a debased mind, to do those things which are not fitting; being filled with all unrighteousness, sexual immorality, wickedness... **Romiyim/Romans 1:28-29a**

Now she knew Mr. Brown soul was lost for eternity. Clemens had suspected that Mr. Brown had become sexually impure. And He did not want to let go of his anger against his pastor and against Yehovah. The following day Clemens went out to see the doctor. That day was a Friday, and she did not have to return to work until Monday. But Sunday afternoon she received a phone call informing her that Mr. Brown had died. She was so sad, and cried a long time, for she knew this man was now in hell! He had refused Yehoshua and the free gift of salvation. He refused to forgive his pastor and returned to his old way of life. She cried many tears, but she could do nothing to change the situation. Mr. Brown made his own choice. How many people hold on to unforgiveness and fight with everybody in anger. They get the attitude everyone is wrong, and they are the only ones who are right. They do not realize they are losing their soul for eternity. This lost sheep did not want to be found by the Shepherd. He refused him, and now he would be living in torment for all eternity.

On another note, later on while working as a nurse's aide at the hospital, she had opportunity to lead many souls to Yehoshua. Anselmo was a man who went through three open heart surgeries. He died during the second surgery but came back to life. However now was almost at the point of death again. He had a life over death experience. He saw himself going to hell, but Yehovah brought him back to life. However, he was told that he had to forgive a relative. He did, but he was told that he also needed to believe and receive Yehoshua. When Clemens asked him if he received Yehoshua as Savior, He answered negatively. Clemens asked him if he wanted to receive Him as Savior, and he said, "Yes." Then she explained the gospel in a few simple words and led him in prayer. He was born again! She was very happy. The following day was her day off. When she returned to work two days later he was already dead. But this time he went up straight to Heaven to be with His Shepherd. This lost sheep found the Shepherd; actually the

Shepherd found him! He had the privilege to know Hell is a real place, and he chose not to go there. The fear of Yehovah came to Anselmo, which helped him to surrender his life completely to Him. Clemens found out many years later that Anselmo had been a very nasty and cruel man, but his family members had been praying for him for many years. When they heard Clemens testimony, his relatives were very happy to hear that Yehovah had answered their prayers. We should never doubt when we pray, for it may take time for us to receive the answer, but the answer will always come. Yehovah is faithful to us and to His Word. His Word cannot become void.

CHAPTER 26

Katrina's Suffering Increases

Years later Clemens left Portland, and came back to Maui. This particular day while she was preparing to go to sleep she decided to wait a little longer. She felt the day's duties were not yet all done. While she was deciding what to do next, the phone rang. Katrina was calling her again. She had been calling Clemens for prayer many times in the last few weeks. She needed prayer for her back. She was desperate! She was having intense pain, and she was hysterically crying very loud like a child. *"I need help, please pray for me." "Sure. Don't cry. Let us agree in prayer. Remember the Word which declares:" "Assuredly, I say to you, whatever you bind on earth will be bound in heaven, and whatever you loose on earth will be loosed in Heaven. Again I say to you that if two of You agree on earth concerning anything that they ask, it will be done for them by My Father in Heaven. For where two or three are gathered together in My Name, I am there in the midst of them."* Both began to pray in tongues for a while, and then in English. Clemens applied the Blood of Yehoshua on her back and the pain little by little subsided.

After a while Katrina seemed to be crying less but was still sobbing and began to share with Clemens her other big problem. She told her that her new husband George asked her to leave after she accused him of having an affair with Margi, another girl. He denied it, but Margi was leaving at his mother's house, and he would see her every day. Margi had rented a room from his mother, and she was loved by the whole family. This girl helped her husband to buy the land to build the house they were now building as husband and wife. Her name actually appeared in the property legal ownership papers. Margi was part owner of the property. Katrina was devastated. Clemens was speechless. She needed to seek Yehovah to know how to help her friend. But her mind raced in many directions. She knew Katrina left Maui and went to that Island in the hope of getting away from her mother. She wanted to be living her life without constant strife. But now she was stuck. George did not love her as she expected it. He was more of a Don Giovanni than a faithful husband! He was a man who liked many women, but committed himself to none. She tried to console her dear friend and prayed again, but this time Katrina needed to repent of her own jealousy and forgive her husband. Hours passed until finally Katrina decided to be more loving and less jealous toward her rival and her husband. She decided to love her enemy! Katrina after it all had no concrete evidence of his adultery. She never saw them together! Maybe she was imagining things. Finally they said good night to one another, and Clemens went to sleep.

The following day very early in the morning Katrina called again. It was still very early, but she said that she did not sleep well the night before. Her husband did not want to be with her, and was still belligerent. They argued for a while, until he went to sleep in the living room far away from her. Her honey moon was over!

Once again Clemens prayed with the new bride and special friend. They prayed for a while. Then Clemens tried to convince the wounded bride to be patient with her new husband. A marriage takes time to become as Yehovah intends it to be. Many times couples do not have the same kind of love for one another, but they learn to live together by lovingly caring for one another. Katrina needed to trust Yehovah, and she prayed and hoped that her husband would forgive her. After it all, they were both followers of Messiah! Time is necessary to have a good marriage. When both, husband and wife, develop a close relationship with their Creator, He will oversee their failures and help them to live victorious lives. However, George was a light hearted Christians. He said he loved Yehovah but was not filled with His Holy Spirit, and lacked consecration. He was a superficial believer, a church going person with not dept. He had no passion, no zeal for his Savior as Katrina had. He was living on the fence. He only try to do the minimum requirement in order to make it to Heaven. He would go to church as a routine duty when he could, but lacked the zeal. However he was faithful in paying his tithes, therefore he was loved at that church. Katrina was in love with her Savior, but she was miss-understood a lot by her husband and the pastor. Somehow he did not believe her when she went to him for counseling. He accused her of been the problem in the marriage. Sure she also needed to tame her tongue, and possibly also trust her husband more. But Katrina was very prophetic and knew the Word very well. She was very discerning in the Spirit, and knew what her husband was doing behind her back. She felt abandoned by all except Clemens and some other far away friend. Clemens understood Katrina and suffered together with her.

Eventually Katrina and George came to visit Clemens on Maui when they came to attend a prophetic conference. Katrina knew in her heart that George was still very immature; however, she expected more of him. He did not want to or was not able to take the responsibility of a husband. He was working only occasionally, but lived on the rentals income of his mother's houses. He never had to struggle to make a living, as Katrina had to do. He did not keep a budget and had little respect for the money. He spent all the money as he desired, being concerned only on his own interests. The money was always there for him to pay his personal bills. Her mother always took care of him, and he did not have to be concerned about anything. He lived a easy life, and did not have to work. No wonder he was not ready to be a husband. And to complicate matters, he knew his wife had bone cancer, and she was given only a maximum seven years to live. That was now the sixth year or so that she discovered to be afflicted with cancer. The burden was too much for him to handle. He probably regretted marrying her soon after their marriage. When both came to see Clemens on Maui, they were arguing with each other. Clemens prepared a dinner for them the following day, and tried to minister to them. He seemed to agree to Clemens counsel, but did not follow through. Once they went back to their home, things did not improve at all, but worsened.

Katrina expected him to be the head of the household, but in reality his mother was handling the family affairs. Clemens remembered that she warned Katrina, before she was married. She had told Katrina to wait al little longer, until she was completely sure he was the one Yehovah had chosen for her. But they had speed up the wedding to avoid falling into sin. Katrina hoped he would be the one who could take care of her now. She knew the diagnosis of her sickness, and did not have any place to go. She no longer wanted to be with her mother. This marriage seemed to be Yehovah's way of caring for her. But things changed drastically very soon.

After a few months the doctor sent her to a special clinic in Arkansas. She was there several months, hoping to be healed from her bone cancer. During that time her mother went to help her. But her husband did not want to stay there after her mother came. Katrina actually believed George tried to deposit poison in the IV because she almost died soon after he left her. Could it be that the cancer had reached her brain and was affecting her thinking? However, it was after this incident that he left her and went to Nevada where allegedly he had an affair. Katrina learned of this escapade while he was still in Nevada.

Finally Katrina returned to Molokai. Both of them tried to work out their problems, but in vain. The differences were too great for them. His immaturity and her sickness were obviously enormous reasons for their separation. But, in the past, while in Molokai, her husband, for tax purposes, added her name to the deed of the house. And when he left her, she rented part of the house to have an income.

When she came back to Maui to be with her mother, she continued to collect the rental's income for several months. That was helpful for a while, but was not sufficient to be able to rent an apartment. The rent for a single apartment is very high on Maui, especially when someone is not in condition to go to work.

Eventually she filed for wife's support, but the judge refused her request because she took the rental's money without her husband's consent. By right she should not have touched the rental income without the consent of her husband. However, He refused to support her. George obviously knowing her physical condition should not have left her without any financial support. Katrina was desperate, and she did what she felt was the right thing to do. When she went to Court the Judge blatantly told her to go to work, and refused her request for wife's support. But can you imagine a righteous judge, saying to Katrina who is battling for her life, "You need to go to work." Knowing her physical condition, how could he say such thing? Well, the world needs to be changed, and the only One who can change each one of us is Yehovah. Without him all of us are Lost Sheep! Katrina had no choice but to return to her mother and brother. Eventually her younger son Clayton came back from Oklahoma to help her. That whole family lived in a very small apartment. Living so close to one another resulted in having many difficult situations to solve. Every day they faced some problems that caused dissensions among them. Katrina knew that soon she would be living this world and wanted to have some financial security for her children. George was not willing to help her situation, and he kept the house for himself.

Chapter 27

Katrina's Home Coming

The cancer continued to grow and many times she had to be taken to Maui Memorial Hospital for treatment. She was having many issues in her whole body. The cancer was spreading over every organ, and could no longer be contained. According to the doctor prognosis she lived much longer than expected. We know that Yehovah gave her extra time to be with her children. We are thankful for His goodness. But now her time was coming to an end, and she would be very soon with her Savior in Heaven. Clemens saw her a few times when Katrina came back to Maui. But, because she lived in Makawao and Clemens did not know her address, she was unable to visit with her. Katrina actually did not want visitors because her mother's house was too small. There was no room to receive visitors and to have a private conversation.

Meanwhile, Clemens had to take a trip to Kentucky for a few months. During this time Katrina illness became more intense. When she returned to Maui Katrina was living her last days on this planet. Her son Clayton was still an introvert and needed his own room, but now he had to share it with others. Plus he did not want to submit to his grandmother and uncle. Katrina was going through great stress and great physical pain. She loved her son; however she needed her own mother to care for her. She no longer was able to do house chores, or cook her own food. She was completely bedridden. During this time her mother did her best to be kind and loving to her daughter. It seems that this sickness brought them closer together and they forgave and loved one another. George would not come to see her, although they were still married. The divorce did not go through, but they lived separated lives. Katrina knowing her time to go to her heavenly home was going to be very short, had already made arrangements for her funeral.

Meanwhile Clemens was also having difficulties with her living situations. She moved from her apartment and was waiting for the manager of the new apartment complex to call her. Presently she was temporarily renting a single room at her friend's apartment. It was during this time that she called her friend Katrina, and found out of her critical condition. Katrina would be in this world only a few more days, after that phone call, and Clemens had no opportunity to see her again. But those last days of Katrina's life were full of drama. When Clemens was able to talk with Katrina for the last time, she had difficulty speaking and was asking for peace. She was very concerned about Clayton who supposedly took her money and was not giving it back. Plus someone said that he had begun to drink alcohol and was using the mother's money to buy beer. Katrina had raised him well, and they never had alcohol in the house. But he was still immature and did not know what to do. He panicked knowing his mother would no longer be there to support him. Although he was an adult, he was not able to live alone. He needed his mother's support, both naturally and spiritually. Sadly, he lacked the experience necessary to be able to provide for himself. His grandmother was upset with him, because she did not understand his pain. His uncle was also not completely mentally well and did not want him to be around his home. His older brother Mitz criticized him for his alleged drinking. No one understood his drama. He was still very naïve in many ways. He felt very much alone and scared of his future. He was in deep need of a touch of Yehovah's love to strengthen him.

Clayton knew Yehovah, and He had a personal relationship with His Savior Yehoshua, therefore he knew how to pray, and I suspect that he prayed. However, losing his mother was something way beyond his ability to comprehend. He felt alone and abandoned, and completely lost. I know Katrina was also concerned about living him with her mother and brother.

Katrina was very sick indeed, and those arguments around her were not suitable for a peaceful passing on to eternal life. Until her last days and moments on this earth she was surrounded with drama. She also had been given large doses of pain killers, which caused her to need rest, but around her, there was no rest. Chaos, stress, and confusion had taken residence. Arguments and contentions ruled.

After Clemens called her she lived only a few days. She was indeed ready to go to be with her Savior. She left this world to enter her home in Heaven where she has now complete peace. She is happy to be with Her Savior that she loved and worshiped. All her pains and struggles are over. She has received her reward. Katrina is now waiting for her resurrection when she will receive her new body cancer free. All her sufferings are over and gone forever. Some day Clemens will see her again, maybe sooner than she thinks. Yehovah also took care of her son Clayton who found a home with an old friend of his mother in the States.

CHAPTER 28

Another Lost Sheep

Clemens woke up suddenly one morning from having a dream. Usually Yehovah spoke to her while awake, or while sleeping. In this dream she saw two branches of black grapes. She tasted one and it was sweet, but that branch was in bad shape. The other was larger and it looked good. Clemens knew Yehovah gave her that particular dream to let her know of her friend Candy's death. When she awoke she was fully convinced that Candy would be going to be with her Elohim that day, but she did not know who the other person would be.

Later in the morning she received a text message from Marisa in California informing her that her mother had passed on to be with Yeshua. The larger grapes that she did not taste concerned that person's death. She did not taste those grapes in her dream, because she never met that lady. Clemens quickly answered the text message giving her condolences promising to be praying for her. Marisa and her mother had been both Jehovah witness. But at some point in their lives they had believed in Yeshua. Therefore Marisa's mother would also be in Heaven that day.

At this point she had no doubt that her friend Candy would be also going to Heaven that day. However she kept busy doing her daily chores without thinking too much about it. Suddenly around five in the afternoon, Michelle, one of her pastors' friends called her. She informed Clemens that Candy had gone to be with Yehoshua. She felt sad and happy at the same time. She had been praying for Candy from the moment she was informed of her imminent death. She also visited her and was praying for Yehovah to help her during the critical last moments of her life. Her daughter had told Clemens that Candy was already talking with her mother who had passed away a few months ago. She seemed to be talking with her as though she was there in the room. Clemens knew that people before they pass on receive visitors from the other realm. They seem to be encouraging them. Usually the person is visited by her dead relatives, Yehoshua, and even angels. The veil between heaven and earth becomes very thin.

Although Clemens was happy for Candy that she was now in Heaven, and was pain free, she still felt a little sad. She went to lie down in her bed trying to sleep, but she could not. Clemens began remembering the first time she met Candy. She also remembered the time she came to help her in ministry while she was ministering in Molokai. Sadly it did not work out because Candy was having some problems with depression and supposedly was taking medication. She slept until noon. Clemens would try to wake her up to get busy doing the ministry. But she would not until later. That was a great concern for Clemens. She had come to help, but had difficulty staying awake. Clemens was perplexed. She had no clue why she slept so late every day.

Finally she informed the senior pastor. Candy left immediately after the senior pastor spoke to her without an explanation. They did not see each other for many years. Clemens did not know that Candy had unforgiveness against her. During those years after they lost contact, when Clemens got her phone number, she tried to contact her many times, but Candy would not respond. Even when she went to the hospital and Clemens went to visit her, she would not open up to talk about her issue.

This situation went on for over twenty years, until Clemens was told from their common friend Linda, that Candy had cancer. At that time Linda did not yet know that she was also very sick with brain cancer. Linda only lived a few months and then passed on unto eternity. About one year later one morning after her prayer time Clemens felt an urgency to get in touch with Candy. She knew in her heart that Candy had unforgiveness in her heart against her, and she needed to forgive Clemens before she would be dying. Unforgiveness is a grave sin, and Yehovah will not forgive us if we do not forgive others. Clemens knew that Candy's would die very soon, and it was imperative for her to forgive.

Unforgiveness is a great block that prevents us from being in the presence of Yehovah. Yehoshua gave us a model prayer, but warned us not to pray repetitious prayers. He also taught us the importance of forgiveness.

"And when you pray, do not use vain repetitions as the heathen do. For they think that they will be heard for their many words. Therefore do not be like them. For your Father knows the things you have need of before you ask Him. In this manner, therefore, pray:

"Our Father in Heaven, Hallowed be Your name,

Your kingdom come.

Your will be done on earth as it is in Heaven.

Give us this day our daily bread.

And forgive us our sins,

As we forgive those who sin against us.

Lead us not into the hand of a test,

But deliver us from all evil.

Amen.

For if you forgive men their trespasses, your heavenly Father will also forgive you. But if you do not forgive men their trespasses, neither will your Father in Heaven forgive your trespasses." **Mattithyahu/Matthew 6:7- 14**

Yehovah will not forgive us, if we do not forgive our brethren. We cannot hold resentment in our hearts, for if we do Heaven is closed to us. We must deal with it. If we as believers do not forgive we are considered as a Lost Sheep. Lost sheep, yes, because Heaven is closed to us, as any other sinner who may have done many terrible sins, such sins as Mina and Katrina who killed their own children. However, any sin prevents us from entering eternity and enjoy our future life with our Savior who redeemed us with His blood.

Moses was a man who spoke to Yehovah and saw His form while on the mountain. But one time he was given an order from Yehovah and he disobeyed. This happened only once, but He could not enter the Promised Land, which was His calling from the beginning. However, he messed up, and was not permitted to enter the Promised Land.

"Take the rod; you and your brother Aaron gather the congregation together. Speak to the rock before their eyes, and it will yield its water; thus you shall bring water for them out of the rock, and give drink to the congregation and their animals. So Mosheh (Moses) took the rod from before Yehovah as He commanded him. And Mosheh and Aaron gathered the assembly together before the rock; and he said to them, "Hear now, you rebels! Must we bring water for you out of this rock?" Then Mosheh lifted his hand and struck the rock twice with his rod; and water came out abundantly, and the congregation and their animals drank. Then Yehovah spoke to Mosheh and Aaron, "Because you did not believe Me, to hallow Me in the eyes of the children of Israel, therefore you shall

not bring this assembly in to the land which I have given them."
Bemidbar/Numbers 20:8-11-12

They angered Him also at the waters of strife, so that it went ill with Mosheh on account of them, because they rebelled against His Spirit, so that he spoke rashly with his lips." **Tehillim/Psalm 106:32-33**

The Scriptures said that Mosheh spoke rashly because the people provoked him. I believe the same spirit that was on the people came upon him, and he lost his temper. We must be always very careful that we do not allow other's people lack of faith, or even their anger, affect us. The sin of Mosheh was unbelief. Unbelief is sin. It is denying the power and ability of Yehovah. Without faith we cannot please Him.

But without faith it is impossible to please Him, for he who comes to Elohim must believe that He is, and that He is a rewarder of those who diligently seek Him. **Ivrim/Hebrews 11:6**

Abused, Delivered And Filled!

Clemens had been not feeling too well for a few weeks, when she visited Miryam, one of her neighbors and long lasting friend. They talked for a few minutes, and when she came out of her apartment a lady who lived across Miryam's apartment, was looking at her and smiling. Clemens never met her before, for this lady was always inside the home. She did not know that she was a new tenant. The other lady who lived there had moved away about a year ago, and this lady had moved in. Clemens herself had moved in after this tenant moved in, therefore she did not know her.

Since Clemens is very friendly she went to speak to this lady who was sitting on a wheelchair. *"Hello, my name is Clemens. I am Miryam's friend."How are you""Oh, I am fine, thank you."*Clemens asked her, *"What is your name? My Name is Annetta.You do Shabbat!""Oh, yes, how do you know? "Miryam told me.""Great, would you like to come?" "Yes."*They continued to speak for a few minutes, and Clemens left telling her that she would have the meeting Friday evening at 6 PM. Annetta agreed to come.

However, things changed. Clemens became hill with a terrible headache and weakness on her whole body, and she had to cancel the meeting until she would feel better. Meanwhile Annetta told her that she loved the garden and especially she loved mint. Clemens immediately brought her a pot of growing mint. Mint was also one the most favored plants to Clemens. One day she visited Annetta and Clemens discovered that Annetta was an ex-Mormon. She actually had married a Pentecostal Believer. Clemens continued to ministered to Annetta to inspire her with faith.

Finally Clemens was healed of her temporary sickness, and on a Wednesday she visited her new friend and set up a date for the Bible Study. Instead of coming to a Shabbat meeting, on Friday evening, which was temporarily off, Annetta agreed to meet on Thursday morning at 9 A.M. However, that morning was a very challenging morning for Clemens, and she prayed to Yehovah, "*I am not in a good spirit to do the Bible Study today, I would like to cancel, but if You want me to do it, Your will be done*" Meanwhile to cheer up she began to play on the keyboard two little songs she had learned how to play. She felt much better after that. Nine o'clock came and Annetta did not come. But she decided to check on her. She went to her apartment and she said, "*Oh, I was trying to call you to come and do the study here in this apartment instead.*""*Oh, sure, I will be right back with the books.*" She went back home to pick up the teaching on the name of Elohim, Yehovah, and of His only Ben/Son, Yehoshua. However, basically, she began to testify to Annetta of some miracles she experienced during her life time. Annetta was amazed. Clemens could see in her face that she believed. Then Clemens asked her if she had ever had experienced the Baptism in the Ruach haQodesh or Holy Spirit. But she answered that she never experienced the fullness of the Ruach haQodesh with the evidence of *glossolalia* which is praying in unknown tongues. When Clemens discovered that she did not, she wondered if she would pray for her later on, and maybe Yehoshua would fill her that day. Clemens continued to share more testimonies, and she told Annetta that she also could be healed, if she believed. Annetta answered, "*I was married and may husband abused me all the time. I couldn't handle it anymore. I became so sick that I was in bed, and went to the doctor but they found nothing wrong with me. However I could not walk. I had been beaten so much, my whole body was so sore from those beatings. But one day I heard a voice saying to me to leave, then I had the energy to get out of bed and I left the house." I left but I took only the little girl with me. The other four children I left behind with my husband.* Clemens asked her if her husband abused her children too, but she answered, *"No, he did not. He only abused me."*

Clemens was shocked to hear such story. Then she asked Annetta, *"What about the four children you left behind, do you speak with them?" "Yes, we are in touch. They are old now and they have their own families. I have seen them. We talk on the phone."* But she added, *"I feel the reason I am in this chair is because I think Elohim has put me here because I left my children. I feel guilty."* Clemens asked her if she repented for leaving her children behind. Annetta answered that she did. Now Clemens assured her that Yehovah did not put her in that chair. Yehoshua is the healer, and He healed everyone who came to Him. *"The devil had been lying to you. Yehovah loves you. He does not put you in this chair. Trust Him, when He forgives He forgets. Yehoshua has shed His precious blood on the cross for you."*

Then Annetta shared that one of her daughters has cancer. She had surgery, but she is very sick, and she is not saved. Immediately Clemens began to share two great testimonies of salvation. She shared about Anselmo who had three open heart surgeries, and during the second surgery he saw himself going to hell. Yeshua told him he had to forgive his brother in law, and to be received him as Savior. However, he forgave the brother in law, but did not yet get saved. Clemens led him to the Yehoshua and he was gloriously saved. The Glory of Yehovah came into that room that day. And two days later he went to Heaven. Clemens shared another testimony, then she prayed in agreement with Annetta for her daughter's salvation. Now Clemens could see that hope had risen in Annetta's heart.

Finally Clemens got up and asked Annetta if she could pray for her. Annetta said, *"Yes."* Clemens began to call upon Yehovah and thank Him for His Blessings. She began to apply the Blood of Yehoshua over Annetta and herself, and the whole apartment. She spoke in other tongues, and then took authority over the spirit of deception and guilt. Then she asked Yehoshua to fill her new friend with the Ruach haQodesh and to give her the prayer language. She asked Annetta to plead the Blood of Yehoshua, And she did likewise. Next she told Annetta to raise her hands up in praise and they praised Yehovah together. Still pleading the Blood of Yehoshua and praising Yehovah. Soon Annetta spoke in the Heavenly language. Both spoke in tongues for a while. It was an awesome moment. The presence of Yehovah was intense. He was there; the Creator of the Universe was there with them. Clemens asked Annetta, *"Can you tell me how you feel?"* Annetta said, *"I felt so light, I feel so good".* Words cannot explain how we feel when the Spirit of Yehovah comes into our lives. He is so marvelous, so pure, so holy, so loving. Yet so many people prefer serving Satan the deceiver who hates them, instead of seeking Yehovah and serve Him only. Now Annetta was equipped to pray with power and great faith for all her children and ex-husband salvation.

Yehoshua has said to His apostles,

"Behold, I send the Promise of My Father upon you; but tarry in the city of Yerushalayim until you are endued with power from on high."Luqas / Luke 24:49.

Before He was taken up to Heaven the apostles asked Him a question,

Therefore, when they came together, they asked Him, saying, "Adonai, will You at this time restore the kingdom to Israel?" And He said to them, "It is not for you to know times or seasons which the Father has put in His own authority. But you shall receive power when the Ruach haQodesh / Holy Spirit has come upon you;

and you shall be witness to Me in Yerushalayim, and in all Judea and Samaria, and to the ends of the earth." Now when He had spoken these things, while they watched, He was taken up, and a cloud received Him out of their sight. **Ma'aseh/Acts1:6-9**

And while they looked steadfastly toward Heaven as He went up, behold, two men stood by them in white apparel, who also said, "Men of Galilee, why do you stand gazing up into Heaven? This same Yehoshua, who was taken up from you into Heaven, will so come in like manner as you saw Him go into heaven." **Ma'aseh/Acts 1:10-11**

Indeed he has lived, died, and rose again, and is coming again to judge the living and the dead. And then His kingdom will be established.

Clemens felt very happy to have witnessed the glory of Yehovah that day. She left her friend Annetta so that she could enjoy the presence of Yehoshua by herself. Such moments are unforgettable! Yehovah is glorious and majestic in splendor and in power! All glory be to Him alone!

Chapter 30

Miryam

Clemens knew Miryam for about twelve years. They met at a prayer meeting. Miryam was known in the past to be a prayer intercessor. When Clemens began to start her radio program with LeSea Radio Broadcast Station, she called Miryam and told her the good news. Miryam immediately said that she would support her ministry with 25.00 Dollars every month. Miryam was very supportive and also began to attend the Friday Evening Shabbat Meetings at Clemens home. She was also very active at her Fellowship in Kihei. They became very good friends. One day Clemens asked her to share her testimony. *"Miryam, tell me where were you born? Were your parents believers in Yehoshua?" "No, actually my father John and my mother Doreen were Catholics and they drank alcohol a lot." "Did anything special happened in your life?" "Yes. When I was five month old while laying in the crib, my two brothers played with my hot milk bottle, and they threw it at me accidentally, and hit my head." "Oh no!" "Yes, then, eventually I got very sick with pneumonia, and the doctor told my parents there was no hope for me to be healed. But a friend of my mother told her to go to a church and ask the visiting Filipino pastor to pray for me. He prayed for me and I got healed. He was Pentecostal and prayed in tongues. And then he ministered to my mother and she accepted Yehoshua" "What about your father? Did He get saved too?" "No. He would not change. He was Catholic and did not want to change." My mother became a fervent believer, and her life style changed. She no longer drank with my father, and because of this fact, my father beat her. He wanted her to go back to the Catholic church, but she would not. She was very busy in her new church."*

Miryam continued to speak about her father John and her mother Doreen. She needed to speak about these things that she usually never spoke to anyone. She remembered minute details of her past life. Doreen eventually had to leave Maui and move to another Island because of her husband abuse, and took all her children. He followed his wife trying to convince her to come back to him, but she refused. She became very active in the Pentecostal church. But He eventually went back to the Philippines to be reconciled with his other wife and children. He had left his wife in the Philippines and married Miryam's mother on Maui when he came to work. But he was still married in the Philippines. I suppose that when Doreen left him, he remembered his other wife and left America to be reunited with her. He had two wives at the same time, he was living a polygamous life. But Doreen did not know about this until after he went back to the Philippines. No wonder the marriage did not work. Miryam eventually met some of his family members who came to Maui from the Philippines. He was a lost sheep, and no one knows for sure if he eventually repented to Yehovah and received Yehoshua as his Savior. I asked Miryam if she forgave her father, she said, *"Yes."*

Miryam was born again at the age of seven. As a teenager she became the youth leader in the fellowship she attended with her mother. She had other sisters but they chose to attend the Catholic Church. Myrna and one of her sisters joined the Baha'i cult, and lives an unrestrained lifestyle. Miryam is very concerned about her sister, and pray for her continually. This cult originated 1863 and had roots in Shea Islam. However, they established their own laws to break away from Islam. They do not give a real name to their god, but they call him Gracious, Helper, All Glorious, Omniscient, and all loving. They prefer call him All Glorious which is Baha in Arabic. They seem to think that they have no sin. Therefore they live together with their partners, as long as they want, and I suppose change partners at will.

Myrna, who is involved with this cult, is living with another man for years, and has no consciousness of sin. Clemens tried to share the gospel to Myrna, letting her know that there is no other way, but one, Yehoshua. But she did not want to listen. However, prayer is going up to Heaven for her salvation and her other Catholic sisters, and one day all of them will be saved in answer to prayers and the love of the Father in Heaven. But for now Miryam sisters are all lost sheep.

Clemens asked Miryam a question, *"Miryam, how was your life at home? "What did you do as a child?" "Well because I was older than the two last babies born to my parents, I ended up being the maid, babysitter and cook. I did every-thing."* She does not have a good memory of her teen years. Probably this was one of the reasons why, although a believer in Yehoshua, and active in the church, she fell in love with a young man and became pregnant. She was only eighteen years old. That was her ticket out. However, her boy friend when he found out that she was pregnant left her. But Miryam contacted his family and his parents arranged for them to get married. However, the marriage was not very successful. She gave birth to six children, with that husband, and after that her husband left her com-pletely. He had been unfaithful with other women during the whole time they were married. But he still was having children with his wife! During those years Miryam did not serve Yehovah. She also drank a lot, and was no longer interested in serving her Savior. But eventually she sensed the need to be in the presence of Yehovah, her Heavenly Father, and she began to seek Him again. She came back to Maui, while five of her chil-dren were, and still are, in California and other states. She became a fervent believer as her mother had become after her conversion.

Presently Miryam is over seventy years old, and together with Clemens pray together for all her family. Miryam is receiving much healing from her past traumas. Many times Clemens prays for her, and Yehoshua heals her. One day, she came to Clemens to visit and she asked her to pray for her neck. Clemens reminded Miryam that she had no ability to heal, but Yehoshua, who lived in her, and in Miryam, was the only Healer. Both began to worship for a few minutes. Then Clemens laid hands on her neck and began to pray, *"In the name of Yehoshua, I curse trauma and I command you to leave; Cellular memory go in Yehoshua's name. All pain go, in Yehoshua's Name."* When she ended the prayer she asked her friend, *"Miryam how is the pain?" "Gone" I have no pain!' Glory, Thank you Yehoshua! Thank you Father Yehovah!"* Both rejoiced and thanked their faithful Elohim.

Yehoshua had said,

"Most assuredly, I say to you, he who believers in Me, the works that I do he will do also; and greater works than these he will do, because I go to My Father. And whatever you ask in My name, that I will do, that the Father may be glorified in the Son. If you ask anything in My name, I will do it." Yochanan/John 14:12-14

"And these signs will follow those who believe; In My name they will cast out demons; they will speak with new tongues; they will take up serpents; and if they drink anything deadly, it will by no means hurt them; they will lay hands on the sick and they will recover." Marqos/Mark 16:17

CHAPTER 31

The Sinful Woman

And now let us read the true story of this sinful woman. Yehoshua was invited to dinner by a Pharisee. This event has required fourteen verses to write it, in order that we would fully understand the lesson in it. It must be very important to Yehovah, for it could not be written with fewer words.

Then one of the Pharisees asked Him to eat with him. And He went to the Pharisee's house, and sat down to eat. And behold, a woman in the city who was a sinner, when she knew that Yeshua sat at the table in the Pharisee's house, brought an alabaster flask of fragrant oil, and stood at His feet behind Him weeping; and she began to wash His feet with her tears, and wiped them with the hair of her head; and she kissed His feet and anointed them with the fragrant oil. Now when the Pharisee who had invited Him saw this, he spoke to himself, saying, "This Man, if He were a prophet, would know who and what manner of woman this is who is touching Him, for she is a sinner." Luqas/Luke 7:36-39

The Pharisee did not recognize Yehoshua to be the Mashiach, or even a Prophet! He was judging Yehoshua and the woman, because he knew her to be a harlot, which means a prostitute. He quickly passed judgment on her life.

Let us read about another incident organized by the Pharisees. Let me share now about this other woman. Yehoshua went to the Mount of Olives.

But Yehoshua went to the Mount of Olives. Now early in the morning He came again into the temple, and all the people came to Him; and He sat down and taught them. Then the scribes and Pharisees brought to Him a woman caught in adultery. And when they had set her in the midst, they said to him, "Teacher, this woman was caught in adultery, in the very act. Now Moses, in the law, commanded us that such should be stoned. But what do You say? **Yochanan/John 8:1-5**

Yehoshua did not answer them immediately, because he knew they would incriminate Him if He would forgive her sin. They persisted in making Him give His decision. Yeshua began to write on the dust of the earth as though He did not hear. (v.6)

So when they continued asking Him, He raised Himself up and said to them, "He who is without sin among you, let him throw a stone at her first." And again He stooped down and wrote on the ground. Then those who heard it, being convicted by their conscience, went out one by one, beginning with the oldest even to the last. And Yehoshua was left alone, and the woman standing in the midst . When Yehoshua had raised Himself up and saw no one but the woman, He said to her, "Woman, where are those accusers of Yours? Has no one condemned you?" She said, "No one Lord." And Yehoshua said to her, "Neither do I condemn you; go and sin no more." Then Yehoshua spoke to them again, saying, "I am the light of the world. He who follows Me shall not walk in darkness, but have the light of life." **Yochanan 8:7-12**

Two women were sinners. This second woman could have been the one who later came to Yehoshua with the alabaster flask of perfume, but we cannot assume who she was, all we know is that she had been accused of adultery. The fact remains that the prostitute went away forgiven, and so did this one caught in adultery. Yehoshua saw the repentance in their hearts, and forgave both of them. Man only looks on appearances, and religion makes a person self-righteous condemning others whom they feel are not as righteous as they are. Sadly this judgmental spirit is seen in the churches as well.

Yehoshua compared idolatry to harlotry.

They did not destroy the peoples, concerning who Yehovah had commanded them, but they mingled with the Gentiles and learned their works; they served their idols, which became a snare to them. They even sacrificed their sons and their daughters to demons, and shed innocent blood, the blood of their sons and daughters, whom they sacrificed to the idols of Canaan; and the land was polluted with blood. Thus they were defiled by their own works, and played the harlot by their own deeds." **Tehillim / Psalm 106:34:39**

"My people ask counsel from their wooden idols, and their staff informs them. For the spirit of harlotry has caused them to stray, and they have played the harlot against their Elohim." **Hoshea / Hosea 4:12**

Religious people do not realize they may be judged as harlots if they, indeed, do not repent. Yehovah's judgment is righteous. He equates idolatry to harlotry. Yehovah is ready to forgive all most vile sinners, if they repent with all their heart with deep sorrow for their sin. Man does not forgive, but holds unforgiveness in his heart, and judges the believers according to their past. This is unrighteousness and Yehovah will judge this self righteous sin. Man is sinful, and we saw how Mosheh could not enter the Promised Land because of one sin; lack of faith. I wonder how many believers lack of faith in obeying

His Commandments? Are they better than a repented sinner? Each of us has fallen big, and each of us deserves to go to Hell forever. We must stop judging the other person thinking we are better than they as the Pharisees had done. We cannot see the heart, but Yehovah sees and knows the heart, and He does not look on appearances.

CHAPTER 32

Idolatry

Clemens spent the day thinking on idolatry. She herself had worshiped idols in the past, and as mentioned earlier she had been also a lost sheep! Actually everyone is a lost sheep until the Good Shepherd saves them. But now she had hate in her heart for this sin, because it denied the very unique existence of her Elohim. She knew there was no other Elohim in the whole Universe. As she was deep in her thoughts concerning idolatry, she remembered her dear friend Akina. She had spoken to her in the past about her faith, and realized that Akina was slipping away from the faith because of her committed attachment to her idolatrous church. She believed her church is the true church. Clemens remembered the conversation she had with her.

"Hello Akina how are you? I was just thinking about you." "Thank you, I am fine, but I am struggling with faith. Please help me to understand. I am feeling that maybe Yehoshua was only a prophet or a good man. I do not believe He is the only way to Yehovah." "You know that maybe there is another way to Elohim, besides Yehoshua, there are other ways, I believe. What about those who do not know the Bible. There cannot be only one way. I am sure there are other ways to Heaven."

Akina had very difficult time believing that Yehovah would send fire from heaven to burn the statue of Miryam and other gods. These and many more questions did Akina mentioned to Clemens. And Clemens was not shocked, for she had gone through some of the same doubts in the past. She began to talk with her friend with great compassion and love, and she began to explain to Akina what her real problem was. She said to Akina, "*Well let me explain to you what I know. I am sure there is something I can do to help you. What is happening to you is only a test to your faith, and you will be set free." Just listen to what I am going to say to you. I love you, and Yehovah loves much more than I do. He will help you."*

Akina had to listen to what Yehovah has to say about idols.

I am Yehovah your Elohim, who brought you out of the land of Mitsrayim / Egypt, out of the house of bondage. You shall have no other gods before Me. You shall not make for yourself a carved image-any likeness of anything that is in Heaven above, or that is in the earth beneath, or that is in the water under the earth; you shall not bow down to them nor serve them. For I, Yehovah your Elohim, am a jealous Elohim, visiting the iniquity of the fathers upon the children the third and fourth generations of those who hate Me, But showing mercy to thousands, to those who love Me and keep My Commandments." Shemot / Exodus 20:1-6

"*Akina Yehovah forbids us to make idols and we cannot bring them into the house. You have statues of idols, Miryam is an idol, and other so called saints are idols, and Yehovah hates it. He wants you to burn them. Listen to what He has said about this.*"

You shall burn the carved images of their gods with fire; you shall not covet the silver or gold that is on them, not take it for yourselves, lest you be snared by it; for it is an abomination to Yehovah your Elohim. Nor shall you bring an abomination into your house, lest you be doomed to destruction like it. You shall utterly detest it an utterly abhor it, for it is an accursed thing. Devarim / Deuteronomy 7:25-26

If you disobey Him in this area means that you do not love Him. Yehoshua said,

"If You love Me, keep My Commandments." Yochanan / John 14:15

Clemens began to talk about the necessity of knowing our true Elohim, and forsaking all other gods, which are not gods at all. Idolatry is forsaking your Elohim with whom you entered into Covenant, and choose to worship and obey the rules of a false god. *"Akina your have learned the truth, why are you now listening to the thought that you may be on the wrong path?" Right now you are under oppression of the devil. He hates you, and he hates Elohim. He wants to destroy you and take you to hell to torment you for eternity. Presently you are being deceived."*

Clemens continued to explain the problem to her friend whom she loved as a sister. Clemens wanted her friend Akina to understand that she was not the only one feeling those doubts. And she tried to make her think for herself, and solve her own problem. Clemens began to speak again.

Why those who are worshiping Satan, Baal, Baha'i, Buddha, Zeus, Astarte, Venus, Ashtoreth, (Virgin Mary), or any other false god, do not realize they are actually worshiping demons? The answer is only one: **Deception.** Because they are been deceived they cannot see Truth. Clemens said, *"I know from experience that idolatry brings forth confusion. I grew up worshiping Miryam / Mary, like all Catholics. I understand how they are deceived. In reality they do not believe Yehoshua is able to save them, and therefore they seek other gods which are not gods at all, but demons. Those people are deluded thinking they are worshiping the mother of Elohim, "God." They pray to her, because they do not have a personal relationship with Yehovah or Yehoshua. They confess their sins to a man, who cannot forgive sins, instead of repenting to Yehovah, in Yeshua's Name. Yehovah alone can help them, but they are blind."*

Akina tried to receive everything Clemens told her. However because she was still involved in a church that worshiped idols, and did not teach the whole Word, as the Word of Yehovah, she could not grasp the Truth. That church does not believe in many fundamental truths, and one of them is Creation. Clemens knew in her heart that she would be resisting principalities and powers in the second heaven. Akina needed to seek Yehovah with all her heart and separate herself from that church. She could not drink from two separate sources. She had to make a choice. Presently she was deeply confused, which is the fruit of Idolatry.

Akina always came to Clemens for prayer for she knew that when Clemens prayed, Yehovah answered. However because she was deeply involved in her church she could not receive truth. Her husband was a deacon at that church.

Satan had her under his thumb. Clemens continued to teach Akina.

"Yehovah only used the womb of Miryam to host His Son and to raise Him as a Hebrew Man, who in the natural had to be descendants of King David. But she is not the mother of Elohim. She is only the natural mother of Yeshua. Elohim did not get married and He did not conceive the Son through the woman. He is the self-existent Elohim. Yeshua existed before He was born through the womb of Miryam. She is not the intercessor and co Savior as that church has elevated to be. She is a false goddess, as Astarte, Ashtoreth the goddess of the Sidonians, Diana, and Ishtar. They all seem to be the same goddess, but with various names, depending on the country they worship her."

Clemens decided to place Akina in Yehovah hands. But let Akina make her own decision. Akina needed to choose whom she would serve. Yehovah has His special ways to reveal Truth, and when He does all deception vanish in to smoke. Clemens continued to pray for Akina and her whole family and trust Elohim to save her.

When a church teaches that the congregation cannot understand the Scriptures by themselves, they are in error. They are preventing them from getting to know Truth, and are keeping them under their control. That church has also removed the second and fourth commandment from the Bible. It is demonic.

The Scriptures are not as difficult to understand. Yehovah instructed the parents to read the Word aloud to their children. The Ruach haQodesh is the real Teacher.

What is so difficult to understand about the following verses?

"I will declare a decree: Yehovah has said to Me, "You are My Ben/Son, Today I have begotten you." "Kiss the Ben/Son Lest He be angry, and you perish in the way when His wrath is kindled but a little. Blessed are all those who put their trust in Him." **Tehillim/Psalms 2:7, 12**.

Clemens also pointed out to Akina the following passage in the Sefer Mishley.

"Who has ascended into heaven, or descended? Who has gathered the wind in His fists / Who has bound the waters in a garment? Who has established all the ends of the earth? What is His name, and what is His Son's name, if you know?" **Mishley/Proverbs 30:4**

Clearly anyone understand that Yehovah has a Son! It is so sad that so many nice people have been deceived by men, and they do not realize they are in danger of losing their lives because of idolatry.

Idolatry is prostitution. Those people who are involved in such sin must repent before they find themselves judged by the Supreme Judge of the whole earth. Miryam is not a virgin, as they made it to be. She conceived and gave birth to boys and girls after the birth of Yehoshua; therefore Yehoshua had half- brothers and half-sisters in the natural. But their natural father is Joseph, while Yehoshua's Father is Yehovah.

While He was still talking to the multitudes, behold, His mother and brothers stood outside, seeking to speak with Him.

Then one said to Him, "Look, Your mother and Your brothers are standing outside, seeking to speak with You." But He answered and said to the one who told Him, "Who is My mother and who are My brothers?" And He stretched out His hand toward His disciples and said, "Here are My mother and My brothers! For however does the will of My Father in heaven is My brother and sister and mother." **Mattithyahu / Matthew 12:46-48**

The statue they venerate is worship to a false god. Yehoshua is our only living Intercessor. They made her to be the substitute of Yehoshua. That statue is an idol and must be burned with fire.

Many so called Christians use tranquilizers and are suicidal. In fact Akina is constantly sick. Deuteronomy 28 should be read constantly by anyone who chooses to doubt there is only one way to salvation. They are living in harlotry, they are prostitutes and they still think that a male or woman who sells his/her body is so terrible, but they are blind and naked and they do not see their own sin. For sure sex immorality is sin, but it is not the only sin. Idolatry is probably at the same level or worse. Prostitutes when Yehoshua touches their heart they quickly respond to Him. While idolaters they resist Him, and make excuses.

We need to pray for those who are still bound in idolatry. Without the Blood of Yehoshua we are all doomed to destruction!

Let us read the parable of the two sons.

"But what do you think? A man had two sons, and he came to the first and said, 'Son, go, work today in my vineyard.' He answered and said, 'I will not,' but afterward he regretted it and went. Then he came to the second and said likewise. And he answered and said, 'I go, sir,' but he did not go. Which of the two did the will of the father? They said to Him, "The first." Yehoshua said to them, "Assuredly, I say to you that tax collectors and harlots enter the

kingdom of Elohim before you. For Yochanan came to you in the way of righteousness, and you did not believe him; but tax collectors and harlots believed him; and when you saw it, you did not afterward relent and believe in him." **Mattithyahu/Matthew 21:28-32**

Many people after listening to the Word of Elohim repent, but Akina did not repent. She continued to worship her beloved Miryam, and other saints. However, Clemens still hopes for her deliverance. Yehovah will reveal truth to Akina and she will be saved and delivered. Yehovah loves her, and He knows how to speak into her life. He can send Yehoshua in the last hour of her life and reveal to her that He his is the only Door, and she cannot enter into Heaven without Him. I know He has visited many unbelievers when they were on the point of death, and I firmly believe He will do something phenomenon for Akina and her family. The day will arrive that she no longer trusts in men for her salvation, but in Elohim alone. Blessed be that day. Clemens continued to pray for Akina believing in her heart for her deliverance and salvation. Akina will come to a point in her life that she will be able to think for herself, instead of believing the lies of the enemy. There are not many ways to Heaven, but only one; one Door, one Way, one Truth, and one Life.

C H A P T E R 3 3

Traditions! Traditions!

Clemens had just moved to a little town on Maui, when the phone rang. To her surprise the caller was Michelle. *"Michelle, how are you? I have not heard from you for a very long time. What is going on? Are you OK? "No, I am not OK. My father in law called my husband and practically forced him to move into his house because he is moving out to be with his girl friend." He is living his wife for good." "Michelle, are you kidding me? You are going to be moving in with your mother in Law?" "Yes, my husband wants to move because he will not pay rent, so he has more money to use for himself! I am so hurt. You know my mother in law is different…than me. I am concerned we will not get along." I told Andre that I only move for a short while. We will not stay longer than three months if do not like it. My husband agreed. So we are preparing to move immediately. I have a bad feeling, I worry my marriage will not last if we move into her house." "Michelle, do not think that way, it may work out well. But what is the reason your father in law is demanding you guys to move into his house?" "Well, she is sick, and he wants me to clean the house, cook for her, and overall help her. And because of that we will not have to pay him or his wife rent." "So he has hired you as a maid!" "Yes, this is what it looks like it."*

Clemens felt so sorry for her friend. But there was nothing she could do to help her. All she could do was to pray and hope things would work well for Michelle. But she could not help but feeling that her husband had done a big mistake. They had just come back to Maui, and were beginning to get to know each other well. They were still newlywed, and needed their own space. Her father in law was doing something he should not do. He was living in adultery for years. He had brought his women even into the house to his wife. He was a *lost sheep,* and needed salvation. He was living his sick wife into the hands of his daughter in law, and they did not yet know each other well. Clemens was very concerned. Besides the fact that she was a foreigner raised in a different culture, and she was adapting to the new customs, all of them were not born again, including Michelle! Without the Holy Spirit would be very challenging for all of them. That situation was not a very good one. Clemens needed to pray for all of them, and she did.

After a long time, Michelle called her again. *"Clemens, I have tried to get along with my mother in law, but she is so picky. She has asthma and I learned to give her injections. This part is good, but I have to be constantly cleaning and cooking for everybody, I am more of a maid than a wife." "Oh, I am so sorry, but be patient. Maybe things will change after a while." "I do not see any way out. My husband is now not even coming home every night. He stays out. He is doing drugs." "Michelle are you sure?" "Yes I am. I saw the battle of cocaine, and he had an elastic tube like the one the nurses use when taking out blood." "Oh, this is really bad news."* Michelle continued to tell Clemens her practically desperate situation. Michelle had no one in America. No relatives at all, except her son. She felt trapped. This situation continued the same way for a few years. Meanwhile, Michelle began to feel depressed, and drank more than she should. She also smoked a lot. She felt lonely for her husband, who just as his father was now an adulterer. She tried New Age, but did not pursue it enough. She also bought one book on witchcraft which her mother in law suggested she buy. She tried to do one of those things they suggested to get money, but it did not work. She felt abandoned because her husband, not only lived his own life away from her, but he hardly gave her money to buy food and clothes. People were giving her their used clothes. She felt humiliated for never before in her life she put on used clothes from other people, except during the Second World War when she was a child. Now she was married, and was a maid to her husband family, and had no income.

During this time her mother in law, Antoinette, asked her to drive her to a Christian Healing Evangelist meeting. She did, and actually she enjoyed. But the next day when she told her brother in law Christopher to go with them, he refused. He said that he had his religion. He was Catholic and Catholic would die. When Michelle heard his speech, she also refused to take her mother in law back, for she also was Catholic. But Antoinette went to the meeting with someone else. That night, the evangelist prayed for her, and she was completely healed of her asthma! It was a miracle! Praise Yehovah! For sure that night she had also given her life to Yehoshua, otherwise the evangelist would not have prayed for her. She stayed healed for one year.

Meanwhile Michelle became completely possessed with evil spirits. She felt miserable, and completely deny the existence of Elohim. This situation lasted for about three months. Then one morning she decided to read a book that Christopher brought home a while ago. This book was teaching of another cult. Michelle refused to read it in the past, but that particular morning she decided to read it. She was looking for answers, and she could find none. To her surprise while flipping the pages, she noticed one page where Elohim (God) and Yehoshua (Jesus) was mentioned. As a Catholic girl she was familiar with those names, and she began to read. To her surprise she read that Yehovah loved her, and that Yehoshua also loved her and that He had died for her sins. Those words began to give her hope. She had believed there was no God, in Heaven or anywhere. And now she was reading that there is an Elohim, and that that Elohim loved her! She was starving for love. She was abandoned by her husband who left her to care for his family, and he was with other women doing drugs. Would there really be an Elohim that loved her? She had to find out. She left the book opened on the kitchen table and she ran into her bedroom to call upon that Elohim. She had to know the truth. She was desperate to know the truth. But in her mind she asked the question, *"Why has no one ever told me that Elohim loved me?"* Indeed she did cried out to Yehovah to reveal himself to her, she wanted to know if He was real. She knelt on the floor in her bedroom and cried out **"Yehovah if you are up there, I want to know. Yehoshua if you are there I want to know now."** That lasted for a few minutes, and suddenly she knew He was real, and Yehoshua was also real. At that point she repented for all her sins. Yehovah spoke to her spirit saying, **"You are been converted."**

She continued to sob uncontrollably for a while. She knew that only He could save her from going to hell! And she knew now that Hell was a real place, just as Heaven is. After a while she felt the presence of the Ruach haQodesh on her left side, and the inner voice told her, **"This is the Ruach haQodesh."** In that precise moment the Ruach haQodesh came inside of her, and she was born again. Now the Spirit of Yehovah was in her and He would be helping her. Yehoshua made this statement,

"No one can come to Me unless the Father who sent Me draws him; and I will rise him up at the last day. It is written in the prophets, 'And they shall all be taught by Elohim.'" Yochanan/ John 6:44-45

Indeed, the Father had taken personally Michelle to His Son Yehoshua, and He married her. Now Michelle was in the Kingdom of Yehovah, and became part of the Bride of Mashiach! What a miracle! That morning Yehovah saved her soul, and delivered her from cigarettes and alcohol! He had indeed set her free!

Now Yehovah is the Spirit; and where the Spirit of Yehovah is, there is liberty. **Qorin'tiyim 2/2 Corinthians 3:17.**

The Spirit of Yehovah taught her many things from that moment on.

He began to give her a desire to know more of Him. And she bought a study Bible that she read for the very first time in her life. Her husband had his grandmother's Bible, but although in the past she tried to read it, she could not grasp what she read. However, now the Spirit of Elohim in her taught her, and the Word made sense. Michelle allowed the Holy Spirit to change her life little by little. One of the changes was that she began to love her mother in law, and forgive her husband. Although nothing changed between her and her husband, she had peace. He continued his new life style, and she began her walk in the Spirit. A few month later she was divorced, and moved into another house with her son. However, Yehovah had told her that her husband was saved. Yehovah lives in eternity, and sees him saved, but Yehovah does not lie, therefore Michelle knows that one day He too will be saved and she will see him in Heaven.

CHAPTER 34

Humility

After having such long conversation with her friend Michelle, she decided to go for a little walk around the block, actually instead of walking she decided to run. After just a few minutes she realized that it would be a real good idea to stop running and simply walk back home. As soon as she arrived the phone rang again. She was not sure if she should answer the call, however she sensed in her spirit that she needed to answer the phone to talk to her old friend Biyu. She was a Chinese lady that she met several years ago at a prayer meeting. Clemens loved her name, which in Chinese means Jasper, precious stone.

"Hello Biyu how are you? I did not hear from you a long time?" "I am fine, I am just warring with a spirit of gluttony. Can you help me? I know I need to fast, but you know it is not easy. I am trying to lose at least 100 pounds because otherwise I cannot do the surgery. The doctor has told me he will not do the surgery unless I lose this weight." "How much do you weigh now?" "Well, I am about 100 pounds overweight." "But I am doing everything Yehovah tells me to do. I am obedient to Him."

Clemens knew her friend, and she knew she was a little boastful at times. Biyu continued to speak negatively about those people who supposedly had been speaking evil against her. She believed she was under a curse. Clemens explained to Biyu that a curse does attach itself to a person unless there is a reason.

Like a flitting sparrow, like a flying swallow, so a curse without cause shall not alight." **Mishley/Proverbs 26:2**

After talking a long time and Clemens realized that Biyu had not completely forgiven those people who were speaking against her. She was actually sending back the curses to those who were supposedly cursing her. At this point Clemens had to correct Biyu with the following verses of Scriptures.

"Blessed are those who are persecuted for righteousness' sake, for theirs is the kingdom of Heaven. 11 Blessed are you when they revile and persecute you, and say all kinds of evil against you falsely for My sake. Rejoice and be exceedingly glad, for great is your reward in Heaven, for so they persecuted the prophets who were before you." **Mattithyahu/Matthew 5:10-12**

Clemens told Biyu, she could not reverse the curse, because by doing this, she herself was cursing them. She was actually sinning against Yehovah and giving Satan more power over her life! She had to pray for them instead, and do good to them. Clemens suggested giving that person a small gift. But she did not answer; it is possible that she could not financially afford any extra expense at that particular time.

You have heard that it was said, 'You shall love your neighbor and hate our enemy.' But I say to you, love your enemies, bless those who curse you, do good to those who hate you, and pray for those who spitefully use you and persecute your, 45 that you may be sons of Your Father in Heaven; for He makes His sun rise on the evil and on the good, and sends rain on the just and on the unjust. 46 For if you love those who love you, what reward have you? Do not even the tax collectors do the same? 47 And if you greet your brethren only, what do you do more than others? Do not even the tax collectors do so? 48 Therefore you shall be perfect, just as your Father in Heaven is perfect." **Mattithyahu/ Matthew 5:43-48**

Clemens also instructed her to refuse the curse and rebuke the spirit of that curse. She also needed to command that demon to not hurt anyone else. After it all, we have been given power over the devil, **(Mattithyahu/Matthew 28:18; Marqos/Mark 16:17),** and we are kings and priests in the kingdom of Yehovah. Satan has to obey when we command him to leave in the all powerful name of Yehoshua.

But you are a chosen generation, a royal priesthood, a holy nation, his own special people, that you may proclaim the praises of Him who called you out of darkness into His marvelous light; who once were not a people but are now the people of Elohim, who had not obtained mercy but now have obtained mercy. **Kepha 2/2 Peter 2:9.**

With many words Clemens spoke to Biyu, and she agreed to stop sending back the curse. She did not realize that by sending it back to that person, she was also cursing a sister in the Kingdom of Yehovah. She repented as both friends prayed together. Yehovah is merciful and forgives us all the time, even when as the followers of Yehoshua behave in the flesh, and are not walking in the power of His Spirit. We are very thankful that He knows our frame; He knows that we are dust, and He knows that we miss the mark many times. However, He is longsuffering and He loves us so much. He is always willing to help us as He is preparing us to reign with Him for eternity.

We must always remember that Satan is the author of all evil. Satan is the one who entices the believers to disobey Yehovah. He uses human instruments because he is a spirit and can do little without a body. His plan is to destroy the Kingdom of Yehovah by destroying us, His children. And if we obey him we will end up with him in the lake of fire and brimstone.

The devil, who deceived them, was cast in to the lake of fire and brimstone where the beast and the false prophet are. And they will be tormented day and night forever and ever. **Chazon/ Revelation 20:10**

Men are ignorant and do not know what they are doing. Yehoshua said this while on the cross,

"Father forgive them, for they do not know what they do." **Luqas/Luke 23:34**

CHAPTER 35

Victories

Clemens went out shopping to Ross, and while on the bus she encountered Michelle. They came out of the bus on Kamehameha Avenue and walked to Whole Foods together. There they bought some snacks, and sat down outside the store to eat and chat. Clemens was curious to find out what had happen to her friend Michelle in the last few years. Because she traveled a lot, she did not know how Michelle lived her life after her salvation experience. Michelle began to tell her story. *"After I got saved, and got divorced, I took several trips. Yehovah began to show me the darkness in the church I had been baptized as a baby. Sometimes I would go to church and run away scare. I did not know how much darkness was in that church until then. Yehovah has delivered me from all idolatry. He actually; literally sent fire from heaven to burn the statue of Miryam, and other false gods."* Clemens was so amazed that Yehovah had done so much for her friend. *"Wow, this is amazing! Our Elohim never changes. What He has done in the past, He can do today, if we trust Him." "Amen!"* **"I am Yehovah, I do not change." Mal'aki / Malachi 3:6**

Because of what He did for me, He was able to sent me to my ex-mother in law Antoinette and warn her. I was led to give her a verse of Scripture.

"As a dog returns to his own vomit, so a fool repeats he folly." Mishley / Proverbs 26:11

Michelle, after she had received the baptism in the Ruach haQodesh/Holy Spirit had led her mother in law in prayer and she also received the power of the Holy Spirit. That same night, she had gotten up and began to speak in other tongues! But she never renounced Miryam's worship. She prayed the rosary and kept to attend service at that church. In other words she did not fully understand that Yehoshua was her only Savior, and He alone could give her eternal life. She still believed the Miryam was co-Savior with Yehoshua! These teachings had been to powerful for her, and she could not let go. She did not want to betray her family and friends; she loved them more than to be loved by her Elohim. She could not let go of her dead and idolatrous religion beliefs. But Michelle continued to pray for her and believed one day she would be set free from her idols. Eventually Antoinette became very sick and the family placed her in the nursing home.

Meanwhile her husband got sick, and went into Maui Memorial Hospital. Michelle went to visit him and he received Yehoshua as His Savior. That was a true miracle. The lost sheep was found by the Shepherd!

Meanwhile Antoinette began to be sick again. For long time she was completely healed, but all sickness returned worse than before. Her house had been cleansed, but left empty, and a worse thing happened to her.

"When an unclean spirit goes out of a man, he goes through dry places, seeking rest, and finds none. Then he says, 'I will return to my house from which I came.' And when he comes, he finds it empty, swept, and put in order. Then he goes and takes with him seven other spirits more wicked than himself, and they enter and dwell there; and the last state of that man is worse than the first. So shall it also be with this wicked generation." **Mattithyahu/ Matthew 12:43-45**

One day Louise, her sister in law, the daughter of her mother in law, came to visit her, and told her that her mother was very sick. Michelle went to the Nursing Home, and visited Antoinette. She was in a coma. Louise asked her if she would not mind staying with her mother, because she needed to go home to rest. She had been there all night. Michelle was so happy to have time alone with her. As soon as Louise left the room, she began to talk with her ex-mother in law. She knew that when a person is in a coma they can hear and understand. Therefore she told her that she needed to renounce worshiping Miryam and consecrate herself completely to Yehovah. Michele let her in a prayer of repentance, and acceptance of Yehoshua. She believed in her heart that she was now saved. After Louise returned she went home a few hours to rest but came back. She was still tired and took a brief nap on a recliner they had placed outside the patient room. She only slept a few minutes and she saw a vision. She saw a dark mountain, but on top of the mountain was a **golden mansion**. She got up knowing Antoinette was going to her mansion in Heaven. Just a few minutes later Antoinette came out from her coma and began her ascension to the mountain. She had difficulty breathing because of her lung problems, but in a few minutes she went home to be with her Savior. Michelle said, *"Yehovah loves us so much that He waits on the right time to minister to us. He already knows the end from the beginning. He waits to be able to be gracious to us."*

Therefore Yehovah will wait, that He may be gracious to you; and therefore He will be exalted, that He may have mercy on you. For Yehovah is an Elohim of justice; blessed are all those who wait for Him. Yeshayahu/Isaiah 30:18

Michelle after leading her ex-father in law to the Savior, and also his wife, she felt her work was done in that household. Now she understood the reason why she had to take care of her mother in law. The times had been difficult for almost five long years. But paid off when she herself was saved, and was used by Elohim to minister to her husband family. Both of them, mother and father in law, who had been lost sheep, were now found by their Savior. Their lives had been changed forever. Now love reign in that family, because LOVE moved in with them.

CHAPTER 36

Pride

———————

Clemens realized that her friend Ai needed to search her heart against pride. At times Ai would speak how much Yehovah was using her, and talked a lot about her prophetic gift. Clemens thought of Yeshua's the parable, *"Two men went up to the temple to pray"*.

"Two men went up to the temple to pray, one a Pharisee and the other a tax collector. The Pharisee stood and prayed thus with himself, 'Elohim I thank You that I am not like other men-extortioners, unjust, adulterers, or even as this tax collector. I fast twice a week; I give tithes of all that I possess.' And the tax collector, standing afar off, would not so much as raise his eyes to heaven, but beat his breast, saying, 'Elohim, be merciful to me a sinner! I tell you, this man went down to his house justified rather than the other; for everyone who exalts himself will be humbled, and he who humbles himself will be exalted." **Luqas/Luke 18:10-14**

Pride and self-righteousness were the sins of the Pharisee, and many times our own sins. *Yehovah resists the proud, but gives grace to the humble.* **Ya'aqov/James 4:6**

Clemens remembered that at the beginning of her ministry, she had to fast to get rid of pride. The pastor used her publicly as an example and bragged about her. He recognized her gifting and praised her publicly, instead of glorifying Elohim who had gifted her. That pastor did not realize that he was not helping her. However, the Ruach haQodesh convicted her of pride. She quickly learned to fast, and when she did the spirit of pride would immediately leave. That went on for a while, until she had complete victory. Yehovah spoke about fasting in His Word. However, we do not fast to be seen by men, or to get our way with Him. But true fasting is done to lose the bonds of wickedness and more.

"Is this not the fast that I have chosen: to lose the bonds of wickedness, to undo the heavy burdens, to let the oppressed go free, and that you break every yoke? 7 Is it not to share your bread with the hungry, and that you bring to your house the poor who are cast out; when you see the naked, that you cover him, and not hide yourself from your own flesh? 8 Then your light shall break forth like the morning, your healing shall spring forth speedily, and your righteousness shall go before you; the glory of Yehovah shall be your rear guard. 9 Then you shall call, and Yehovah will answer; you shall cry, and He will say, 'Here I am.' **Yeshayahu/ Isaiah 58:6-9**

Clemens learned to fast to lose herself from her own bondage, and Yehovah was there to answer her request. Eventually at times she would give the money that she would use to eat on that fast day to the poor. Fasting is not the means to save money or to lose weight. But if we fast for the right motives Yehovah is pleased and will answer us.

However, a very proud man will be arising into power, *That* person will say that he is Yeshua in the flesh. If you are a born again, believer, you will know that he is a liar. He will demand complete submission, and most of the world will follow him. Be not deceived. Remember Yehovah declares all men unrighteous; there is none who does good. This man of sin, as the Scriptures calls him, will ridicule the true Elohim, and deny His Existence because he will declare that he is god.

Clemens was shocked to hear a prominent leader speaking things contrary to the Word of Yehovah. He is a world religious leader, but he is very deceived and is deceiving the world. She saw one of his services on YouTube, and the cantor was singing in Latin praises to Satan, instead of Yehovah.

This man is denying that Yehovah created the world in six days. He also denies the Scriptures to be the Word of Elohim. He is proclaiming that there are many ways to Heaven. He says that all gods are one god with many names, which is false. He also says that everyone will be saved and go to Heaven no matter what name they call their god. He is an imposter and an apostate. These and many more lies he will continue to speak to deceive many. He is deceived and will deceive all who do not have a close relationship with Elohim. He is turning away weak believers from the true Elohim. He may eventually deny the existence of Elohim Yehovah, and of His Ben/ Son Yehoshua.

***The fool has said in His heart, "There is no Elohim." They are corrupt, they have done abominable works, there is none who does good.* Tehillim/Psalm 14:1; 53:1**

When a man expects obedience to his doctrine, and says that he can prevent you from going to Heaven if you disobey him, he is not speaking truth. He is filled with Satan, and he is an impostor, an adulterer, and a harlot. Flee from such person for he is greatly deceived. If you encounter such person or you see him on television, run away from him, for he is a false prophet.

The man of sin, also called the Anti-Messiah, as already mentioned, will demand complete obedience. He will have the false prophet to help him. He will also be a homosexual; he will not care for the love of women. Eventually he will persecute the saints who will not bow their knee to worship him.

"I was watching; and the same horn was making war against the saints, and prevailing against them; 25 He shall speak pompous words against the Most High, shall persecute the saints of the Most High." Daniel 7:21, 25

Believers, now is the time to repent of any sin, and be consecrated to Yehovah in Yehoshua's Name. Repent of lukewarmness, and serve Yehovah with all your heart. The time is very short before the tribulation and the return of Yehoshua. Be ready for any test you may have to go through. Yehoshua said that we must be watching.

But take heed to yourselves, lest your hearts be weighed down with carousing, drunkenness, and cares of this life, and that day come on you unexpectedly. For it will come as a snare on all those who dwell on the face of the whole earth. Watch therefore, and pray always that you may be counted worthy to escape all these things that will come to pass, and to stand before the Son of Man." **Luqas/Luke 21:34**

Clemens has been praying to be counted worthy to escape the tribulation that is coming on this earth. Yehovah will judge this planet because of many sins, and **especially** because the murdering of the innocent. The sin of abortion is an abomination to Him, together with the same- sex marriage new law, which is conceived to mock Yehovah. **But He will not be mocked.**

Do not be deceived, Elohim is not mocked; for whatever a man sows, that he will also reap. For he who sows to his flesh will of the flesh reap corruption, but he who sows to the Spirit will of the Spirit reap everlasting life. **Galatiyim/Galatians 6:7-8**

Yehovah knows our heart.

The Christian sinners usually when they are sinning say: But God knows my heart. What does the Scripture say on this subject?

The heart is deceitful above all things, and desperately wicked; who can know it? I, Yehovah, search the heart, I test the mind, even to give every man according to his ways, according to the fruit of his doings. **Yirmeyahu/Jeremiah 17:9-10**

Yehovah knows us intimately. We cannot fake devotion. Either we love Yehovah or we do not. But if we are faithful to Him, he can take us home before His judgment to the unrighteous comes down the earth in its fullness. His Hand of protection toward America is distancing more and more because He loves us, and He allows some things to happen to test our faith. But He does not to judge the believers. We judge ourselves when we come to Him in repentance.

I am not Yehovah. I do not know how He is going to deal with the believers who are becoming more concerned with the world than with what pleases Him. I know He hates lukewarmness, for He says, that He will spit them out of His mouth!

"I know your works, that you are neither cold nor hot. I could wish you were cold or hot. So then because you are lukewarm, and neither cold or hot, I will vomit you out of My mouth." **Chazon/Revelation 3:15-16**

All of us must seek Him and repent, or we will be lost for eternity. Do not be deceived. Know your Elohim now. Study His Word, and keep his Commandments. Fill your soul and mind with the Truth, and when deception comes your way, you will discern it and will not fall into the trap. Keep on seeking Yehovah and Yehoshua. Do not venture into some new thing, for there is nothing new under the sun. The Ruach haQodesh will give you the discernment when you need it. Elohim alone can protect you from the deceiver. Remember Yehoshua's Word,

"I am the Way, the Truth, and the Life. No one comes to the Father except through Me. Yochanan/John 14:6

"Then the Son of Man will appear in Heaven, and then all the tribes of the earth will mourn, and they will see the Son of Man coming on the clouds of Heaven with power and great glory." Mattithyahu/Matthew 24:30

CHAPTER 37

The Defiled

It was a Sabbath day and Clemens was resting and praying all day. Then she decided to call a friend, but that person was not available. Eventually she just sent a text to the daughter or her close friend who had gone into eternity recently. Suddenly she tried to call her long lost friend Danielle, a very old friend that she had lost contact with. To her surprise Danielle answered the phone! *"Danielle is it you? Wow! Got you! How are you!" "Well, I recognized the number and I answered. Then I heard you speaking in tongues, How are you? It is such a long time since we talked."* Clemens began to share how she had been spending a lot of more time in prayer, and how Yehoshua had been giving her revelations. She told Danielle that Yehoshua is raising up prayer warriors in these last day, for the days that we are going to approach will be challenging to many followers of the Mashiach. The Spirit of the Antichrist is raising to power very fast and Yehovah needs to equip us to be able to stand against the works of Satan. Danielle listened intently and then both began to intercede in tongues for while. While praying in tongues Clemens saw a vision of Danielle dressed in white long dress with a red drape from the right shoulder to the left foot. The vision spoke to the purity of the faith of Danielle, and the covering of the regal mantle. But also speaks of the Blood of Yehoshua that is covering her life. Danielle told Clemens that she saw the earth tremble when she prayed. Demons was being defeated, she was like a general commending the enemy to flee. They continued to pray in tongues for long times. Then Clemens shared how she went through a spiritual attack, she thought her time to go to Heaven was near. But after much prayer, she had gotten the victory. Then Danielle told Clemens that she needed to ask a person to cover her with prayer continually. When a person is in ministry needs strong prayer covering. Clemens offered to pray for Danielle, and now Danielle will intercede regularly for Clemens. At this point Danielle shared with Clemens that one of her daughters, Irma, had left her faith in Yehovah and Yehoshua, and is now performing gay weddings. She had been raised at the same church that her mother and father had been for many years, yet she has backslidden. Danielle is heartbroken. Then she shared about the fourth daughter whose name is Aurora and is now married to an older woman! Danielle shared how Aurora had been involved in the Youth Ministry. She would bring her friends to church, and was on fire for Yehovah. Then she went to the College of a Big Christian Organization, but she left because she saw the hypocrisy and went to a women's College. That brought her downfall. Her Basket Ball Coach, an elderly lesbian woman courted Aurora, who was very innocent, and defiled her. She never recovered. And as soon as the same sex marriages law passed, they were married! How devious is Satan to trap such young Christian? Whose fault is it? Did not the Youth Group Leader warn the youth to be on guard against predators?

Actually, in the eyes of Yehovah, the family is the most important guardian of their children. Yehovah holds parents responsible to teach their children, especially Christians and Messianic parents. Did they warn the girls to protect their virginity? Did the parents not warn their daughters of the dangers in the world? Certainly they never thought their daughters were in danger of losing their faith. Maybe they were naïve. They trusted them because they went to church with them and could never imagine such thing would happen to them. We do not know why, except that Satan is as a roaring lion seeking whom he may devour. He is no respecter of person, and loves to entice the believers in Yehoshua. We must be continually be on guard.

Many parents think that because their children know Yehovah they will be fine. But they forget that the devil is waiting for the right opportunity to destroy their family. He has nothing good in him, and will harass the virgins, so that he can control them and destroy their lives.

Danielle is a fervent worshiper. She hears Yehovah's Word. She if faithful. But her husband, Antonio, is not fulfilling his role as the priest and king in the home.

"But I want you to know that the head of every man is Mashiach, the head of woman is man, and the head of Mashiach is Yehovah." **Qorin'tiyim 1/1 Corinthians 11:3**

Yes, apparently, he has never completely surrendered his life to the Savior, Yehoshua. He is still, to some extent, on the fence. While praying for him, Clemens discerned that Antonio is resisting the calling upon his life, and may have some secret sin. This sin is keeping him away from Him who can set him free. That sin may be simple trust in Yehovah, but it is hindering him from fulfilling his destiny according to what is written in his books in Heaven. Danielle believes in her hearth, that when her husband surrenders his life to the leadership of Yehovah, the whole family will come to faith. But presently there are three lost sheep in one household! Irma and Aurora are kept in bondage by the enemy, and so is their father. Clemens as promised to pray for this family on a daily bases. She encouraged Danielle with two Scriptures.

"All your children shall be taught by Yehovah, and great shall be the shalom of Your children. **Yeshayahu/Isaiah 54:13**

"As for Me," says Yehovah, "This is My covenant with them: My Spirit who is upon you, and My words which I have put in Your mouth, shall not depart from your mouth, nor from the mouth of Your descendants, nor from the mouth of Your descendants' descendants," Says Yehovah, "from this time and forevermore." Yeshayahu/Isaiah 59:21

"And whatever you ask in My name, that I will do, that the Father may be glorified in the Son. If you ask anything in My name, I will do it." Yochanan/John 14:13-14

Yehoshua adds the following words, *"If you love Me, keep My commandments." (v. 15)*

Together with prayer, He expects us to be obedient to His Word, and this part it is difficult for some. But Clemens knew Danielle would obey Him in every area of her life. Danielle is in love with Yehoshua, and she is very attentive to hear His voice and also to obey it. However, Clemens continued to share the Word of Yehovah to Danielle to encourage her. She is convinced that His Word is the anchor of our faith, for His Word does not return void.

Seek Yehovah while He may be found, Call upon Him while He is near. Let the wicked forsake his way, and the unrighteous man his thoughts; let him return to Yehovah and He will have mercy on him; and to our Elohim, for He will abundantly pardon. "For My thoughts are not your thoughts, nor are your ways My ways," says Yehovah. "For as the heavens are higher than the earth, so are My ways higher than your ways, and My thoughts than your thoughts. For as the rain comes down, and the snow from Heaven, and do not return there, but water the earth, and make it bring forth and bud, that it may give seed to the sower and bread to the eater; so shall My Word be that goes forth from

My mouth; it shall not return to Me void, but it shall accomplish what I please, and it shall prosper in the thing for which I sent it." **Yeshayahu 55:6-11**

They continued to intercede in tongues and in English for a long while, and finally said their good nights. Yehovah will answer their prayers prayed in complete unity.

Chapter 38

Defilement

Clemens decided to help her close friend Adriana who lived up country. She was living at her home for a few months. She had been asked to come up to help her because Adriana had surgery and needed help until she would recover. Clemens also needed a good place to stay for she had been waiting for her apartment to open up. She felt it would be a great opportunity to be together with Adriana and her family. But now Adriana was beginning to feel better, and the atmosphere in the home changed drastically. Adriana could not endure Clemens diet. But the special diet that Clemens was following was the biblical diet of Leviticus 11, which teaches us to know what is good for our health and what is not. Pig is an unclean animal and therefore is not supposed to be eaten. Some of the other unclean animals are shrimp, lobster, and clams, and many more. Adriana loved those animals, while but Clemens refused to eat them. One day as Clemens was cooking dinner Adriana came in with the open Bible and she said, *"The priest said Jesus said we can eat everything now."* Then she took the bible and showed Clemens the Scriptures. Now Clemens knew a battle was on. She was calm and listened to what Adriana read in the Bible.

"Are you thus without understanding also? Do you not perceive that whatever enters a man from outside cannot defile him,

because it does no enter his heart but his stomach, and is elimi-nated, thus purifying all foods." **Marqos/Mark 7:18-19**

Clemens knew she was attacked by her friend because she kept the Sabbath day holy, and obeyed the teaching in the Bible, which Adriana, as a Catholic girl would not. Actually her church taught that the Bible was not even the Word of Elohim, but the words of man, and they should only obey what their leader says. We are not to fear man, but Elohim alone. When a leader expects to be called father, he is usurping the title that belongs to Yehovah alone. There is only one Father we must obey and honor: Yehovah. Yehoshua also warns us about this false teaching.

"Do not call anyone on earth you father; for One is your Father, He who is in Heaven." **Mattithyahu/Matthew 23:9**

Of course He was not saying we cannot call our earthly father, father. He is our parent, and we supposed to honor our parents.

"Honor your father and your mother, that your days may be long upon the land which Yehovah your Elohim is giving you." **Shemot/Exodus 20:12**

When reading the whole chapter in the gospel of Marqos we learn that Yehoshua was not speaking of foods, but of words we speak,

Yehoshua was speaking of defilement because the Pharisees accused the apostles to eat with unwashed hands. First and fore-most there is no Commandment that says to wash our hands before we eat. Secondly the Pharisees had and still have many added teachings that Yehovah never gave us. They wash hands not as we do, they do it as a tradition and a ceremony, and Yehoshua would not do that, because it was not His Commandment, but a com-mandment of men. 23 verses of Marqos are needed to explain away that according to the priest we can eat anything, but this is not the teaching. Yehoshua clearly says that what we put in our mouths does not defile us, but what comes out. When we curse, gossip, murder, we speak harshly to someone, and we do all types of sin, those things defile us. In other words those are sinful, but it is not sinful and does not defile us if we do not wash our hands ceremonially as they were doing. They did not wash their hands with soap and water to get clean. They just poured a little of water on their hands and prayed saying that Yehovah commanded them to do it. But He did not. And Yehoshua and the apostles would not do that because that was not a commandment of Yehovah. Yehoshua was exposing their man made traditions (See Deuteronomy 4:2). We could get sick if we did not wash our hands with soap and water after touching something dirty, which would make us sick, but would not defile our spirit. We would not go to hell because of it. Yehovah would not condemn us. This is the true teaching. However, the churches take it to mean that Yehovah changed the dietary Commandment, which He never did.

"Do not think that I came to destroy the Law of the Prophets. I did not come to destroy but to fulfill. For assuredly, I say to you, till heaven and earth pass away, one jot or one title will by no means pass from the law till all be fulfilled. Whoever therefore breaks one of the least of these commandments, and teaches men so, shall be called least in the kingdom of Heaven; but whoever does and teaches them, he shall be called great in the kingdom of Heaven. For I say to you, that unless your righteousness exceeds the righteousness of the scribes and Pharisees, you will by no means enter the kingdom of Heaven." **Mattithyahu/ Matthew 5:17-20**

Indeed, Yehoshua is the Word of Elohim made Flesh. He is the author of the Torah, which is called Law in English. Therefore He could not destroy any one of His own Rules or He could not judge the Pharisees and the scribes.

In Marqos/Mark 7 and Mattithyahu/Matthew 15 He is speaking of defilement, which is a spiritual issue, and not about food that we eat and is eliminated. Words we speak are enduring and hurt people and ourselves for eternity unless we stop and repent.

Defilement comes from within

At this point is proper to remember that our words do make us unclean or defiled, and even sick. Our words indeed can cause a lot or problems. Please read the teaching concerning Lashon hara. Open the book of Leviticus chapters 13-14. Our words can hurt us and make us unclean or spiritually defiled.

Beware of the traditions of men.

Then the scribes and Pharisees who were from Yerushalayim/ Jerusalem came to Yeshua, saying, Why do Your disciples transgress the tradition of the elders? For they do not wash their hands when they eat bread." He answered and said to them, "Why do you also transgress the Commandments of Elohim because of Your tradition? For Elohim commanded, saying, 'Honor your father and your mother" and 'He who curses father or mother, let him be put to death. But you say, 'Whoever says to his father or mother, "Whatever profit you might have received from me is a gift to Elohim"- then he need not honor his father or mother.'" Thus you have made the Commandment of Elohim of no effect by your tradition. Hypocrites! Well did Yeshayahu/Isaiah prophesy about you, saying:'These people draw near to Me with their mouth, and honor Me with their lips, but their heart is far from Me. And in vain they worship Me, teaching as doctrines the commandments of men." When He had called the multitude to Himself, He said to them, "Hear and understand: Not what goes into the mouth defiles a man; but what comes out of the mouth, this defiles a man." **Mattithyahu / Matthew 15:1-11**

Once again food does not defile us. However, our own words that we speak to others will defile us and them, if they are not spoken in love. They, indeed, will defile us. Eating pig or lobster will not defile us, but can hurt physically because Yehovah has not created those animals for consumption. Some are created to clean up the mess the clean animal leave behind. Those animals are not "Food."

Now Yehovah spoke to Mosheh / Moses and Aaron, saying to them, 'Speak to the children of Israel, saying, "These are the animals which you may eat among all the animals that are on the earth: Among the animals, whatever divides the hoof, having cloven hooves and chewing the cud-that you may eat. Nevertheless these you shall not eat among those that chew the cud or those that have cloven hooves: the camel, because it chews the cud but does not have cloven hooves, is unclean to you; the rock hyrax, because it chews the cud but does not have cloven hooves, is unclean to you; the hare, because it chews the cud but does not have cloven hooves, is unclean to you; and the swine, thought it divides the hoof, having cloven hooves, yet does not chew the cud, is unclean to you. Their flesh you shall not eat, and their carcasses you shall not touch. They are unclean to you. **Wayyiqra / Leviticus 11:1-8**

Yehoshua said, "I say to you, till Heaven and earth pass away, one jot or one tittle will by no means pass from the law till all is fulfilled." **Mattithyahu 5:18.**

Why the churches refuse to misuse the Word to eliminate anything that the "Jews" do? Because it is anti-Semitism. The church cannot survive without the root, yet they disdain the Root.

For if the firstfruit is holy, the lump is also holy; and if the root is holy, so are the branches. And if some of the branches were broken off, and you, being a wild olive tree, were grafted in among them, and with them became a partaker of the root and fatness of the olive tree, do not boast against the branches. But if you do boast, remember that you do not support the root, but the root supports you. You will say then, "Branches were broken off that I might be grafted in. Well said. Because of unbelief they were broken off, and you stand by faith. Do not be haughty, but fear. For if Elohim did not spare the natural branches, He may not spare you either. Therefore consider the goodness and severity of Elohim: on those who fell, severity; but toward you, goodness. If you continue in His goodness. Otherwise you also will be cut off." **Romiyim/ Romans 11:16-22**

The church stopped from obeying the Commands because of anti-Semitism, and has chosen never to recover from her mistakes. Yehovah is longsuffering. However, now He is choosing those who will obey Him, and He will use them in these last days before His return. Others may fall away.

Sadly Clemens was not able to convince Adriana. Eventually their relationship became stronger again, but Adriana has chosen to eat what she wants, and to believe the false teachers. Clemens prays for her and her family. Some day, she hopes, that all family will be set free from the traditions of men. Yehovah alone can convince a soul of sin, and consequently change and obey His Word. Adriana could be much healthier if she would obey the Creator who created the animals we are able to eat, and refuse those He created to be used ecologically. But pride and traditions are very difficult, for some people, to let go. However, Yehovah will answer the prayer of the saints as they intercede for those who are still blind. Nothing is impossible to those who believe. He will destroy the wisdom of the wise and bring the nothing the understanding of the prudent.

"Therefore, behold, I will again do a marvelous work among this people, a marvelous work and a wonder; for the wisdom of their wise men shall perish, and the understanding of their prudent men shall be hidden." **Yeshayahu/Isaiah 29:14**

C H A P T E R 39

Asham

———————

Someone knocked on the living room door while Clemens was taking a much needed nap. Reluctantly she went to open the door. To her great surprise the visitor was Alison, one of her best friends.

*"Alison, how nice you come to visit. I missed you. I have not seen you for such a long time, come in!"*Both embraced and cried a little bit. So much had taken place since they had seen each other. Alison began to speak. *"Clemens I came to talk with you because I have to let this out. Please help me to get rid of this guilt. "What happened? What have you done Alison? But first, please sit down. Then you can tell me what you have done that keeps you in such state of guilt.""By the way, can I offer you a cup of hot coco" " Sure Clemens."* While the coco was being prepared, Alison burst into tears. Clemens could not grasp the gravity of the problem. Gently, but firmly, she asked Alison again, *"What is the problem, tell me already!"* Clemens knew Alison very well, and could not picture in her mind that her friend could have done something so horrible to cause her to cry. However, Alison had a wonderful walk with her Master, Yehoshua, and whatever she had done, must hurt her very much, because she sinned against her Savior.

Finally Alison spoke. *"Yesterday, I was speaking to my neighbor Himari and was explaining to her that her son cannot come to pick from the mango tree all the fruit he wants without asking permission from the office, because this is the rule. I read the monthly bulletin and this what it says. He has been coming all the time since the tree has ripened mengoes. I also told her that because she is a Christian if she disobeys the rule, she is sinning. I told her that, and much more."* In the course of the conversation I also told her not to take yoga because yoga is a cult. I do not want her to go to hell, if she will not repent. But she gave me a dirty look, like satan was looking at me. However, I prayed for her and for her memory because she has dementia."

"The following day two guys with yellow shirts came to the mango tree by my apartment and they began picking mangoes. I took for granted they were workers here in this facility. So I asked them to give me some mangoes. They were very nice and asked me if I wanted them green. I answered no. I like them ripe. So I only took four although the tree was loaded with many mangoes. Then I took two mangoes to Himari, but she refused saying she had plenty, which I am sure it is true." "Well what is wrong about this?* Clemens could not yet understand, and asked her, *"What is the point?"The point is that maybe the two workers were not working in our facility and they did not have permission to pick from the tree.We have been given the notice from the office that we cannot pick from the tree, but if we want to pick we have to ask for permission from the office and we can pick only two or three."This is why I am crying because if they were illegally picking I took the mangoes illegally too."* Now Clemens began to understand the problem. Alison is very sensitive and very attentive on keeping the Commandments, and the office rules are the same as the Commandments in the Bible, because by disobeying them there would be a penalty. Rules are rules and need to be obeyed. *"OK, Alison, now I understand. But you did not know and still do not know if they were true workers of your facility or not. This sin was taken care with an offering called Asham, which was a guilt offering. Have you repented to Yehovah about this? Have you received your forgiveness and asked for the Blood of Yehoshua to be applied?"Well, I have but I still feel guilty."*

Clemens knows now how to calm and encourage her dear friend. *"Alison you have already repented of Your sin to Yehovah, therefore you must* believe the Word, He has forgiven you for He knows all about your sin, and He loves you."

For as the heavens are high above the earth, so great is His mercy toward those who fear Him; As far as the east is from the west, so far has He removed our transgressions from us. As a father pities His children, so Yehovah pities those who fear Him. For He knows our frame; He remembers that we are dust. Tehillim/Psalm 103:11-14

In the Book of Wayyiqra/ Leviticus there are recorded all the various Offerings. Yehoshua fulfilled those sacrifices. There was one offering called Asham which was a guilt offering. This offering was done *"If a person sins, and commits any of these things which are forbidden to be done by the Commandments of Yehovah, though he does not know it, yet he is guilty and shall bear his iniquity. And he shall bring to the priest a ram without blemish from the flock, with your valuation, as a trespass offering. So the priest shall make atonement for him regarding his ignorance in which he erred and did not know it, and it shall be forgiven him. It is a trespass offering; he has certainly trespassed against Yehovah."* **Wayyiqra/Leviticus 5:17-19.**

"After you took the mangoes you were attacked by guilt. Yet you did not know for sure, and you continue to feel guilty. Yehoshua paid the penalty for all types of guilt. He has become our Asham/guilt offering."

"Yeshayahu/Isaiah 53 says it all. He paid the full price for our sins, for our transgressions, for our iniquities, for our healing, for our guilt, for our Shalom, even for our free will offering. He is our Olah/free will offering. Our Minchah/meal offering. Our Shelamim/peace offering. Our Shalmei Todah/ thank offerings. Our Chatat/ sin offering. Our Asham/guilt offering".

"Yehoshua offered Himself freely to die for us taking our place on the cross. His Blood was shed for you and me, therefore today you can be at peace.

*He paid the price in full, and you do not have to feel guilty. In fact if you persists on **feeling** guilty you offend Him. Stop feeling guilty. Did you give away the same amount of mangoes those guys gave you? "Yes, I gave much more than that. But still I could not get rid of the guilt until now. Now I feel free. I can worship Him and be thankful again. Thank you Clemens for helping me to understand, you are a real good friend. Thank you for teaching me and loving me. I love you."*

Alison left with restored joy and peace. And Clemens went to the keyboard to practice her piano lesson. She also felt strengthened in her spirit and thankful to Yehoshua for what He has done for her. However the following day Alison called her and told Clemens that the two boys who gave her the mangoes were new workers at the facility, and they work in the kitchen. Therefore she did not sin at all. They had the legal right to give her the mangoes. She was so happy and rejoiced once again. She was truly free, and very thankful to Yehovah that she did not sin against her Savior.

C H A P T E R   40

Lashon Hara

Clemens was teaching the Parashah of the week which includes the following passage. *"You shall not go about as a talebearer among your people; nor shall you take a stand against the life of Your neighbor: I am Yehovah. 17 You shall not hate your brother in your heart. You shall surely rebuke your neighbor, and not bear sin because of him. 18 You shall not take vengeance, nor bear any grudge against the children of Your people, but you shall love your neighbor as yourself; I am Yehovah."* **Wayyiqra /Leviticus 19:16-18**

Lashon Hara means "the evil tongue," but it is not only when someone is slandering someone or using profanity. Lashon hara means saying something bad about another person *even if it happens to be true. Lashon hara* is gossip. When someone is speaking about another person with a critical spirit it is *Lashon hara,* or evil tongue. The consequence of this sin, and some other sins, in Israel was that they became affected by Tsara'at, which was a sickness of the skin. The translators translated Tsara'at as leprosy. However, it was not as the leprosy we know. It was a chastisement Yehovah released to those who could not forgive and spoke evil or critical of another person that was not present. *Tsara'at* was not only the punishment for gossip, but also other kinds of sin, such as pride, theft, a vain oath, adultery, murder,

191

but most of all was the punishment for the sin of *lashon hara,* or the evil tongue. When a person realized to be afflicted had to go to the priest. The priest had to inspect that person and if afflicted by *Tsara'at* it had to be quarantine outside the camp, until that person would repent and be healed.

Now the leper whom the sore is, his clothes shall be torn and his head bare; and he shall cover his mustache, and cry, "Unclean!" Unclean!" 46 He shall be unclean (tamei'). All the days he has the sore he shall be unclean. He is unclean, ad he shall dwell alone; his dwelling shall be outside the camp. **Wayyiqra/ Leviticus 13:45-46**

The law of been alienated outside the camp was called *metzorah* (dwelling outside the camp).

He would not be allowed to speak to anyone during the time of his punishment. He had plenty time to repent. Once the leper was healed as in the case of the leper Yehoshua healed, he had to present himself to the priest again.

Then Yehovah spoke to Mosheh / Moses, saying, This is the law of the leper for the day of his cleansing" He shall be brought to the priest. And the priest shall go out of the camp, and the priest shall examine him; and indeed, if the leprosy (tzara'at) is healed in the leper, then the priest shall command to take for him who is to be cleansed two living and clean birds, cedar wood, scarlet, and hyssop. And the priest shall command that one of the birds be killed in an earthen vessel over running water. As for the living bird, he shall take it, the cedar wood shend the scarlet and the hyssop, and dip them and the living bird in the blood of the bird that was killed over the running water. And he shall sprinkle it seven times on him, who is to be cleansed from the leprosy, and shall pronounce him clean, and shall let the living bird loose in the open field. He who is to be cleansed shall wash his clothes, shave off all his hair, and wash himself in water, that he may be clean. After that he shall come into the camp, and shall stay outside his tent seven days. But on the seventh day he shall shave all the hair off his head and his beard and his eyebrows-all his hair he shall shave off. He shall wash his clothes and wash his body in water, and he shall be clean. **Wayyiqra 14:1-9**

We see that blood has to be shed for his cleansing. The two birds, one had to die, and one had to be covered with the blood of the dead bird. I believe in this act we can picture the Mashiach, who came to die for us, and was covered with blood, but He rose from the dead. The live birth represents the resurrection of Mashiach. The water is a type of the Word of Elohim. Yehoshua is the Word made flesh. But the Scriptures continue to say that ex-leper after eight days, had to bring two male lambs of the first year. The lambs once again remind us on the Passover Lamb, Yehoshua our Sacrifice! Space does not allow me to write all the verses, but I suggest you will read this whole chapter. What we learn is that lashon hara or the evil tongue is a grave sin. We sing against Yehovah and our neighbor, and repentance is necessary for us to be made whole again.

Clemens, the teacher, while she read the Scriptures she realized that she also had been affected by **lashon hara.** Just a few days before the Shabbat bible teaching, she had complained about a friend who had her somehow hurt her feelings. It was not a big deal, but she related the offense to two other friends. She also talked with the person who had offended her, in obedience to the Word of Yehovah, explaining that she would not be able to do what she wanted her to do.

"Moreover if your brother sins against you, go and tell him his fault between you and him alone" **Mattithyahu/Matthew 18:15-16**

However she needed to make some corrections in her own life. Repentance was necessary. She did not get afflicted with *tzara'at,* on her skin, but in her spirit she felt guilty and needed to repent there at the presence of her friends. Each one in the Bible study was convicted that day. We are all guilty, but as followers of our Mashiach Yehoshua who gave His life to redeem us from our sin, we can repent. We must come to Him, who is our Priest and let Him inspect us. When we repent He is faithful and forgiving. The Father loves us and forgives us, but we cannot continue to repent for the same sin. Once we repent, we must stop doing it. Some Christians are living with their boy friend and repent occasionally, but continue to do the something day after day. They never stop the relationship with the saying, *"We are going to get married."* Beloved, this is not repentance. Repentance means to stop going the wrong way, and choose to obey our Creator with all our hearts. If they are going to get married, they have to wait to live as husband and wife until they are legally married. This is righteousness. But until them while they are sinning, they are lost sheep. They have to choose to want to obey Yehovah, for His grace is sufficient to each of us to obey Him. Al glory is to Him alone, our King and our Savior! Sometimes we have to cut relationships with unrepented sexually immoral people.

But now I have written to you not to keep company with anyone named a brother, who is sexually immoral, or covetous, or an idolater, or a reviler, or a drunkard, or an extortioner-not even to eat with such a person. For what have I do with judging those also who are outside? Do you not judge those who are inside? But those who are outside Elohim judges. Therefore "Put away from yourselves the evil person." Qorin'tiyim 1/1 Corinthians 5:11-13

Fornicators will not inherit the Kingdom of Elohim (6:9).

The same rule is for the gossipers who destroy their neighbor by killing their reputation. Let us be Holy, for Yehovah is holy. We must judge ourselves so that Yehovah will not judge us. Repentance from the heart must be made. Yehovah is merciful and loving and He will grant us His forgiveness on the bases of the shed Blood of Yehoshua haMashiach, our Messiah, on Calvary.

Chapter 41

Holiness

Clemens was talking on the telephone with one of her friends and the conversation subject was Holiness. *"Atara, do you know that Yehovah has called us to be holy?" "O Yes, I know." "Really?" "Do you understand what it means to be holy?" "Well, yes, I know, it is to go to church on Sunday and to obey Him." "Well Yehovah does not say to go to church on Sunday, but to keep the Sabbath day holy, which is Saturday, not Sunday!"*

Atara was shocked! *"What did you say?" "We have to keep the Sabbath day holy, and not Sunday?" "That is right." "However, you do not sin if you worship any day of the week, but obey His Commandments."*

Clemens began to tell Atara about the fourth Commandment and share other verses of Scripture. We must, through the grace of Yehovah, fulfill His calling upon our lives. And what is our calling? Our calling is to be HOLY, or to be consecrated unto Him.

"You shall not make yourselves abominable with any creeping thing that creeps; nor shall you make yourselves unclean with them, lest you be defiled by them. For I am Yehovah your Elohim. You shall therefore consecrate yourselves, and you shall be holy; for I am holy." Wayyiqra/Leviticus 11:43-44

To be consecrated means we yield our whole life to Him without reserving anything to be done according to our own will. Our whole life has to reflect Him, and not ourselves. No idols are allowed. Self will is sin and it defiles us. Consecration is basically when we take up the cross daily and follow Him. All sin defiles us, and becomes an obstacle between us and our Heavenly Father in Heaven.

The apostle Kepha, who lived with Mashiach and learned His ways, made the following declaration in his epistle.

"but as He who called you is holy, you also be holy in all your conduct, because it is written "Be holy, for I am holy." And if you call on the Father, who without partiality judges according to each one's work, conduct yourselves throughout the time of Your stay here in fear; knowing you were not redeemed with corruptible things, like silver or gold, from yours fathers, but with the precious blood of Messiah, as of a lamb without blemish and without spot. **Kepha 1/1 Peter 1:15-19**

When a brother or sister sins against us we must quickly forgive him/her. Yehoshua spoke about this sin because He knew that forgiving is not easy when we have been offended. The best thing we should do is not to receive the offense. We must immediately forgive and pray for that person who is hurting us. Leave that person to Yehovah and He will take care of the situation. However if the problem persists, and that person continues to harass us, then we must have a loving confrontation. Yehoshua has given us the teaching that we must practice.

"Moreover it your brother sins against you, go and tell him his fault between you and him alone. If he hears you, you have gained your brother. But if he will not hear, take with you one or two more, that 'by the mouth of two or three witnesses every word may be established'. And if he refuses to hear them, tell it to the congregation. But if he refuses even to hear the congregation, let him be to you like a heathen and a tax collector." **Mattithyahu/ Matthew 18:15-17**

We know that Yehoshua is the only Ben/Son of Elohim, and He is Elohim.

"I and My Father are one." **Yochanan/John10:30**

We must follow His teachings to be blessed. Remember when Kepha/Peter asked Him how many times he had to forgive a person?

"Lord, how often shall my brother sin against me, and I forgive him? Up to seven times?" Yehoshua said to him, "I do not say to you, up to seven times, but up to seventy times seven. Therefore the kingdom of Heaven is like a certain king who wanted to settle accounts with his servants. And when he had begun to settle accounts, one was brought to him who owed him ten thousands talents. But as he was not able to pay, his master commanded that he be sold , with his wife and children and all that he had, and that payment be made. The servant therefore fell down before him, saying 'Master, have patience with me, and I will pay you all.' Then the master of that servant was moved with compassion, released him, and forgave him the debt." **Mattithyahu/ Matthew 18:21-27**

Because He forgives us, we must also forgive our neighbors when they offend us. This parable relates to each one of us. Yehovah has given us His Commandments. When we disobey him, we cannot pay Him back. Unforgiveness is sin, and sin has no place in Heaven. Most of us have trouble with unforgiveness, but we can overcome. Satan uses this weapon to cause the saints, who are the set apart believers, to stumble and to be separated from Yehovah. We must be consecrated unto Him and live according to His Divine Commandments. Consecration is when a person chooses to separate his whole being; body, soul, and spirit to Yehovah. When Yehovah speaks to that person, he or she must quickly obey. When a person is consecrated to Yehovah, the world has no longer power to control his mind or his finances.

Yehovah becomes the complete source of their lives. That person will do nothing that would separate him/her from Elohim, but will quickly repent if falling into sin. Here is an example of a prayer of consecration, *"Father Yehovah in Yehoshua's Name I consecrate myself to you now, body, soul, and spirit. I am completely Yours. From this moment on, I want to do only Your perfect will. Fill me with your Spirit and use me according to Your Holy will." Amen.*

If you have prayed this prayer from your heart, expect Him to reveal Himself to you from this moment on. He will release His blessings to you, and you will feel free. All struggles will be over. You will have that peace you have been searching for it. You will no longer desire to run into trouble. You made a commitment to serve Him alone, and He will honor your request and bless you abundantly. His holy angels will help you to walk the narrow way of life. Yehoshua will be on your side to help you. He will let you know His will for your life, and all confusion will disappear.

Holiness is a command, and forgiveness is a necessity for each of us. You cannot be holy if you have unforgiveness in your heart, or any other sin for that matter. In fact even if you are a born again believer, and if you die with unforgiveness, or any other sin in your heart, you will not go to Heaven! Heaven will be closed to you forever.

Let us remember that sin separate us from our Elohim.

"When you spread out your hand, I will hide My eyes from you; even though you make many prayers, I will not hear. Your hands are filled with blood." **Yeshayahu/Isaiah 1:15**

"Behold, Yehovah's hand is not shortened, that it cannot save; nor His ear heavy, that it cannot hear. But your iniquities have separated you from your Elohim; and your sins have hidden His face from you, so that He will not hear. For your hands are filled with blood, and your fingers with iniquity; Your lips have spoken lies, your tongue has muttered perversity." **Yeshayahu/Isaiah 59:1-2**

The above verses also speak of speaking lies and perversity. When a person is very sensitive and takes an offense, he or she always blames the other person, and refuse to take responsibility for his or her actions. Therefore anyone who is offended rarely repents of his sin, because believes they are innocent. They are deceived and also speak lies. But the Ruach haQodesh will be able to convict the most stiff-necked sinners, when prayer is lifted up on their behalf. Yehovah loves the sinner, for Yehoshua died for sinners, and all of us qualify.

The hand filled with blood is a statement that can be attributed to all sin. When we are holding unforgiveness we are oblivious to the sin in the land. We are concerned about our own hurts, and we do not care very much on the sin of the nations, and do not speak up for righteousness. Therefore our hands are also filled with blood. But most of all, we- made –Yehoshua- bleed, and His Blood is on our hands! Our sin crucified Him!

Yehovah knows how many blessings we have lost because we chose to hold unforgiveness in our hearts. How many years of joy and peace, we traded in for resentment and cutting off people. Never considering our own sin, but attributing all guilt to the other person. All of us have sinned in one way or another.

But when we choose to consecrate ourselves to Yehovah, He will help us to be Holy as He is Holy, for He provided the Atonement.

The Black Cat

Zoe had been having conversations with her son Thomas concerning the last name of his daughter. He suggested that Cathy, the mother of his daughter had her daughter Fiorella adopted by her second husband, because she was now called by his name, Atzeni. She was very concerned about her son. He had been taken for a fool. With these thoughts in mind she decided to call Clemens to pray in agreement about this situation.

Clemens lived far away from Zoe. She lived in Idaho, while Clemens was living in Hawaii. However they were prayer partners; distance did not lessen the effectiveness of their prayers, for there is not distance in prayer.

Clemens was washing the dishes when the phone rang. She ran to answer it and was surprised to hear her friend calling her at that time. Usually Zoe went to sleep very early in the evening, while now was almost eight PM! *"Shalom Zoe, how are you?"* Shalom Clemens, I am *not doing too good." "Oh, are you sick? What is going on?" "No, I am not sick, but I am very concerned about my son. Do you mind if I take a little of Your time this evening to talk and pray?" "Not at all. Please let me know what is bothering you."*

Zoe began to speak. *"My son has to still pay over eighteen thousand dollars to child support. You know that He made a big mistake in his life. He was driving all over the country as truck driver, and on his days off he would go to his father's house to spend the weekend and vacations. Across his house lived a divorced woman with three children. They got involved in a relationship and she became pregnant and gave birth to a beautiful little girl. In the beginning he was fine with the idea of having a child at his late years. However, when she began to pursue him to do the DNA test, he got scared and run away from that state."*

Clemens interrupted Zoe saying, *"I remember this. He lost his job and had no income for almost one year."* Zoe continued speaking, *"Yes, and it was then that he met his present wife Corinne. As you remember I asked you to pray because they were immediately living together. Corinne had also been married twice as my son, and she seemed to be the right person, but they did not want to get married. That caused a lot of anguish to my heart if your remember. We prayed so much for them to get married, and exactly one year later they did, and asked me to do the ceremony. Remember that I was scare to death. It was a big deal to me."* *"Yes, I remember, you said that from then on you would stop marrying anyone!"* *"But it was during the time they were living together unmarried that Cathy changed the last name of my son's daughter, without any explanation, while at the same time she was pursuing him to pay child support."* *"Previously Fiorella had another last name, probably the name of her first husband that she carried, which was also wrong"* Clemens was speechless! How can a professing Christian do such things?

Zoe was calling Cathy and sending her emails but she was ignoring Zoe. Finally after sending three emails to Cathy, Zoe had a dream. Cathy was in the dream, and she seemed sad. At the same time in that dream Zoe was holding a black cat in her arms and she was lovingly caressing the black cat. But suddenly the cat became vicious and became very angry at Zoe grinding her teeth! That very morning Cathy answered her and said that all Zoe wanted to do was to stop the child support. That was not true. Zoe continued to talk with Clemens about this matter.

Finally Cathy answered the email, but she was very defensive, and tried to hurt Zoe with accusations. Plus she lied to Zoe. *"She also said that she had sent the paper work to my son concerning the name change. But she did not. She lied. Her new husband became a father to her daughter, but she wanted possibly to punish my son for not wanting to care for his daughter soon after she was born."Indeed he did wrong. Both sinned. However, her action has caused my son to be in this big debt."*Clemens asked Zoe if she asked Cathy to drop the child support charges." *"Yes, I have. And I told her that my son would be paying her personally. That would help him because the government is charging 6 to 8 % interest on that bill. But she does not want to do it. She ignores the request."*

Zoe said, *"It is difficult not to become suspicious. She seems to be taking vengeance on my son. And Thomas loves his daughter and does not want to make waves…because he does not want to stop that relationship." "I want to pray with you about this problem.""Thomas income is much less than hers. She is a teacher and has a much larger income than Thomas. Plus she is now remarried with a wealthy man. They have bought a villa on the lake, because her new husband is in real estate.* Clemens agreed. *"Meanwhile, Mr. Atzeni died, and now my son is still paying child support for a girl who has been practically adopted by another man." "Yes, I see the problem,"*said Clemens.

Zoe continued to share her concerns with Clemens. Zoe hoped that Cathy would agree to receive the money personally from Thomas. But so far, she ignored her request. The bill was not going down because he could not pay that much more over the monthly child support Cathy requested. Zoe was concerned because of the national situation being so precarious; Thomas could be in big trouble owing so much money if indeed a war broke up, or inflation took place soon. His whole life is insolved trying to catch up with the child support charges. He has paid thousands and thousands of dollars for high interests which benefits no one, except the State. Thomas income was much less than Cathy's, who was a teacher. Indeed there is a consequence for sin. Only Yehovah in His mercy could solve this dilemma. Zoe and Clemens prayed for His mercy on both of them.

Cathy is a lost sheep. She claims to be a Christians but is not a living proof of the teachings of Yehovah. Zoe prayed and she felt Yehovah gave her the victory. Fiorella will have her real father's name. It may take some time, but it will happen. Meanwhile though, Zoe has not been able to speak with her granddaughter Fiorella. And this is the reason why she called Clemens to agree in prayer that Cathy will not prevent Zoe to connect with her granddaughter.

Cathy needs to consecrate herself to Yehovah and listen to His voice and obey Him. Zoe needs to love Cathy no matter if she will obey Yehovah or not. He has to be in full control of the situation. Zoe feels that legally her son could go to court and win, but again, He does not want to lose his daughter. He wants to live in harmony with everyone. Yehovah will bless him for his choice.

Zoe has prayed for these issues in tongues and in English. She believes the Word of Elohim.

The Scriptures declare,

"Trust in Yehovah, and do good; dwell in the land, and feed on His faithfulness. Delight yourself also in Yehovah, and He shall give you the desires of Your heart. Commit your way to Yehovah, trust also in Him, and He shall bring it to pass. He shall bring forth your righteousness as the light, and your justice as the noonday. **Tehillim/Psalms 37:3-5**

Thomas is beginning to live righteously and love his Savior. Zoe is helping her son to bring down that horrible debt, and their relationship has greatly improved. He finally realized how much his mother loves him. She is doing all she can to help him. Soon she may be going to Heaven, and everything she will leave behind will be for her son.

Yehovah has blessed her abundantly. Cathy does not realize that all her actions have a consequence.

Do not be deceived, Elohim is not mocked; for whatever a man sows, that he will also reap. For he who sows to his flesh will of the flesh reap corruption, but he who sows to the Spirit will of the Spirit will of the Spirit reap everlasting life. And let us not grow weary while doing good, for I due season we shall reap if we do not lose heart. Therefore, as we have opportunity, let us do good to all, especially to those who are of the household of faith. **Galatiyim/Galatians 6:7-10**

Can we as believers live according to the Scriptures? Yes, we can with the power of the Ruach haQodesh in us. We must yield all concerns to Him, and He will solve the most difficult problem according to His perfect will.

Zoe told Cathy that she no longer will talk with her about this issue, but is praying for her, and told her that she let Yehovah be in control of this situation. Zoe still prays for her and her family. Yehovah will give complete victory.

CHAPTER 43

The Perfect Lamb

Leon, Clemens cousin, called her to find out about the Feasts of Yehovah. He said, *"Clemens I know you keep the Feasts of Yehovah. You know that in Germany my parents never kept the Passover. But I am interested in learning about them. Can you help me?" "Sure Leon. Write down some Scriptures that I will give you now. OK?" "Done, I have pen and paper with me. Thank you cousin." "By the way you are Jewish, am I also Jewish?" "Well, of course, If I am you are too. Our fathers were brothers." "That is great, I have to learn all I can, and maybe if you let me come to visit you, we can pass the Passover together sometime." Sure Passover is in about two weeks, if you can come it will be awesome! I will invite some other family members to join us." "Great. Thank you very much, you are always so* **helpful**. *"Should I bring something from Germany?"* Clemens jokingly said, *"Sure, bring the snow!"* Both laughed! *"Alright I am ready to start, are you ready to write?" "Yes, go for it."*

Now Yehovah spoke to Mosheh / Moses and Aaron in the land of Egypt, saying, "This month shall be your beginning of months; it shall be the first month of the year to you. Speak to all the congregation of Israel, saying: "On the tenth of this month every man shall take for himself a lamb, according to the house of his father a lamb for a household."

"Your lamb shall be without blemish, a male of the first year. You may take it from the sheep or from the goats. Now you shall

keep it until the fourteenth day of the same month. Then the whole assembly of the congregation of Israel shall kill it at twilight. And they shall take some of the blood and put it on the two doorposts and on the lintel of the houses where they eat it. Then they shall eat the flesh on that night; roasted in fire, with unleavened bread and with bitter herbs they shall eat it". **Shemot/Exodus 12:1-3, 5-8**

Leon interrupted with a good question, *"Do we still apply the blood on the lintels and doorposts?" "Not really, because Yehoshua has fulfilled the Passover, but we can apply the blood of Yehoshua always symbolically."* "OK, thank you Clemens."

The Passover was fulfilled in Mashiach Yehoshua who is the sinless Lamb.

For He made Him who knew no sin, to be sin for us, that we might become the righteousness of Elohim in Him. **Qorin'tiyim 1/1Corinthians 5:21**

Yehoshua/Yeshua was blameless, and His Blood was shed on the cross for our redemption. Some people have said that Yehoshua was a failure because He did not fulfill the Scriptures by establishing peace on this earth. However, He came first as our suffering Servant, to be our Passover Sacrifice, to set us free from our sin. He offered Himself, who was Elohim in the Flesh.

Let us listen to Yochanan testimony.

"Behold! The Lamb of Elohim who takes away the sin of the world!" **Yochanan/John 1:29**

Let us also read the prophecy of the prophet Yeshayahu.

"Behold, My Servant shall deal prudently; He shall be exalted and extolled and be very high. Just as many were astonished at you, So His visage was marred more than any man, And His form

more than the sons of men; So shall He sprinkle many nations. Kings shall shut their mouths at Him; for what had not been told them they shall see, and what they had not heard they shall consider. **Yeshayahu/Isaiah 52:13-15.**

Who has believed our report? And to whom has the arm of Yehovah been revealed? 2 For He shall grow up before Him as a tender plant, and as a root out of dry ground. He has no form or comeliness; and when we see Him, there is no beauty that we should desire Him. 3 He is despised and rejected by men, a Man of sorrows and acquainted with grief. And we hid, as it were, our faces from Him; He was despised, and we did not esteem Him. 4 Surely He has borne our griefs and carried our sparrows; Yet we esteemed him stricken, smitten by Elohim, and afflicted. 5 But He was wounded for our transgressions, He was bruised for our iniquities; The chastisement for our peace was upon him, and by His stripes we are healed. 6 All we like sheep have gone astray; we have turned, every one, to his own way; and Yehovah has laid on Him the iniquity of us all. 7 He was oppressed and He was afflicted, Yet He opened not His mouth. 8 He was taken from prison and from judgment, and who will declare His generation? For He was cut off from the land of the living; for the transgressions of My people He was stricken. 9 And they made His grave with the wicked-but with the rich at His death, because He had done no violence, nor was any deceit in His mouth. 10 Yet it pleased Yehovah to bruise Him; He has put Him to grief. When You make His soul an offering for sin, He shall see His seed, He shall prolong His days, And the pleasure of Yehovah shall prosper in his hand. 11 He shall see the labor of His soul, and be satisfied. By His knowledge My righteous Servant shall justify many, for He shall bear their iniquities. 12 "Therefore I will divide Him a portion with the great, and He shall divide the spoil with the strong, because He poured out His soul unto death, and He was numbered with the transgressors, and He bore the sin of many, and made intercession for the transgressors." **Yeshayahu 53:1-12**

Sadly many people never read this passage of Scripture and are not aware how much truth is in the Word. Yehovah spoke this passage several hundred years before Yehoshua was born, and only if a person refuses to believe Yehovah can say, *'I do not believe."* Yehovah knows the end from the beginning, and we cannot but believe His Word.

The Commandments are our guide for life. But we have broken them all. Sin is in our heart because of the fall of man, we have been born with the propensity to sin, and each of us has sinned.

For all have sinned and fall short of the glory of Elohim. **Romiyim/Romans 3:23**

All but One Being; Yehoshua the Ben of Adam, the Ben of Elohim, the Lamb of Elohim, Yehoshua haMashiach, the Messiah. Elohim alone could qualify to be our Sacrifice because He is spotless, unblemished, and completely righteous.

"Behold! The Lamb of Elohim who came to takes away the sin of the world!" **Yochanan/John 1:29**

Sin earns bad wages. When we serve Satan he rewards to us with sorrow in this life and hell when we die. Spiritual death is our reward for our sin if we do not repent.

"Behold all souls are mine; The soul of the father as well as the soul of the son is Mine; The soul who sins shall die. **Yechezqel/Ezekiel 18:4**

Yehoshua was born of a virgin to be the sin bearer and King of Israel

The Angel Gabriel was sent from Yehovah to Miryam, a virgin of the Tribe of Yahudah/Judah.

Now in the sixth month the angel Gabriel was sent by Elohim to a city of Galilee named Nazareth, to a virgin betrothed to a man whose name was Yoseph, of the house of David. The virgin's name was Miryam. And having come in, the angel said to her, "Rejoice, highly favored one, Yehovah is with you; blessed are you among women! But when she saw him, she was troubled at his saying, and considered what manner of greeting this was. Then the angel said to her, "Do not be afraid, Miryam, for you have found favor with Elohim. And behold, you will conceive in your womb and bring forth a Son, and shall call His name Yehoshua. He will be great, and will be called the Son of the Highest; and Yehovah will give Him the throne of His father David. And He will reign over the house of Ya'aqov forever, and of His Kingdom there will be no end." Then Miryam said to the angel, "How can this be, since I do not know a man" And the angel answered and said to her, "The Ruach haQodesh/Holy Spirit will come upon you, and the power of the Highest will overshadow you; therefore, also, that Holy One who is to be born will be called the Ben/Son of Elohim." **Luqas/Luke 1:26-35**

Yeshayahu spoke about Him.

"Behold, the virgin shall conceive and bear a Son, and shall call His name Immanuel." **Yeshayahu/Isaiah 7:14**

Immanuel means **"Elohim with us."** Yehovah became man in His Son, Yehoshua, and would be born to the tribe of Yahudah, of the King of David lineage, to be the Mashiach, the King of Israel.

Clemens spoke to Leon saying, *"Call me again, and we can talk more. However, when you will come we can go through many more verses in the Scriptures that will help you understand."Thank you Clemens. I missed out so much in this life, not knowing this wonderful truth." "I know Leon, I felt the same way when I discover the Word for the first time." Give my love to uncle and aunty and your whole family, I will see you soon. Shalom." "I will. Shalom Clemens."*

Clemens thanked her Savior for her cousin Leon who now was on his way to be used in the Kingdom of Yehovah. She was so blessed to know her family was coming to faith in Mashiach.

Chapter 44

The Father Revealed

Clemens, shortly after her salvation experience had some problems concerning the true identity of Yehoshua. The reason for that is the she opened the door to sin, and Satan took advantage of her life. She came under demonic attack, but did not know that she was. She went through a time of questioning the true identity of Yehoshua, and of Yehovah. But the Word came alive to her as she continued to search the Scriptures. Yehoshua revealed the Father to the apostle Thomas and to you and me.

Let not your heart be troubled; you believe in Elohim, believe also in Me. In My father's house are many mansions, if it were not so, I would have told you. I go to prepare a place for you. And if I go and prepare a place for you, I will come again and receive you to Myself; that where I am, there you may be also. And where I go you know, and the way you know." Thomas said to Him, "Adonai, we do not know where You are going, and how can we know the way?

Yehoshua said to him, "I am the Way, the Truth, and the Life. No one comes to the Father except through Me. If you had known Me, you would have known My Father also; and from now on you know Him and have seen Him." Philip said to Him, "Adonai, show us the Father , and it is sufficient for us. "Yehoshua said to Him, "Have I been with you so long, and yet you have not know me, Philip? He who has seen Me has seen the Father; so how can you say, 'Show us the father'? Do you not believe that I am in the Father, and the Father in Me? The words that I speak to you I do not speak on My own authority; but the Father who dwells in Me does the works. Believe me that I am in the Father and the Father in Me, or else believe Me for the works themselves. Yochanan 14:1-11

Yeshua did nothing apart from His Father *and He is Elohim in the Flesh.*

"Most assuredly, I say to you, the Son can do nothing of Himself, but what He sees the Father do; for whatever He does, the Son also does in like manner." Yochanan/John 5:19

Thomas had also a little doubt of Yehoshua resurrection, for the resurrection was the final proof that Yehoshua was and is Elohim. Yehoshua after His resurrection appeared first to all the apostles, but Thomas was absent.

Now Thomas, called the Twin, one of the twelve, was not with them when Yeshua came. The other disciples therefore said to Him, "We have seen Adonai." So he said to them, "Unless I see in His hand the print of the nails, and put my finger into the print of the nails, and put my hand into His side, I will not believe." And after eight days His disciples were again inside, and Thomas with them. Yehoshua came, the doors being shut, and stood in the midst, and said, "Shalom Aleichem! (Peace to you). Then He said to Thomas, "Reach your finger here, and look at My hands; and reach your hand here, and put it into My side. Do not be unbelieving, but believing." And Thomas answered and said to Him, "My Adonai and my Elohim!" Yehoshua said to him, "Thomas, because you have seen Me, you have believed. Blessed are those who have not seen and yet have believed." Yochanan 20:24- 29

We are blessed because we have not seen Him, but we have believed!

Yehoshua is also our Shepherd, Indeed, He is our **Good Shepherd.**

"Yehovah is My Shepherd" **Tehillim/Psalm 23:1**

Yehoshua declares to be our Shepherd, and the Father also is our Shepherd, therefore both Yehovah and Yehoshua is one Shepherd, one Elohim. The very title Elohim is plural. When we see Yehoshua, we see the Father. Yehovah became Man in His Ben/Son to save us from our sins. Yehoshua spoke about His identity continually, but the majority of the people could not grasp it, until after His death and resurrection. When we see the Ben, we see the Father.

Shema Israel, Yehovah Eloheinu, Yehovah Echad. Hear Israel, Yehovah our Elohim, Yehovah is One. **Devarim/Deuteronomy 6:4**

We do not worship many gods, but only one Elohim. **Yehoshua is Shepherd, Door, and Savior**

Once you know that He is real, you immediately will recognize that you are a **sinner,** or a **lost sheep**, and that He is the **True Shepherd** who loves you; His sheep.

Then Yehoshua said to them, "Most assuredly, I say to you, I am the door of the sheep. All who ever came before Me are thieves and robbers, but the sheep did not hear them. I am the door. If anyone enters by Me, he will be saved, and will go in and out and find pasture. The thief does not come except to steal, and to kill, and to destroy. I have come that they may have life, and that they may have it more abundantly. I am the good shepherd. The good shepherd gives His life for the sheep. But a hireling, he who is not the shepherd, one who does not own the sheep, sees the wolf coming and leaves the sheep and flees; and the wolf catches the sheep and scatters them. The hireling flees because he is a hireling and does not care about the sheep. I am the good shepherd; and I know My sheep, and am known by My own. 15 As the Father knows Me, even so I know the Father; and I lay down My life for the sheep. 16 And other sheep I have which are not of this fold; them also I must bring, and they will hear My voice; and there will be one flock and one shepherd. 17 Therefore My Father loves Me, because I lay down My life that I may take it again. 18 No one takes it from Me, but I lay it down of Myself. I have power to lay it down, and I have power to take it again. This command I have received from my Father. Yochanan/John 10:7-18

He is our Shepherd. When they pressured Him to tell them if He was the Mashiach, or the Messiah, *Yehoshua answered them "I told you, and you do not believe. The works that I do in My Father's name, they bear witness of Me. But you do not believe, because you are not of My sheep, as I said to you. My sheep hear My voice, and I know them, and they follow Me. And I give them eternal life, and they shall never perish; neither shall anyone snatch them out of My hand. My Father, who has given them to Me, is greater than all; and no one is able to snatch them out of My Father's hand. I and My Father are one.* Yochanan/John 10:25-30

Clemens had to learn the most important lessons of the faith by the teaching of the Ruach haQodesh/Holy Spirit. She did not learn it from the church that she had been going all her life. And later on when she got involved at a Pentecostal Church she learned much more. But her spiritual maturity came mostly by her personal encounters with the Living Elohim. Yehovah chose to teach her and many times allowed her to make some mistakes in order to learn very important lessons.

For all things work out together for good, to those who love Yehovah, to those who are called according to His purpose. **Romiyim/Romans 8:28**

CHAPTER 45

In The Beginning

Clemens grew up not knowing the Scriptures. The priest of the congregation her parents regularly frequented forbade the reading of the Word of Elohim. But eventually she went away from home, and after she surrendered her life to Yehovah, and believed in Yehoshua, His only Ben, she discovered the Word of Elohim, which completely changed her life. She began to read the Scriptures with great fervor. She also began to memorize many chapters. Meditating on the Scriptures became her favorite time of the day, together with prayer and worship.

She found the Word of Yehovah as a treasure that needed to be discovered. The very first few chapters of the Word of Elohim were very interesting and fascinating to the virgin soil of her mind. She read and re-read until she could find the hidden treasures in it.

There she realized how special our Creator is, and how much love and care He has for us humans. It was so amazing to her to learn how this Universe came to be. She spent a lot of time thinking on this wonderful and mighty Elohim who decided to create a Universe, and to create us humans with such great details. The smallest cell in our bodies is so complete and unique and so special that human being cannot duplicate. We are finite, but He is infinite. He creates, but we cannot create. He knows all things, but we do not. We have limitations, but

He has not limits. We are also limited by space, but He is not, He can be anywhere any time. He does not live according to our time schedule, for He creates time, and can bend time. He is so marvelous, yet man does not fear Him.

Yehovah Eloheinu created the Heaven and the earth, the sun, the moon, the stars, the animals. **(Bereshith/Genesis 1:1-25).**

And then Elohim also created Adam; a man from the earth.

Then Elohim said, "Let Us make man in Our image, according to Our likeness; let them have dominion over the fish of the sea, over the birds of the air, and over the cattle, over all the earth and over every creeping thing that creeps on the earth. So Elohim created man in His own image; in the image of Elohim He created him; male and female He created them. Then Elohim blessed them, and Elohim said to them, "Be fruitful and multiply; fill the earth and subdue it; have dominion over the fish of the sea, over the birds of the air, and over every living thing that moves on the earth." Bereshit/Genesis 1:26-27

Elohim created man in His image, but man is not a god. He created man to have dominion over the created animals, and gave him abilities which animals cannot possess. He gave him a soul and the ability to know when he has sinned. He also placed in him a spirit in order to be able to commune with his Creator. And he also gave him a job.

Then Yehovah Elohim took the man and put him in the Garden of Eden to tender and to keep it. Bereshit/Genesis 2:15

Adam was to till the ground and cause it to produce fruit in order for him to have food to eat, and also to keep him busy, and not to become idle. Man needs to use his faculties and his body, or he will self-destruct. Clemens knew very well, how easy it is to become a sluggard. Man has to keep busy, and be productive.

And Elohim said, "See, I have given you every herb that yields seed which is on the face of all the earth, and every tree whose fruit yields seed; to you it shall be for food. Also to every beast of the earth, to every bird of the air, and to everything that creeps on the earth, in which there is life, I have given every green herb for food." And it was so. Then Elohim saw everything that He had made, and indeed it was very good. So the evening and the morning were the sixth day. **Bereshit/Genesis 1:29-31**

Yehovah has created man with the ability to think for himself. Yehovah has given us humans the ability to choose, to obey or to disobey Him. We have been given a free will. This has caused us a lot of problems beginning with Adam and Chava, whom Yehovah created from him, and for him. Yehovah took a rib of Adam and created Chava to be his wife. **(Bereshit/Genesis 2:21-25).**

Yehovah Elohim after He created the world in six literal days, He rested.

Thus the heavens and the earth, and all the host of them, were finished. And on the seventh day Elohim ended His work which He had done, and He rested on the seventh day from all His work which He had done. Then Elohim blessed the seventh day and sanctified it, because in it He rested from all His work which Elohim had created and made. **Bereshit/Genesis 2:1-3**

Clemens had begun to keep the seventh day, or the Sabbath day or rest, many years after her salvation experience. The reason for that is that the congregation she had been attending, although very charismatic, did not keep the Sabbath and the Feasts of Yehovah according to the Scriptures. They also taught Replacement Theology, which does not recognize Israel to be the true Israel. These teachings are very damaging to them, for they are missing on the blessing.

One day she asked her pastor, *"Pastor why are we not keeping the Sabbath?"* *"Oh, the Sabbath is now Sunday."* She thought it was strange. He also added that because Yeshua rose on a Sunday now we worship on Sunday. Clemens was a new believer and could not say much on the subject until many years later. However, she read her Bible and Sabbath is Sabbath not Sunday. Sunday is the first day of the week. Yehovah never change. Yehoshua did not change the Commandment.

But after Clemens left that Assembly, Yehovah led her to begin to obey all the Commandments, which include keeping the Sabbath Day Holy. She knows that she is saved by grace through faith, However, she also knows Yehovah has never changed the Commandments.

"For by grace you have been saved through faith, and that not of Yourselves; it is the gift of Elohim, not of works, lest anyone should boast. Eph'siyim/Ephesians 2:8, 9

(But please see Ya'aqov/James 2:8-14)

We had to be saved because we broke the Commandments, but once we come into the Kingdom of Yehovah He helps us by His grace to obey Him. Yehovah never removed the Sabbath from the Word.

Remember the Sabbath day, to keep it holy. Six days you shall labor and do all your work, but the seventh day is the Sabbath of Yehovah your Elohim. In it you shall do no work: you, nor your son, nor your daughter, nor your male servant, nor your female servant, nor your cattle, nor your stranger who is within your gates. For in six days Yehovah made the Heavens and the earth, the sea, and all that is in them, and rested the seventh day. Therefore Yehovah blessed the Sabbath day and hallowed it. Shemot/ Exodus 20:8-11

Adam and Chava and all mankind kept the Sabbath. While in Mitsrayim Israel could not keep the Sabbath because they were slaves, but after they were redeemed, Yehovah reminded them. They could pick the manna six days of the week, but the seventh day was the Sabbath, and on the sixth day they picked double portion to prepare for the seventh day and it did not stink. **(Please see Shemot 16)** By reading the Scriptures Clemens learned to trust Yehovah; obey Him and He would provide for all her needs.

But man listened to Satan and fell from His grace.

Clemens could never understand how Chava, who is called Eve in the English language, could be tempted to eat the forbidden fruit, and cause her husband also to sin against Her Elohim. **(Bereshit/Genesis 3:1-7).** However, she also realized that man wants to be god, and fails miserably in the process. She read in the Scriptures that Yehovah gave to Adam only one Command, besides the work orders.

"And Yehovah Elohim commanded the man, saying, "Of every tree of the garden you may freely eat; but of the tree of the knowledge of good and evil you shall not eat, for in the day that you eat of it you shall surely die." **Bereshit/Genesis 2:16**

Clemens as she read the story about the fall of man, and tried to imagine herself in the Garden of Eden. Knowing the Command of Yehovah to abstain eating the fruit of that tree, what would she have done? To be honest, thinking about it for a while, she came to the conclusion that maybe she would have done the same thing as Chava. She would have listened to the serpent and disobeyed Yehovah without considering that she would suffer the consequences to her actions, and with her all humanity would also suffer. Women are more inquisitive than men in many ways. It is possible that she also would have eaten of the fruit. Sad!

But she was very glad that she was not the one who caused the fall of man by instigating her husband to eat of the forbidden fruit. That thought was overwhelming her, and she decided to continue reading the Scriptures.

She now agreed with the Scriptures that declares all of us guilty. When she read the Brit Chadashah, (New Testament), while reading one of the letters of Shaul/ Paul, she read the following verse.

But now the righteousness of Elohim apart from the law is revealed, being witnessed by the Law and the Prophets, even the righteousness of Elohim, through faith in Yehoshua haMashiach, to all and on all who believe. For there is no difference; for all have sinned and fall short of the glory of Elohim, being justified freely by His grace through the redemption that is in Mashiach Yehoshua. **Romiyim/Romans 3:21-23**

"Behold all souls are Mine; the soul of the father as well as the soul of the son is Mine; the soul who sins shall die." **Yechezqel/ Ezekiel 18:4**

"It is amazing how much truth is in the Scriptures," Clemens thought. *"I wonder why so many people pass judgment on Elohim about the Holocaust, thinking that He did that. However, He did not do that. Evil man conceived to wipe out one whole human race; the Jewish people. They did it simply to elevate self above all others. However the reason for it is bigger than that. The reason is that the Jewish people are the Chosen People of Elohim and they have received His Oracles to teach all the nations."*

Clemens thought, *"Indeed, the penalty for my sin is death." "But I am so glad that Yehoshua paid the price for my salvation. If I only think on the horrible pain He suffered to be my substitute, it is too much for me to handle. They falsely accused Him of blasphemy, they spat upon Him, beaten Him, they pulled His beard, they placed a crown of thorns on his head, they mocked Him, and crucified Him! Oh, how much He loved me! He willingly gave up His life for me. I do not deserve to be saved. I am so unworthy!"* With that thought racing in her mind, she could not stop crying. She was sorry for any sin she had committed, and for any unconffessed sin she may have forgotten to repent and be forgiven of. She wanted to be sure every sin was forgiven. Yehoshua had suffered such horrible pain because of her sin. She knew the Jews did not kill him, and neither did the Romans. They were the instruments, but He offered Himself as their sacrificial offering to re-connect them to the Father. They did it in ignorance. They did not know He was their expected Mashiach, their Savior!

Clemens knew her sin has caused His death! She cried for a long time, until she sensed His presence coming close to her and comforting her, letting her know that she was forgiven. She felt wave after wave of Yehovah's love enveloping her! She sensed the presence of Yehoshua in the room, who was assuring her of her salvation. She was born again, and He had a place prepared for her in Heaven

(See Mattithyahu/Matthew 26-47-75; 27:1-66; 28:1-20; Marqos 14:43-72 -15:1-47; 16:1-20; Luqas /Luke 23:1-56; 24:1-53; Yochanan/John 18:1-40' 19"1-42; 20:1-31; 21:1-25)

Clemens knew that one day; she also would rise from the dead, as Yehoshua rose from the dead after three days and three nights! And then she would live forever with Him for all eternity. This was her sure hope, and no one could convince her of the contrary. She would serve Him now with all her heart all the days of her life, and eventually she would serve Him in Heaven for eternity!

Chapter 46

Revelations

Clemens was looking at the weather outside and was beginning to wonder when her friend Akako would arrive. She usually would come around five in the afternoon, after she did all her shopping. Akako lived up country in Kula, and because of the gas prices she could not come down as she would desire. She loved Clemens as an older sister, or even as a mother, for she was much younger than Clemens. Akako was also Japanese, and Clemens French! But the common love for their Father in heaven, and the presence of the Ruach haQodesh in their lives, united them in a very special way. Akako came to Maui as an adult. She fell in love with a young Canadian man and got married in a very short time. He is much taller than she is, but just as skinny as she is. She has given birth to a son and she home schools him.

Well, five o' clock is now, and Akako is right at the door. Clemens runs to open the door for her, for she is bringing some gifts to Clemens. She never seem to want to come empty handed.

"Akako, you made it! I was concerned for I saw the dark clouds coming up, and was concerned about you been caught in the rain on your way home." "O no, I do not think so. It has been like this all day." "Well, I hope so. I do not want you to be caught in the rain. Come Akako sit down. Do you want me to make you some mint tea?" "Oh yes, I love mint tea. You do not have green tea, do you?" O No, I am sorry, you know that I do not drink tea, except some mint tea some-

times! However, I can also give you some grape juice, do you want some?" "No, no, thank you Clemens. I am fine with the mint tea. Thank you."

While they talked about this and that, suddenly Akako began to talk about the last news she heard on You Tube. She also listens to a special true news program, and reports to Clemens what she finds out. Clemens is not very interested in the news, for she considers all fake news. Actually she did listen to the news in the past until one day Yehoshua told her to stop listening to the news; pray more and listen to Him alone. Her life changed dramatically after she obeyed Him and stopped listen to the fake news!

It did not take long until He began to share with her what is going on in the world, and what is going to come to pass. He had told her that we are entering the end of this era. America will experience many cataclysmic events. Several states will burn with fire. California, Nevada, and partially Oregon, and also some of Washington state and New York city would be affected. No counting other disasters in the central of the US. Akako answered her, that someone had already prophesied these things. Clemens was happy to hear that, because it meant she heard correctly. And she continued sharing with Akako what Yehoshua told her another day during her prayer time.

"It is going to be an overthrow of government that will shake the world. It is going to be from the inside, not outside." When Clemens asked Him, *"Can you avert that?"* *"No. I will not. The world has forsaken Me, the fountain of living water, and dig up cisterns that can hold no water. The water is polluted, mud, it stinks to My nostrils. Beware of a change soon. My Word is forsaken. The climate has changed. The waves are rising. Rejection. Be not dismayed at the outcome. The whole world is in chaos. The smell is so putrid, it stinks." He also had said that there is idolatry in the House."* Clemens specified that this word came to her February 22, 2020

Clemens also said to Akako that He has given her a *vision of the White House crumbling down.* She saw this June 13, 2020. And He told her, "*Insurrection. All Hell is arising against the Government. Anarchy until the dictator will arise. Beware of deception in high places. Believe no one. Satan's fury is released to destroy any one who opposes him." Pray for Trump for his sanity. The devil wants to dismantle him.*"

Satan is the one who is going to be doing all these things, not Yehovah. Satan has legal rights because of our corporate sin. But we, the Body of Mashiach can repent, and much damage can be stopped.

Akako listened and understood. She could compare to what she was listening on the news. However, the news is not perfect. Yehovah alone is Truth. We cannot believe anyone, except Him. Yehovah is coming to eventually judge the world, as we read in the Book of Revelation. But if we repent of our sin, He will help us in the middle of chaos because He loves us.

He also had said that something worse than corona virus would come to America. In fact China is our enemy, and will try to hit us with another virus worse than corona virus. This last word was given to another evangelist recently.

We must pray that we, His followers, the children of Elohim, will not be affected. And pray also for the lost that they repent, instead of cursing. But the end is not yet. However our faith is going to be tested.

We know what is written in the Word. It is a matter of time until all those things will come to pass. Many will die. Many saints will be martyred, but they will receive eternal life. This life is only for a season. Our goal is that we pass the tests and trust Yehovah. He is with us in the midst of the fire.

Akako prayed together with Clemens for Yehovah to send His Holy Spirit to refresh the Body of Messiah, and cause each of us to be ignited with new Holy Spirit fire. They prayed that their zeal for Him would increase in them.

Certainly each of us needs to be alert and spiritually alive, and we must fear nothing, only Him, Yehovah. But He is with us, and will be with us, even to the end of the age.

CHAPTER 47

The Messenger

Clemens was resting laying on her sofa in her living room, however she was thinking on a conversation she had with Giselle the previous month. They talked about the riots that were taking place all over the world. *"Certainly"* Giselle said, *"those riots must have been organized by the elite to be the beginning of the future overthrow of the government in America."* Clemens agreed that this chaos manifesting all over the world may have been organized in order to facilitate the establishment of the One World Order. The enemy had been working since the birth of the United States to form a "One World Government." Anyone can see that by simply looking at the One Dollar Bill. Below the Pyramid with the cap stone in the air, the Dollar Bill has the following defining words written in them, **"Novus Ordo Seclorum."** Charles Thompson translated these words to mean, **"A new order of the ages,"** which is a correct translation. When they wrote this motto they were declaring that as of the date of the Declaration of Independence on July 4, 1776 there would begin a new era. I suppose they were first of all detaching themselves from Britain. We can hear on the news all the time that this is the plan.

"By the way, according to my search on "Google" said Giselle, "13 colonies met on July 1, 1776 in Philadelphia, and on the following day 12 of the 13 colonies voted motion for independence. The delegates spent the next 2 days

*debating and revising the language of a statement drafted by Thomas Jefferson.
I am sure they probably had a few arguments. Finally on July 4 Congress offi-
cially adopted the Declaration of Independence. As a result of the Declaration
of Independence on July 9, 1776 had a riot! Today we have riots because they
do not want the rules of the Declaration of Independence and the Constitution
of the United States of America."*

As believers in Yehovah and Yehoshua we ought to not concentrate
on the government's faults or on its plans, but on the Kingdom of
Elohim. As followers of Yehoshua we need to change our perspective,
and our focus. Yehoshua when He came to this world did not speak
against Caesar, but against the religious leaders who were not teaching
His Word correctly. He called them hypocrite and brood of vipers. He
confronted sin. This is our calling. We may have to be confronting false
teachings, because those teachings will take people to hell if they do
not repent. We know what is going on in the world, but we are not
of this world. Our focus has to remain on Him, and on the lives who
are now perishing. We must preach the gospel in the power of the
Holy Spirit that Yehoshua has commanded us to preach. We cannot
be distracted and loose our focus. While Clemens was thinking on
these things, she remembered that Giselle had called her a week ago
asking if she could come over. And now was almost the time that she
should be coming. She quickly changed her pajamas, and shortly after
she heard the knock on the door. Quickly she walked to the door and
open it. Clemens was so happy to see her special Messianic Jewish
friend again. They exchanged embraces and walked together to the
Sofa and sat down.

*"Giselle, how are you? You look so young, what have you done?""Oh, Clemens,
I am doing so well lately. Yehovah is so good to me. I am so happy to be alive. I
thank Him every day for His goodness to me and His many blessings." Clemens
asked her friend if Yehoshua had spoken to her lately. "O Yes, He has been
speaking to me about these last days.""Can you share with me? "Of course."*

"He spoke to me this morning too.""What did He say to you?" "This is what I sense He is saying to me." "Prepare for incoming disaster. The rich will not be rich anymore. Cataclysmic events all over the world. Famines, droughts, **floods,** pestilences." "And He also said to me, 'I am trying to wake up the church to respond to the call: Repentance. The proud will be humbled and the humble will be exalted. I will use those who have their hearts broken because of the sin of My people. They claim to love Me, but disobey My laws. They are indeed broken cisterns that can hold no water."

Clemens interrupted Giselle by quoting the Scripture.

"For My people have committed two evils; They have forsaken Me, the fountain of living waters, and hewn themselves cisterns—broken cisterns that can hold no water." Yirmeyahu/Jeremiah 2:13

"Truly" said Clemens, "in America and the World we have become idolaters. In the previous verses 11 and 12 we read, "Has a nation changed its gods, which are not gods? But My people have changed their Glory for what does not profit. Be astonished, O heavens, at this, and be horribly afraid; be very desolate," says Yehovah.**

"America is in big trouble. We have seen the rebirth of false gods, Ashtoreth and Zeus were always here, but now we see images of Satan himself. Some young children are declaring they have given their lives to Satan. The churches are lukewarm to say the least, but they too are silent and do not speak up against sin. I am sorry, please continue Giselle."

Giselle continued declaring the word she has received from Yehoshua.

"Will you warn My people for impending disaster? The greatest revival the world has ever known is going to come to pass in the midst of terror and bloodshed. Fast and pray that you be able to escape what is coming to pass."

"Yehovah allows us oppressive government because of our disobedience, said Giselle", and she quoted some verses of scriptures.

"Tehillim 78 speaks of all of us, even though the Word was given to Israel applies to all of us. He gave us the Commandments, but we have not obeyed them."

"Therefore thus says Adonai Yehovah; 'Because you have multiplied disobedience more than the nations that are all around you, have not walked in My statutes nor kept My judgments, nor even done according to the judgments of the nations that are all around you'—Therefore thus says Adonai Yehovah: 'Indeed I, even I, am against you and will execute judgments in your midst in the sight of the nations." Yechezqel/Ezekiel 5:7-8

"But we know that the judgment of Elohim is according to truth against those who practice such things. And do you think this, O man, you who judge those practicing such things, and doing the same, that you will escape the judgment of Elohim? Or do you despise the riches of His goodness, forbearance, and longsuffering, not knowing that the goodness of Elohim leads you to repentance? But in accordance with you hardness and your impenitent heart you are treasuring up for yourself wrath in the day of wrath and revelation of the righteous judgment of Elohim, who "will render to each one according to his deeds," eternal life to those who by patient continuance in doing good seek for glory, honor, and immortality; but to those who are self-seeking and do not obey the truth, but obey unrighteousness-indignation and wrath, tribulation and anguish, on every soul of man who does evil, of the Jew first and also of the Greek; but glory, honor, and peace to everyone who works what is good, to the Jew first and also to the Greek. For there is no partiality with Elohim. Romiyim/Romans 2:2-11

Yehovah knows our deeds. He is righteous. He has made provision for our salvation through Yehoshua who died and rose again for our justification.

All we like sheep have gone astray; we have turned, every one to, to his own way; and Yehovah has laid on Him the iniquity of us all. **Yeshayahu/Isaiah 53:6**

"What we need is massive repentance to take place in the whole world," said Giselle. *"Anarchism has taken hold of the world. This is a political philosophy that rejects all involuntary coercive forms of hierarchy .What they want is to bring down the Government. The sheep has gone its own way, and unless we repent we will be in big trouble. ButYehoshua has told us that we can pray to be removed from this planet individually, if we are counted worthy to escape."That means to go to heaven before the tribulation! And I sayYes to this!"*

Watch therefore, and pray always that you may be counted worthy to escape all these things that will come to pass, and to stand before the Son of Man." Luqas/Luke 21:36

"We also read in the book of Revelation," **"Because you have kept My Command to persevere, I also will keep you from the hour of trial which shall come upon the whole world to test those who dwell on the earth," Chazon/Revelation 3:10**

"I believe I will go to the Heaven before all those terrible things happen ***if,*** *as He has said, I obey him.The church does not keep the Sabbath who is one of the Ten Commandments.Yehovah is not happy about this. Because the Sabbath is the visible sign of the follower of Mashiach, in same way as the Rainbow is to the world. A sign has to be seen. I think the church does not read the First Covenant. He said,*

"Surely My Sabbaths you shall keep, for it is a sign between Me and you throughout your generations, that you may know that I am Yehovah who sanctifies you. You shall keep the Sabbath, therefore, for it is holy to you. Everyone who profanes it shall surely be put to death; for whoever does any work on it, that person shall be cut off from among his people. Work shall be done in six days, but the seventh is the Sabbath of rest, holy to Yehovah. Whoever

does any work on the Sabbath day, he shall surely be put to death.
Shemot/Exodus 31:13-15

Clemens completely agreed. Giselle continued to share the message of Yehoshua.

"The Church is sitting like a queen thinking 'I am the favored one' but she does not know her time of leisure is up. It is time to repent and to seek My Face. I am waiting on those who will choose the narrow way, to the pleasures. The pleasures will end suddenly. The lies and deceptions will be exposed to all to see. I am the Way, the Truth, and the Life. No one comes to the Father except through Me. I expect obedience to My Word. Every Word has a value. Every Command I gave I expect to be obeyed. Picking and choosing only the blessings is over. Choose to obey and the blessing will flow. The false gospel of prosperity which has enriched some preachers will dissolve into nothing. The greed, the pride, the arrogance in the churches is about to end. What I am doing is a cleansing of the Bride before the wedding. She has to be washed clean. My soap is effective. Those who submit to the cleansing will be purified and made white. The others will be left behind. In My House there is no room for compromise. I expect obedience. I expect purity".

Let the wicked forsake his way, and the unrighteous his thoughts; let him return to Yehovah and He will have mercy on him; and to our Elohim, for He will abundantly pardon. Yeshayahu/Isaiah 55:7

Giselle stopped talking. Clemens spoke, *"Wow, Giselle, Yehovah is using you so much. He is speaking to you even more now than in the beginning of your salvation experience. You are so blessed."*

Giselle answered Clemens. *"Remember what He had told me the very same day He filled me with His Ruach haQodesh? You were there too, He had said,* **"Prophesy, Elijah is, Prophesy.'** *"Yes, I remember, and He had you prophesy immediately judgment against the very world church that you were in that very moment."*

"I know that many church goers do not want to listen to you. But be consoled, that the prophets were many times rejected and also killed. I pray Yehovah takes you to heaven before that takes place."

Giselle continued to tell Clemens of another Word Yehoshua had spoken to her.

"Yehoshua told me to get some extra food because there will be a blackout. To also be prepared to have lamps that do not require electricity. Get batteries, and get a transistor radio.' I did get the transistor radio immediately, but I have to stock up on dry foods that do not require refrigeration. Things such as cereal, dry milk, dry fruits and vegetables, dry tomatoes, tuna, corned beef, or chicken in the can may be good to storage.

Clemens was amazed to hear such counsel from Yehovah. He really cares for us. He wants us to trust Him with all our hearts, and no matter what takes place in this world He is going to be with us. But he requires obedience. Yehoshua said it this way,

"If you love me, keep my Commandments. And I will pray the Father, and He will give you another Helper that He may abide with you forever, the Spirit of truth, whom the world cannot receive, because it neither sees Him nor knows Him; but you know Him, for He dwells with you and will be in you. I will not leave you orphans; I will come to you." Yochanan/John 14:15-18

Clemens was so thankful to Yehovah for giving her such friend as Giselle. Both had experienced the presence of Yehovah and were living their lives exclusively to serve Him. They had chosen to walk the narrow way, and they would not compromise their walk for what the world had to offer. They kept their eyes looking up for their redemption that was coming near. They were satisfied and lived in harmony with themselves and Yehovah. His peace was evident in their lives. They never seem to worry. The riots continued but they felt secure in him. He promised them and all of us, that He will never leave us nor forsake us.

Both took His Command seriously.

And Yehoshua came and spoke to them, saying, "All authority has been given to Me in Heaven and on earth. "Go therefore and make disciples of all the nations, baptizing them in the name of the Father and of the Son and of the Holy Spirit, teaching them to observe all things that I have commanded you; and lo, I am with you always, even to the end of the age. **Mattithyahu/Matthew 28:18-20**

Clemens stood up to prepare some dinner. While she was busy in the kitchen Giselle went to keyboard and began to play a song that she loved. She worshiped as she played. The presence of Yehovah came sweetly into the room, and soon they sensed him saying, *"I have called you for such time as this, My hand is on you. Be not dismayed, listen to My voice and say what I put in your mouth. The times of refreshing are coming for you. Do not cease worshiping. I am in your midst. Open your hearts to listen to My heart. Soon you will be in Heaven with me. Do not fret what people may say to you. I am in complete control over your lives. You are Mine. I have purchased you with My own Blood, and no weapon formed against you will prosper. Soon things will change, but you have nothing to fear. My peace I leave you. Speak my message to the world, for I am going to cause this great revival to come about. Many will be wonderfully changed and transformed. Others will reject Me, but do not fear. I am here with you always. My love is sufficient for you, even if the world reject you. Be not dismayed for your names are written in Heaven. I love you. I care for you. I am your Father. My love is in you now. Give My love away. Hate must bow down to Love. You are carrying my Love, and My love is your safety."*

Clemens and Giselle worshiped a little longer. They were no longer hungry, however they ate some food, and took Communion together.

Then Yehoshua said to them, "Most assuredly, I say to you, unless you eat the flesh of the Son of Man and drink His blood , you have no life in you. Whoever eats My flesh and drinks My blood has eternal life, and I will raise him up at the last day. For My flesh is food indeed, and My blood is drink indeed. He who eats My flesh and drinks My blood abides in Me, and I in him."
Yochanan/John 6:53-56

When Yehoshua knew in Himself that His disciples complained about this, He said to them, "Does this offend You? What then if you should see the Son of Man ascend where He was before? It is the Spirit who gives life; The flesh profits nothing. The words that I speak to you they are spirit, and they are life."
Yochanan 6:61-63

Please know that we should not kill Him and eat Him up, that is cannibalism. He meant spiritually we must eat or partake of Him, in order to obtain eternal life.

Remember that the Passover Sacrifice had to be eaten. He was telling them that He was their true Passover sacrifice, and that He would be giving His own body to be sacrificed for their redemption. We must be born again, and we are born again when His spirit enters our body and only then we have eternal life. We still have some time before His judgment will be released to this sinful world. However, we must live our lives as though each day could be the last on this earth. Our sins need to be repented of daily, and we must be filled with His Spirit and His love.

C H A P T E R 48

The Narrow Way

Clemens was reading the Word of Yehovah and the following passage caused her to pause for a moment.

"Enter by the narrow way; for wide is the gate and broad is the way that leads to destruction, and there are many who go in by it. Because narrow is the gate and difficult is the way which leads to life, and here are few who find it." Mattithyahu/Matthew 7:13-14

Clemens continued to meditate on the Word. *"Yeshua our Mashiach has spoken these words. His words are self explanatory. Not many people will choose to leave their own evil desires to purse and obey His desire for their lives. Men want to be in control of their lives, they want to be their own god, but make a big mess of it. The point is that we are all lost sheep, and we need the Shepherd to lead us. Our pride must be abased, and Him alone exalted."*

She was still engulfed meditating on these things when the phone rang. She quickly went to answer and on the line she heard the voice of Giselle.

"Hello Giselle, I was reading the Word and began thinking on so many religious ministers who are not preaching the truth. Have you listened to your pastor lately?" "Yes I have." "Has he been speaking on the subject of holiness, and on the words of Yehoshua when He spoke on the narrow way?" "No, he has not,

*he only wants to make the people feel good, but he has not been addressing sin."
Clemens added, "There are some religious ministers, without be condemning
them, that would not pass the test according to the following scriptures."*

**"Not everyone who says to Me, 'Lord, Lord, shall enter the
kingdom of heaven, but he who does the will of My Father in
heaven. Many will say to Me in that day, 'Lord, Lord, have we not
prophesied in Your name, cast out demons in Your name, and done
many wonders in Your name?' And then I will declare to them, 'I
never knew you; depart from Me, you who practice lawlessness!"
Mattithyahu/Matthew 7:21-23**

Clemens continued, *"I am very concerned that many preachers will
hear the words 'I never knew you. Depart from Me, you who practice lawlessness!"* Giselle said, *"This is scary, not for the good shepherds, but for the
bad shepherds!"*And she continued, *"Imagine how Yehoshua must feel seeing
such sinful preachers."* Clemens added, *"It seems to be very clear that He is
speaking of preachers in the healing ministry, or any person who is casting out
devils, and prophesying, however, they do not realize that they need deliverance
themselves."*

Giselle said, *"Preachers do not think they are sinning of lawlessness."*
Clemens said, *"They think they are preaching the whole Word, but are practicing lawlessness, which means 'without Law." They choose what to obey, but
other commandments they discard as belong only for the Jews. This is so sinful.
They thing they are special and above the whole Law."* Giselle continued,
*"Yehoshua told me to pray for the churches. Hopefully not all churches practice
lawlessness, but He knows who is and who is not. We do not have to know. All we
need to do is to pray for the church."*

Giselle added, *"Do all the churches keep the fourth Commandment? I
know they do not. Those who do not, according to Yehoshua's own Word, they are
practicing lawlessness. Lawlessness is disobeying the law therefore is anarchy.
Many so called 'believers' do not keep Torah, or the Commandments, which are*

the Rules of the Kingdom of Yehovah. In the English language the word Torah is called the Law. The Scriptures declare that if we disobey in one point we are guilty of all.

For whoever shall keep the whole law, and yet stumble in one point, he is guilty of all." Ya'aqov / James 2:10

Clemens and Giselle continued to discuss the condition of the churches. They already had talked about the Sabbath the last time they visited. But they felt so sad to deny Yehovah the privilege to want to spend time with them on that special day. It is a very special time of fellowship with Yehovah. And the Sabbath has been given to the man in order to rest, and rest in Him. He gave us the Sabbath to be refreshed physically and spiritually. Giselle added, *"It is sad that traditions of men keep many people from obeying Yehovah. It is such a great blessing every Sabbath! I wait for that day to come. Sometimes I wish I had one extra Sabbath. But actually we do have the extra Sabbath days, when we celebrate the Feasts. Passover and Sukkot; Sukkot is the Feast of Tabernacles, and both feasts have two extra Sabbaths. There are also two more Sabbaths every year, on the Feast of Yom Teruah, (Day of Shouting, or Feast of Trumpets) which is on the first day of the seventh biblical Month. And on the tenth day of the Seventh Biblical month is another Sabbath; the Day of Atonement." "Yes, Amen"* said Clemens, and she added that besides not keeping the Sabbaths, the Body of Mashiach needs to be cleansed from other sins. Many other sins are commonly practiced by many believers: Gossip, lying, compromising, cheating, and avoiding paying taxes, misuse of finances, greed, gluttony, addictions and many others sins. Here is small list of things Yehovah hates.

These six things Yehovah hates, yes, seven are an abomination to Him; a proud look, a lying tongue, hands that shed innocent blood, a heart that devises wicked plans, feet that are swift in running to evil, a false witness who speaks lies, and one who sows discord among brethren. Mishley / Proverbs 6:16-19

Let us remember that Yehovah and Yehoshua taught on love.

"You shall not take vengeance, nor bear any grudge against the children of Your people, but you shall love your neighbor as yourself: I am Yehovah." **Wayyiqra/Leviticus 19:18**

"You shall love Yehovah your Elohim with all your heart, with all your soul, and with all your mind.' This is the first and great Commandment. And the second is like it: You shall love your neighbor as yourself.' On these two Commandments hang all the Law and the Prophets. **Mattithyahu/Matthew 22:37-40**

Yehoshua had quoted the Shema'

Hear O Yisrael! Yehovah is our Elohim, Yehovah is One. You shall love Yehovah your Elohim with all your heart and with all your soul and with all your might. **Devarim/Deuteronomy 6:4**

If we love Him with all our hearts, we will also obey Him. **(See Yochanan/John 14:15**) But if we do not love Yehovah with all our heart, we cannot have a relationship with Him, and we also cannot love our neighbor as ourselves. Gossip is a lack of love. Most times gossip is done because they have not forgiven whoever they became offended with. Instead of love they have hate in their hearts. Gossip is like murdering a person identity.

Each of us needs to know Yehovah personally. And we can do that when we receive His Ruach/ Spirit in our heart at salvation.

Some people that are going to church every Sunday, they forget Yehovah on Monday, and do what they please the rest of the week. To be a believer is to walk the narrow way. Which means is to be in the world, but not be doing as the things of world. It means consecration unto Yehovah, who is holy. It means not to commit adultery, and not to abort their babies, and so forth.

Habitual sinners, although born again, are backslidden when they choose not to abstain from habitual sin. They fall into the category of a lost sheep! Such persons need to repent, for if they die in that condition they will not be part the kingdom of Yehovah. They cannot go to Heaven. They need deliverance from evil spirits. But sadly many churches do not obey this commandment, and avoid ministering deliverance. The reason for this may be that they themselves may need to be delivered from some secret sin. However, if they do not repent, they will be rejected by Yehoshua on the Last Day because of their personal and congregation sinful condition. Pastors and all ministers are called to be watchmen.

"Son of man, I have made you a watchman for the house of Israel; therefore hear a word from My mouth, and give them warning from Me: When I say to the wicked, 'You shall surely die,' and you give him no warning, nor speak to warn the wicked from his wicked way, to save his life, that same wicked man shall die in his iniquity; but his blood I will require at your hand. Yet, if you warn the wicked, and he does not turn from his wickedness, nor from his wicked way, he shall die in his iniquity; but you have delivered your soul." **Yechezqel/Ezekiel 3:17-19**

I hope you realize that the way to heaven is indeed narrow. I know that knowing these things will help all of us to stop judging someone's sins, and first and foremost inspect ourselves. We may be surprised how much trash we may find in the process! My prayer is that each of us sincerely asks Yehovah to cleanse and purify our hearts, and to fill us with His love and compassion. Only then, after we offer our hearts to be circumcised and let Him cut off the flesh, we will walk in humility, for indeed…

All we like sheep have gone astray; we have turned, every one, to his own way; and Yehovah has laid on Him the iniquity of us all." **Yeshayahu/Isaiah 53:6**

Our hope is only in Yehovah and His Son Yehoshua. No one else can help us. He is the only way. Each of us needs to work out our salvation with fear and trembling.

Yeshua had died for all our sins. He paid the price in full. He is the Good Shepherd who lives the 99 sheep to search for the lost one. He cares for the children, for the spiritually immature, and for all His sheep.

"Take Heed that you do not despise one of these little ones, for I say to you that in Heaven their angels always see the face of My father who is in Heaven. For the Son of Man has come to save that which was lost. What do you think? If a man has a hundred sheep, and one of them goes astray, does he not leave the ninety-nine and go to the mountains to seek the one that is straying? And if he should find it, assuredly, I say to you, he rejoices more over that sheep than over the ninety-nine that did not go astray. Even so it is not the will of Your Father who is in Heaven that one of these little ones should perish." **Mattithyahu / Matthew 18:10-14**

There is hope for all of us. Remember the prodigal son when he came home, how much his Father rejoiced over his return. This is how He will rejoice each time you and I choose to return to Him who loves us so much. He yearns for each of us to do right so that the enemy of our soul does not take us away from Him for all eternity. Yehovah has such great love for each of us, and yes, He is a Jealous Elohim. How can we disobey him any longer? Let us come running to Him and never go away from Him again! He is the eternal Husband that loves and cares for us. Yeshua is waiting for each of us to come to Him and acknowledge Him as our only Saviour. He is the only One who took upon Himself the penalty of death that belongs to each of us because of our sins. Let us honor Him and embrace Him. Let us give to Him all our devotion and passionately love Him. Yes, passionately, not lukewarmly, but ardently, fervently, with all our hearts, because this is how He loves us!

Let us trust Him, for He is our true Shepherd who loves us.

Yehovah is my Shepherd;

I shall not want.

He makes me to lie down in green pastures;

He leads me beside the still waters.

He restores my soul;

He leads me in the paths of righteousness for His name sake.

Yea, though I walk through the valley of the shadow of death,

I will fear not evil;

For You are with me;

Your rod and Your staff, they comfort me.

You prepare a table before me in the presence of my enemies;

You anoint my head with oil;

My cup runs over.

Surely goodness and mercy shall follow me

All the days of my life;

And I will dwell in the house of Yehovah

Forever.

Tellim/Psalm 23

C H A P T E R 49

Know Your Destination

Clemens is preparing a teaching for her Bible Study Group. Her students are mostly young believers. She begins by reminding the group that the Word declares all of us are sinners. Each of us has inherited the sin of Adam. We cannot deny our sinfulness, for if we do, we are denying Yehovah, who declares all an unclean thing. The prophet Yeshayahu writes our condition in his Book,

"But we are all like an unclean thing, and all our righteousness are like filthy rags; we all fade as a leaf, and our iniquities, like the wind, have taken us away. And there is no one who calls on Your name, who stirs himself up to take hold of You; For You have hidden Your face from us, and have consumed us because of our iniquities." **Yeshayahu/Isaiah 64:6-7**

"This Scripture is generally speaking the condition of the world at this present time. But what do you feel in your heart? Do you feel that you have need of nothing, or do you feel empty and are looking for something to feel that void?"

That class knows their condition. One of them replied,

"I know my condition, I have done so many wrong things in life; things that I should not have done. When I take the bread and wine, I am always heartbroken over my sins. He had to suffer so much because of my own sin.

And there is nothing I can do to repay Him. Nothing in this world can pay for my salvation, except Yehoshua's own Blood. I know that we humans are all spiritually bankrupt. Without Him, we would all go to eternal perdition. Oh, the wonder of His love. How thankful I am that He has saved me, and will also save my whole family because of my prayers."

Clemens asked the rest of the class specific questions. *"You may have tried pornography, homosexuality, eastern religions, witchcraft, and you may have been possessed by demons and have experienced astral -projection and think you are untouchable because Satan is using you to do evil in this world. But today you know you need to fill that unrest in your soul."*

Everyone in the class understood the danger of sin, but she continued with the lesson. You may be a person as some of those that I have mentioned in other lessons, who have murdered their own children in the womb. You may have not honored your parents as Yehovah commands us. You may have committed adultery; or pedophilia. You may have stolen and murdered to make a living, but today you are sensing that you cannot continue to live that life style. You need a chance or you may commit suicide. Now suicide is out of the question, for that is not the answer. Death in not the end of life, but it is the beginning of eternity, either in Heaven or in Hell. If you would kill yourself, your problems would be just beginning and would never end.

Yehovah said: **"You shall not murder."** Shemot/Exodus 20:13

Life is sacred to Yehovah. Satan is the one who tempts people to end their lives knowing they will go to his future home, which is the lake of fire. But he does not want you to know it.

Let me mention some verses of Scriptures.

"Behold, all souls are Mine; The soul of the father as well as the soul of the sons is Mine; the soul who sins shall die". Yechezqel/Ezekiel 18:4

For the wages of sin is death, but the gift of Elohim is eternal life in Mashiach/Messiah Yehoshua our Master. **Romiyim/ Romans 6:23**

Yehoshua spoke of Hell as a place where the sinners went after death. He spoke about Hell, and also told the story of the rich man and Lazarus.

"There was a certain rich man who was clothed in purple and fine linen and fared sumptuously every day. But there was a certain beggar named Lazarus, full of sores, who was laid at his gate, desiring to be fed with the crumbs which fell from the rich man's table. Moreover the dogs came and licked his sores. So it was that the beggar died, and was carried by the angels to Abraham's bosom. The rich man also died and was buried. And being in torments in Hades, he lifted up his eyes and saw Abraham afar off, and Lazarus in his boson. Then he cried and said, "Father Abraham, have mercy on me, and send Lazarus that he may dip the tip of his finger in water and cool my tongue; for I am tormented in this flame. But Abraham said, 'Son, remember that in your lifetime you received your good things, and likewise Lazarus evil things; but now he is comforted and you are tormented. And besides all this , between us and you there is a great gulf fixed, so that those who want to pass from there to you cannot, nor can those from there pass to us." **Luqas/Luke 16:19-26**

Hades was a place like Sheol, but here it is described as a real hell for the rich man was in the fire. The rich man asked Abraham to send Lazarus to go back to his brothers and warn them. He still had no respect for Lazarus, he wanted to use him as a slave. **(v.27-28)** He was commanding even in hell, but could not be obeyed. Please also realize that after physical death, our soul lives forever, and has memory. In hell they remember every sin they committed and took them there. to torment them forever and ever.

Abraham could not help that man. He had chosen his destiny while alive. He did not seek Yehovah while he lived, but now he tried to get help from a man he had despised while alive.

29 Abraham said to him, "They have Moses and the prophets; let them hear them.' And he said, 'No, father Abraham; but if one goes to them from the dead, they will repent.' But he said to him, 'If they do not hear Moses and the prophets, neither will they be persuaded though one rise from the dead.'" **Luqas/Luqas 16: 29-31**

The righteous were separated from the unrighteous, and after the Resurrection of Yehoshua they went to Heaven.

"When He ascended on High, He led captivity captive, and gave gifts to men." **Eph'siyim/Ephesians 4:8**

And Yehoshua cried out again with a loud voice, and yielded up His spirit. Then, behold, the veil of the temple was torn in two from top to bottom; and the earth quaked, and the rocks were split, and the graves were opened; and many bodies of the saints who had fallen asleep were raised; and coming out of the graves after His resurrection, they went into the holy city and appeared to many. **Mattithyahu/Matthew 27:51-53**

Be certain and understand that there is a Heaven and a Hell. Life does not end here, but continues. We make the choice here and now while we live.

The devil, who deceived them, was cast into the lake of fire and brimstone where the beast and the false prophet are. And they will be tormented day and night forever and ever. **Chazon/ Revelation 20:10**

6 And He said to me, "It is done! I am the Aleph and the Tav, the Beginning and the End. I will give of the fountain of the water of life freely to him who thirsts. He who overcomes shall inherit all things, and I will be his Elohim, and he shall be My son. But the cowardly, unbelieving, abominable, murderers, sexually immoral, sorcerers, idolaters, and all liars shall have their part in the lake which burns with fire and brimstone, which is the second death. **Chazon 21:6-8**

This list covers all kinds of sin. Sin is disobedience to the Rules He has given us, His Commandments. Love Yehovah and our neighbor is the key to life. Sin is not loving Him with all our heart, and not loving our neighbor as ourselves, which include all the Commandments.

Salvation is a free gift from Elohim to us when we repent of our sin of disobedience. We cannot earn it by doing anything that we think it is good enough to earn us eternal life in Heaven.

For by grace you have been saved through faith, and that not of Yourselves; it is the gift of Elohim, not of works, lest anyone should boast. **Eph'siyim/Ephesians 2:8-9**

It is impossible for us to be saved by obeying the Commandments alone. Because if we break one of them, we are already disqualified to go to Heaven, and the penalty of sin is death. In the Garden of Eden, Yehovah revealed the magnitude of sin. A life had to die to cover Adam's and Cava's sin. Blood had to be shed. Eventually He gave the animal sacrifices to cover us, but could not take away the sin. Yehoshua had to come and give His life for us. We could not give our lives because we are unclean. Besides the fact that Yehovah does not accept human sacrifice. Yehovah Himself had to die to cleanse us and make us righteous. There was no other way.

Your may like to read in the Scriptures when Yehovah made a covenant with Avraham. He told him to cut the animals except the birds, and placed the pieces opposite each other on two stones. This is how they made the Covenants in ancient times. Once the animals were cut they were placed opposite of each other. Then the two parties had to pass between the broken pieces on the blood that was running mean-ing, if they would break the Covenant, they would die as those animals. But Yehovah placed Abram to sleep knowing his descendants would break the Covenant. Therefore He took the responsibility and passed between the pieces Himself as a smoking oven and a burning torch. Yehovah was and is the only qualified One who can pay the penalty for our disobedience, and He did it in Mashiach. **(See Bereshit 15:9-18)**

"As the Father knows Me, even so I know the Father; and I lay down My life for the sheep. And other sheep I have which are no of this fold; them also I must bring, and they will hear My voice; and here will be one flock and one shepherd. Therefore my Father loves Me, because I lay down My life that I may take it again. No one takes it from Me, but I lay it down of Myself. I have power to lay it down, and I have power to take it again. This command I have received from My Father." **Yochanan/John 10:15-18**

The class was very thankful for Clemens teachings. They had been lost sheep, but now they believed in their Savior and wanted to know Him better and obey Him . They were learning the basics of life in the Spirit. But now they were very thankful to Yehovah for sending His only Son to be their Shepherd and for saving them.

Clemens felt the need to continue the class a little longer that day to talk about the Ruach haQodesh. She asked a simple question.

"Have you read in the Scriptures about the coming of the Ruach haQodesh/ Holy Spirit?"

One of the ladies said, *"Yes, but I do not understand. I know the Spirit of Yehoshua comes into my life at Salvation, right? Do I have to have more of Him?"*

"Well, you can receive more fillings. Yes, He comes into the believer at sal-vation, but you can receive a deeper filling of His Spirit the same day, or later on. Personally I received more of His Presence and the gift of tongues after

salvation." But you can receive the prayer language the same day, if you ask Him." "Oh, OK, Do you want to know how I get the gift of speaking in other tongues?"

Clemens began to share the Scriptures. Yehoshua promised the apostles they would receive Power.

"But you shall receive power when the Ruach haQodesh has come upon you; and you shall be witnesses to Me in Yerushalayim, and in all Judea and Samaria, and to the ends of the earth." Ma'aseh/Acts 1:8

Yochanan the Immerser said this of Yehoshua. The scriptures calls it a baptism or an immersion.

"I Indeed baptize you with water unto repentance, but He who is coming after me is mightier than I, whose sandals I am not worthy to carry. He will baptize you with the Ruach haQodesh (Holy Spirit) and fire." Mattithyahu/Matthew 3:11

"The apostles had to wait until the day of Shavuot, which is called Pentecost in English. You see Yehoshua had to fulfill all the Feasts. Yehoshua went back to Heaven forty days after His resurrection, But Pentecost was to be 50 days after Passover, or seven weeks later counting from the weekly Sabbath, and the following day after the 49th day, or 50th day they celebrated Shavuot." **(Wayyiqra/Leviticus 23:15-22).**

When the day of Shavuot (Pentecost) had fully come, they were all with one accord in one place. And suddenly there came a sound from heaven, as of a rushing mighty wind, and it filled the whole house where they were sitting. Then there appeared to them divided tongues, as of fire, and one sat upon each of them. And they were all filled with the Ruach haQodesh and began to speak with other tongues, as the Ruach gave them utterance. Ma'aseh/Acts 2:1-4

"The apostles were in the Temple, where they needed to celebrate the feast. They had to offer sacrifices and offer the first fruits of the grain harvest."

A believer has to be holy as He is holy. He sent His Ruach haQodesh to empower the believer to live a holy life. Sinners cannot enter into heaven with unconfessed sin. Daily repentance still needs to continue after the first experience of being saved. We are imperfect, and sin in many ways. We must continually, daily repent, and when we do, His presence will manifest in our lives. And He will be able to help us to serve Him in His power and abilities He has given us.

Let us live according to our Father's Commands, which will ensure us eternal life. After the study she had written the following little notes that she will ask the group to repeat after her on the next session.

"Father Elohim, I repent for breaking all Your Commandments. I repent for not loving you with all my heart, soul, and my whole strength, and for not loving my neighbor as myself. I ask You that You set me free from all demons that I have served in the past. I repent for getting involved in New Age, and other occult practices. I renounce and reject the demons of New Age, Astrology, Ouija board, Witchcraft, and astral projection. I also repent for wanting to kill myself, and others. I repent for doing an abortion and for telling others to do the same. I repent for rebellion against You, my Heavenly Father Yehovah, and for rebelling against my parents. I repent for all known and unknown sin, and I plead the Blood of Yehoshua now and I ask Him to wash me clean. I consecrate myself to you forever and by your grace I will be able to live a holy life from now on. Thank you for delivering me, and for writing my name in the Book of Life. And now I ask you, Yehoshua to give me the free gift of the Ruach haQodesh, Your Holy Spirit, that I be able to speak in Your heavenly tongues as the believers did on Pentecost. And I promise that I will pray in your heavenly language all the time. Let also the Baptism of Holy Fire be released to me now. Make me to be all you desire that I become

according to what is written in my books in Heaven. Thank you. I receive You and your gifts now. Amen."

Clemens knew that after they would pray that prayer, they would have His shalom, and live for Him by the Help of His Ruach haQodesh. Repentance of all sin is the key to become intimate with the Father. She expected great things to happen at the next Bible Study. They ended the class with a prayer of thanksgiving and sang praises to Yehovah in Yehoshua's Name.

C HAPTER 50

To The Jew First

Clemens had a Jewish friend that she wanted to share the gospel with. However, she seemed to feel a little bit insecure, and had difficulty approaching him. She decided to pray and to prepare herself on how to approach him or any other Jew. She sat down and wrote this imaginary conversation that she would use to minister life to the Jews. First of all she read the scriptures which convinced her of the great importance to minister to the Chosen People, and her own brethren.

"For I am not ashamed of the gospel of Mashiach, for it is the power of Elohim to salvation for everyone who believes, for the Jew first and also for the Greek. For in it the righteousness of Elohim is revealed from faith to faith; as it is written, "The just shall live by faith." Romiyim/Romans 1:16

She also read,

"I tell you the truth in Mashiach, I am not lying, my con-science also bearing me witness in the Ruach haQodesh, that I have great sorrow and continual grief in my heart. For I could wish that I myself were accursed from Mashiach for my breth-ren, my countrymen according to the flesh, Who are Israelites, to whom pertain the adoption, the glory, the Covenants, the giving of the law, the service of Elohim, and the promises; of whom are the fathers and from whom, according to the flesh, Mashi-

ach came, who is over all, the eternally blessed Elohim. Amen".
Romiyim 9:1-5

Yehoshua came to the Jews, who were the lost sheep of Israel, and He sent His apostles to them first.

***These twelve Yeshua sent out and commanded them saying; "Do not go to the Gentiles, and do not enter a city of the Samaritans. But go first to the lost sheep of the house of Israel."*Mattithyahu/Matthew 10:5-6**

After His death and resurrection, before He went back to Heaven, again He sent them to the Jew first, but after they received the Ruach haQodesh, He told them to witness in Jerusalem first, in all Judea and Samaria, and to the end of the earth. **(Ma'aseh/Acts 1:8)**

The Gospel spread all over the world from the Jewish people and many were killed in the process. The Gentiles owe their salvation to the obedience of the Jews. The Jews are indeed the Chosen People of Elohim, but at the first coming of Mashiach many did not receive Him.

Many Jews today have never heard the Name Yeshua, and if they have they have been forbidden to believe in Him, and they are also forbidden to read the B'rit Chadashah/New Covenant. They have erroneously been told that because many so called "Christians" killed the Jews, the B'rit Chadashah must be teaching about Yehoshua instructing how the kill the Jews. They have been forbidden to talk to the followers of Yehoshua believing those lies. Yes it is true that false Christians, who did not even know Yehovah or Yehovah personally, who had no knowledge of the Word, have indeed massacred the Jews on AD 70 and also destroyed their Temple. They have done great evil to them because of hate and anti-Semitism. What a disaster! If those religious leaders had read the Word they would have known that to touch the Jews is as touching the apple of Yehovah's eye. They have literally cursed themselves! It is understandable that the Jewish leader would warn their children against Yehoshua, because they also had been taught lies.

Also in modern times many so called Christians call the Jews "Christ killers!" Those children who are constantly attached never heard the name of Yehoshua much less killed Him! Sadly that church inspires such wrong teachings to its followers, and this is the reason young children harass the Jewish people. And the end result is that Jews do not want to worship a foreign Elohim called Yehoshua. His name has been also hijacked and replaced with Jesus which is not a Hebrew name and means nothing. Names in Hebrew have meaning.

No wonder parents told their children to stay away from the Christians. This is Satan's plan to forbid Yehovah's Chosen People to come to faith in Yehoshua. Because Yehoshua is coming back to Yerushalayim to reign for a thousand years after He fights the Enemies of Israel. They will know Him, and mourn for Him whom they pierced. **(Zechariah 12:8-11; Chazon/Revelation 20:4-6).**

Yes, His true Name is Yehoshua, which in English is the Name Joshua. The Hebrew alphabet lacks the letter J. Therefore it is already impossible for the Mashiach who was Jewish, born to a Jewish family, to be called Jesus. The English language also invented the letter J about 500 years ago. Therefore the name Jesus is a new invention. But He, Yehoshua, was born in Israel and in Bethlehem of Judea about 2000 years ago!

The Correct biblical Name of the only Ben of Yehovah is Yehoshua, and it means, Yehovah saves. The contracted form is Yeshua, which means Salvation.

Clemens understood all these things, and sadly we cannot change the damage done to the Jews in the name of Yehoshua! The church has a lot to repent for.

Thinking on all these things, Clemens prepared herself how to approach her friend Hoshea. She would make an appointment and begin a conversation.

"Hoshea, I need to ask you a question, I know you are Jewish, but have you ever considered the fact that your Mashiach has already come and is coming again?"

Hoshea would not answer quickly, but then he may say, *"Really, and who is he?" "Oh, his name is Yehoshua." "You mean the Catholic Jesus?" "Yes and no. The Christians call Him Jesus because they do not know his real name, but He was not Catholic, He was Jewish, born in Israel to a Jewish family, descendant to King David, and His Name is Yehoshua."* Hoshea was a Lawyer, and loved to argue his case. *"Tell me about the Holocaust. Where was Elohim at that time? Why did He let it happen?" "Ask Yehovah. He will answer you. I do not know."* And she would continued to share with Him beginning with the birth of Yehoshua. She would read to him the Genealogy of Yehoshua in the first chapter of the gospel of Mattithyahu/Matthew. She had to let Hoshea know that the New Testament was a Jewish Book and that Yehoshua was indeed Jewish, not a Gentile false god. She proceeded by reading parts of the book of Luqas.

For unto us a Child is born, Unto us a Son is given; And the government will be upon His shoulder. And His name will be called Wonderful, Counselor, Mighty Elohim, Everlasting Father, Prince of Peace, "Of the increase of His government and peace there will be no end, upon the throne of David and over His kingdom, to order it and establish it with judgment and justice from that time forward, even forever. The zeal of Yehovah of hosts will perform this." Yeshayahu/Isaiah 9:6-7

Clemens decided that she would also speak of the angel Gabriel visit to Miryam which fulfilled the above prophecy.

"Now in the sixth month the angel Gabriel was sent by Elohim to a city of Galilee named Nazareth, to a virgin betrothed to a man whose name was Yoseph, of the house of David. The virgin's name was Miryam. And having come in, the angel said to her, "Rejoice, highly favored, Yehovah is with you; blessed are you among women! But when she saw him, she was troubled at his saying, and considered what manner of greeting this was. Then the angel said to her, "Do not be afraid, Miryam, for you have found favor with Elohim. And behold, you will conceive in your womb and bring forth a Son, and shall call His name Yehoshua. He will be great, and will be called the Son of the Highest; and Yehovah Elohim will give Him the throne of His father David. And He will reign over the house of Ya'aqov forever, and of His kingdom there will be no end." **Luqas/Luke 1:26**

Hoshea would probably simply listen to her friend Clemens. She thought that she would continue reading the Scriptures, and let the Ruach haQodesh speak to his heart.

"Your throne, O Elohim, is forever and ever, a scepter of righteousness is the scepter of Your kingdom. You love righteousness and hate wickedness, therefore Elohim Your Elohim, has anointed You with the oil of gladness more than Your companions." **Tehillim/Psalm 45:6-7**

"Of old You laid the foundation of the earth, and the Heavens are the work of Your hands. They will perish, but You will endure; yes, all of them will grow old like a garment, like a cloak You will change them, and they will be changed. But You are the same, and Your years will have no end." **Tehillim 102:25-27**

Yehoshua is the fulfillment of these prophesies.

"But to the Son He says, "Your throne, O Elohim, is forever and ever; a scepter of righteousness is the scepter of Your

*kingdom. You have loved righteousness; therefore Elohim, Your Elohim, has anointed You with the oil of gladness more than Your companions." And "You, Yehovah, in the beginning laid the foundation of the earth, and the heavens are the work of Your hands; they will perish, but You remain; And they will all grow old like a garment; like a cloak You will fold them up, and they will be changed. But You are the same, and Your years will not fail." **Ivrim/Hebrews 1:8-12**

By this time Hoshea would say: *"I never read this in the Tanakh. But you are saying the B'rit Chadashah has also quoted this passage? I thought this book was only to worship a false Gentile god." "Hoshea let me continue to give you more Scriptures. You will be surprised what the B'rit Chadashah teaches. It is a Jewish book, not a heathen book."*

Clemens would continue to say, when He began His ministry, He made Himself known to Israel and went into the synagogue.

He found the place where it was written: "The Spirit of Yehovah is upon me, because He has anointed Me to preach the gospel to the poor; He has sent me to heal the brokenhearted, to proclaim liberty to the captives and recovery of sight to the blind, to set a liberty those who are oppressed; to proclaim the acceptable year of Yehovah." Then He closed the book, and gave it back to the attendant and sat down. And the eyes of all who were in the synagogue were fixed on Him. And He began to say to them, "Today this Scripture is fulfilled in your hearing." **Luqas/Luke 4:18-21**

He was saying that Scripture in the Sefer *Yeshayahu/Isaiah 61:1-3* was speaking about Him.

Hoshea probably would have difficulty accepting the truth. Leaders lied to him about the identity of "Jesus" all his life, and it seemed strange that he never read those verses in his own Tanakh.

She already knew that Hoshea had a lot of problems believing that Yehovah had a Ben/Son. However Clemens would confidently continue ministering to him.

"I will declare the decree; Yehovah has said to Me, 'You are My Son, today I have begotten You. Ask of Me, and I will give You the nations for Your inheritance, and the ends of the earth for Your possession. You shall break them with a rod of iron; You shall dash them to pieces like a potter's vessel.'" Now therefore, be wise, O kings; be instructed, you judges of the earth. Serve Yehovah with fear, and rejoice with trembling. Kiss the Son, lest He be angry, and you perish in the way, when His wrath is kindled but a little. Blessed are all those who put their trust in Him." **Tehillim/ Psalm 2:7-12**

Clemens would read the Scripture in Sefer Mishley.

Who has ascended into Heaven, or descended? Who has gathered the wind in His fists? Who has bound the waters in a garment? Who has established all the ends of the earth? What is His name, and what is his Son's name if you know?" **Mishley/Proverbs 30:4**

At this point, Clemens thought that the Lawyer would be speechless. He had never read these verses before in his Tanakh. Therefore he would search the Tanakh on His own, and surely He would find those verses there. He probably would say, *"Wow! Yehovah has a Son! It is amazing!" "Well, what about his birth place, He was supposed to be born in Beit Lechem."*

"Yes, We read this prophecy in the Bible, **"But you, Beit Lechem (Bethlehem), Ephrathah, though you are little among the thousands of Yahudah, yet out of You shall come forth to Me the One to be ruler in Israel, whose goings forth have been from of old, from everlasting. Mikhah/Micah 5:2**

It was fulfilled according to the record, on the First Day of the First Biblical month of Yehovah's Calendar.

"And Yoseph also went up from Galilee, out of the city of Nazareth, into Yahudah, to the city of David, which is called Beit Lechem, because He was of the house and lineage of David, to be registered with Miryam , his betrothed wife, who was with child. And she brought forth her firstborn Son, and wrapped Him in swaddling cloths, and laid Him in a Manger, because there was no room for them in the inn." **Luqas/Luke 2:4, 5, 7**

Clemens knew Hoshea, very well, and he would have great difficulty taking this all in. And he, as a lawyer, would make another attempt to try to discourage Clemens. He probably would ask:

"What about Mosheh, he never said anything about this, or did he?" *"Yes he did,"* said Clemens.

"Yehovah your Elohim will raise up for you a Prophet like me from your midst, from you brethren. Him you shall hear, according to all you desired of Yehovah your Elohim in Horev in the day of the assembly, saying, 'Let me not hear again the voice of Yehovah my Elohim, nor let me see this great fire anymore, lest I die.' And Yehovah said to me: 'What they have spoken is good. I will raise up for them a Prophet like you from among their brethren, and will put My words in His mouth, and He shall speak to them all that I command Him. And it shall be that whoever will not hear My words, which He speaks in My name, I will require it of him." **Devarim/Deuteronomy 18:15-19**

Hoshea may say:

"Oh, I do not remember reading this before." *"Hoshea, there are many more prophecies in your Tanakh. Please read the Scriptures together with the B'rit Chadashah (New Testament) and you will realize that Yehoshua is indeed your Mashiach. He is the only Way to the Father in Heaven. He said,*

"I am the way, the truth, and the life. No one comes to the Father except through Me." Yochanan/John 14:6

"You cannot have a relationship with our Heavenly Father apart from His only Son Yehoshua. He is the Door to the Father. When you pray you have to pray in His Name." "Remember Mosheh said Yehovah told him that He would put His Word in His mouth, and what He would speak had to be obeyed. We must believe this for we cannot deny the Word" "We need Him because He died for our sins to reconcile us to the Father. Without Him we cannot come to the Father. This is the reason you cannot communicate personally with Yehovah, you must be born again by the Spirit of Yehovah. This is truth."

Clemens would be led by the Ruach haQodesh and speak only what she heard in the Spirit. And after talking with him for long time, she hoped he would believe the Word and be willing to submit to the truth and would say something like this, *"He said that He is the way. How do I do it? How can I talk with Yehovah as you do?" I never heard the rabbis speak to Yehovah as you do. How can you do that? He is My Elohim, and You talk with Him on first Name basis! This is shocking to me." Even the Gentiles can talk to Him by calling Him by Name! This is amazing."Why have I not been able to do this?"*

However Hoshea would take time to digest all this information, and he would probably say what he always say: *"I have to go to work now, but we continue next time. Call me."*

He would call her saying, *"Shalom Clemens, can you now finish telling me the answer to my question? How can I talk to Yehovah as you do?"*

Clemens would explain to him that he needed to be born again by the Spirit of Yehovah. Each of us sin, and sin has consequences, which are separation, and death.

Behold, Yehovah's hand is not shortened, that it cannot save; nor His ear heavy, that it cannot hear. But your iniquities have

separated you from your Elohim; And your sins have hidden His face from you. So that He will not hear. But you hands are defiled with blood, and your fingers with iniquity; your lips have spoken lies, your tongue has muttered perversity. **Yeshayahu/Isaiah 59:1-3**

The B'rit Chadashah declares,

For the wages of sin is death, but the gift of Elohim is eternal life in Mashiach Yehoshua our Elohim. **Romiyim/Romans 6:23**

She also would mention, *"Behold, all souls are Mine; the soul of the father as well as the soul of the son is Mine; the soul who sins shall die."* **Yechezqel/Ezekiel 18:4**

Hoshea would remembered reading this verse in his Tanakh in the past. Clemens would continue to explain to Hoshea our position as sinners. We cannot pay our way to heaven by doing good works. Even if a person could keep all the Commandments, which no one has, except Yehoshua, he would be unworthy to go to Heaven, because the penalty for our sin is death. We are saved by His grace.

For by grace you have been saved through faith and that not of Yourselves; it is the gift of Elohim, not of works, lest anyone should boast. **Eph'siyim/Ephesians 2:8-9**

"OK, so in the past we had the temple sacrifices, but now the rabbis say that all we need to do is: do good deeds, do charity and pray, and we are accepted." "No, Hoshea, prayer and good works are not accepted to atone for your sin. Yehovah has given us the Perfect Sacrifice, Yehoshua. Listen to the next verse of Scripture."

Surely He has borne our griefs and carried our sorrows; Yet we esteemed Him stricken, smitten by Elohim, and afflicted. But He was wounded for our transgressions, He was bruised of or our iniquities; the chastisement for our peace was upon Him, and by His stripes we are healed. **Yeshayahu/Isaiah 53:4-6**

She thought that Hoshea would say, "Are your reading from the B'rit Chadashah? You are describing Yehoshua."

"No, I am reading from the Prophets in your Tanakh." "I never read that before." "Yes, I know because the rabbis forbade the Jews to read it, and you also did not read most of the other verses I read you today." "You mean they did it on purpose?" "Looks like it!" Oh, wow!" I have to get the complete Bible as you have and read it for myself. Thank you so much for the time you have taken in talking with me. I so appreciate this very much. But now I have to go. I have to work for living you know!" "Yes, Hoshea, I know. But let me tell you first how you can be saved." "OK. I listen, I do want to know."

"Please read the whole chapter of Yeshayahu 53 and learn how much Mashiach has suffered for your salvation." Clemens would give him time to read it all, and then she would ask him the question:

"Do you believe that He is your Mashiach now?"

"Yes, I do believe." "Will you ask the Father to forgive your sin and receive Yehoshua in your life. Are you willing to surrender your life to Him?"

Yehoshua said in the gospel of Mattithyahu the following words…

"Repent, for the kingdom of Heaven is at hand." Mattithyahu/ Matthew 4: 17

If we confess our sins, He is faithful and just to forgive us our sins and to cleanse us from all unrighteousness. Yochanan 1/1 John 1:9

"Believe and receive Him."

He was in the world, and the world was made through Him, and the world did not know Him. He came to His own, and His own did not receive Him. But as many as received Him, to them He gave the right to become children of Elohim, to those who believe in His name: Who were born, not of blood, nor of the will of the flesh, nor of the will of man, but of Elohim." Yochanan/John 1:10-13

She was sure that her friend Hoshea would be saved. She thanked Yehovah for giving her the plan on how to minister to her friend. And she also prayed for the Ruach haQodesh/Holy Spirit to lead her when to do the phone call. She already rejoiced in her spirit, for she knew in her heart that Hoshea would receive the truth, and be found by the Good Shepherd. That day there would be great joy in Heaven!

CHAPTER 51

Great Joy in Heaven

What a great joy is in Heaven when a lost sheep comes to the Shepherd! Clemens continued to share the Word of Elohim to anyone who would listen. One day she began to teach her good friend Minerva. She had been having difficulty believing that Yehovah would love her so much. She had been taught that Yehovah was an austere Elohim and that He always wanted to kill everyone. This was the reason she, as a Catholic girl had preferred to be consecrated to Miryam instead of Yehoshua or the Sacred Heart of "God." She asked Clemens the following question:

"Clemens how do I know that Elohim really loves me?" Clemens began to read some verses from the Bible to her, and the first verses were what He Himself said to Mosheh when He wanted to see His glory, **(Shemot/Exodus 33:12-13)** Yehovah assured Mosheh that He would make His goodness pass before him. Yehovah is a good Elohim.

Now Yehovah descended in the cloud and stood with him there, and proclaimed the name of Yehovah. And Yehovah passed before him and proclaimed, "Yehovah, Yehovah Elohim, merciful and gracious, longsuffering, and abounding I goodness and truth, keeping mercy for thousands, forgiving iniquity and transgression and sin, by no means clearing the guilty, visiting the iniquity of the fathers upon the children and the

children's children to the third and the fourth generation."
Shemot 34:5-7

"Minerva do you know that Yehovah is a good Elohim, but of course, He is righteous and cannot condone sin. Do you understand this?" "Yes, I do." He is a forgiving Elohim, and He sent His only Son to die for you and me. You know already that you and I have sinned." "Yes, I know." "Can you imagine His great love He has for you and me that He sent His only Son, Yehoshua, to become a human being in order to be able to die as a human being for our sins? He came to undo what the first man did when he disobeyed Yehovah. Yehoshua came to be the way to restore us to the Father in Heaven." You know the scriptures that say, I am the way, the truth and the life, and no one comes to the Father except through Me." "Yes, I kind of know a bit about it." "Well, it was the love of the Father manifesting in Person."

"But Elohim demonstrates His own love toward us, in that while we were sinners, Messiah died for us." Romiyim / Romans 5:8

Think about the great love of Yehoshua.

This is my commandment, that you love one another as I have loved you. Greater love has no one than this, than to lay down one's life for his friends." Yochanan / John 15:12-13

Minerva was beginning to believe and accept the fact that Yehovah loved her. How could the most powerful Being in the Universe leave Heaven, and come down to earth to be killed in order to save His own people. He not only saved them but also adopted them as His own children. Yes His children, in fact we become His children when we believe and received Yehoshua.

But as many as received Him, to them He gave the right to become children of Elohim, to those who believe in His name; Who were born, not of blood, nor of the will of the flesh, nor of the will of man, but of Elohim. Yochanan 1:12-13

"Behold what manner of love the father has bestowed on us, that we should be called children of Elohim! Beloved, now we are the children of Elohim; and it has not yet been revealed what we shall be, but we know that when He is revealed, we shall be like Him, for we shall see Him as He is. And everyone who has this hope in Him purifies himself, just as He is pure." **Yochanan 1/1 John 3:1-3**

Minerva was now overwhelmed by the presence of Yehovah and could hardly speak. She never read these Scriptures before. Yehovah manifested Himself in His own Son, Yehoshua. Amazing. She understood that sin has a consequence, and Yehoshua came to remove the sin that was blocking her from coming into the presence of Yehovah, the Father in Heaven. Clemens read the following words to her,

"What man of You having a hundred sheep, if he loses one of them, does not leave the ninety-nine in the wilderness, and go after the one which is lost until he finds it? And when he has found it, he lays it on his shoulders, rejoicing. And when he comes home, he calls together his friends and neighbors, saying to them, 'Rejoice with me, for I have found my sheep which was lost!' I say to you that likewise there will be more joy in heaven over one sinner who repents than over ninety-nine just persons who need no repentance." 10 Likewise, I say to you, there is joy in the presence of the angels of Elohim over one sinner who repents." **Luqas/ Luke 15:4-7; 10**

Yehovah rejoices when sinners repents, and so do the angels. He rejoices because that person has become part of His Kingdom, and part of His family, and has been saved from the fires of hell. Every time a sinner receives Yehoshua as Savior after repenting of his sins, the sinner rejoices, but in Heaven they rejoice even much more. What a blessing it is to know our Creator personally and to live in

His presence all the days of our lives now on the earth, and later on in Heaven for eternity. There is reason to rejoice indeed!

Minerva was overwhelmed with thanksgiving. *"I am so ashamed of myself to doubt the fact that Yehovah loves me, a sinner. What can I do to please Him?" "Return His love by obeying Him and receive Yehoshua as your Sacrifice. Repent of Your sin, and ask the Father to forgive you. Talk to Him with your own words. He is here now."*

Minerva knelt down and received Yehovah. Joy came into her heart and she experienced great peace. The Shepherd had found His lost sheep, and the angels rejoiced with Him.

CHAPTER 52

The Fence

Clemens had witnessed to many people who loved and served Yehovah with all their heart. However, she also encountered many people who did only what they felt it was necessary to be saved. They did not try to learn and understand the Word, and certainly did not spend time getting to know Him through prayer and the reading of the Word.

Most churches do not preach consecration to Yehovah. They teach that once a person prays the sinners is guaranteed entrance into Heaven. That is reality, if they continue to serve Him the rest of their lives, but if they go back into the world, they will not be able to enter Heaven unless they repent and stop their wandering in the cesspool of sin.

Many believers stand on the fence of life. They have one foot in the world, and one foot in religion.

They do only what they think is necessary to enter into Heaven. But they may never enter in because they are lukewarm, and Yehoshua said that He will spit them out of His mouth! A Christian may go to church on Sunday, and each time the church is open, but at her apartment is the boy friend waiting for her return. *"Well, He is going to marry me soon when he gets the money."* But the money never comes and they stay in such condition for a very long time. Such women are deceived and are taken advantage by smart boys. They do not want to believe that their friend is lying. Their boyfriend has no intention to take a wife as long as she is living as a wife with him, and many times supporting him. Clemens saw this happening many times.

Clemens has ministered to several Christians, who were in this is very sad situation. One of them is Rosella, who could not be faithful to Yehovah. She was so excited at times when the Ruach haQodesh touched her, but it did not last. Soon when temptation came around she opened the door to sin and became trapped again.

She could not understand how Rosella could change so quickly. Finally Clemens prayed to Yehovah to reveal her the problem. He revealed to her that she was never personally discipled. She never knew the love of the Father and of His only Son, Yehoshua. Her understanding of the gospel was superficial. She was thought once saved always saved. She also had never forgiven her mother who had been a very promiscuous woman. She left her father for another man, and did not raise her daughter. Rosella never received real personal love from her mother or from her father. She did not understand what love is all about except in a sexual relationship. But that is a poor surrogate to pure love. She also had iniquity in her blood line. Her own mother sin was now working in her own life. She needed to go to the Courts of Heaven and repent, and ask for the Blood of Yehoshua to speak on her behalf. She had to ask that her repentance would be recorded in the books of Heaven, and ask for a divorce from the accuser of the brethren, Satan himself, would be granted to her.

Then I heard a loud voice saying in Heaven, "Now salvation, and strength, and the kingdom of our Elohim, and the power of His Mashiach have come, for the accuser of our brethren, who accused them before our Elohim day and night, has been cast down. And they overcame him by the blood of the Lamb and by the word of their testimony, and they did not love their lives to the death. **Chazon/Revelation 12:10-11**

Believers who live on the fence are fearful of staying single, and they do what they think needs to be done in order to keep a man. However, they find themselves disappointed again and again, with their hearts broken in thousands pieces. They want to be good Christians, but lack perseverance and do only what seemed good to them to do. They go to church, but forget to read the Bible and pray. *"That is too much work. As long as I go church and I do not hurt anybody I am OK."* But they are hurting someone: Yehovah, the assembly, and themselves.

Those living on the fence will not fully embrace His love and be consecrated unto Him! Clemens had to deal with many such people. Those people lack love. It is sad that the churches they attend regularly do not notice the need of their sheep. Many churches are like the following assembly.

***And the angel of the assembly (church) in Sardis write, 'These things says He who has the seven Spirits of Elohim and the seven stars: "I know your works, that you have a name that you are alive, but you are dead. Be watchful and strengthen the things which remain, that are ready to die, for I have not found your works perfect before Elohim. Remember therefore how you have received and heard; hold fast and repent. Therefore if you will not watch, I will come upon you as a thief, and you will not know what hour I will come upon you."* Chazon/Revelation 3:1-3**

Yehoshua obeyed the Father to the fullest. He went on the cross to die for us. How can we take for granted Salvation, when He paid such high price for it? Assemblies, wake up! He will return when you are not ready. Clemens had very difficult time understanding such believers, but she kept praying for them, and herself. She wanted to be always filled with zeal for Him, who died and rose again that she may have eternal life.

Living on the fence is not the way to serve Yehovah. Many believers will fall into Hell because they do not live the sacrificed life that is required of them. They refuse to pick up the cross and follow Him.

"If anyone desires to come after Me, let deny himself, and take up his cross, and follow Me. For whoever desires to save his life will lose it, but whoever loses his life for My sake will find it. For what profit is it to a man if he gains the whole world, and loses his own soul? For the Son of Man will come in the glory of His Father with His angels, and then He will reward each according to his works. **Mattithyahu / Matthew 16:24-27**

Sadly the cross is not preached lately from most pulpits of the world. The preaching concerns more how to get rich, and how to live a happy life. But this is not the message of the cross. When the test will come many will fall away because they have not prepared themselves to negate self for the sake of the gospel of the Kingdom of Elohim. The way of the Kingdom is no longer popular, but it is the most rewarding way of life. Will you be one who chooses to live a sacrificial life, in order to obtain eternal life? Will you choose the narrow way instead of the wide way that leads to destruction? Which road will you choose to walk in it? You may want to ask me, what is a sacrificial life?

To live a sacrificial life is to avoid sin, and choose to live holy unto Yehovah by the power of His Ruach haQodesh who lives in each one of us believers. It is loving and obeying Him at the cost of giving up our own life. It is complete surrender to do His perfect will, instead of wanting to gratify ourselves. But the rewards will be extravagantly beautiful in His Kingdom.

CHAPTER 53

One Blood and One Savior

Giselle came to visit Clemens and was very concerned about the riots going on all over the United States. *"Clemens can you pray with me about this concern I have in my heart?" "Sure, what about it?" "Well, I need to get some peace about my neighbors. They are Black, and I am White. They are beginning to look at me as their enemy." 'What? Are you kidding me? You are good friends with them for such a long time."Yes, this is the reason why I am concerned." "Listen Giselle, you have Yehoshua in your heart. Why do you not invite them into your home to share a meal, and reassure them of Your love. They need to receive Yehoshua too. If they are not in the Kingdom, they could be a problem because of the bad news they hear."*

Clemens continued to explain to Giselle how to speak to her friends. She needed to let them understand that she consider them equal to her, because each of us has the same Father who created us. The problem at times is that it is not only the skin color, but also the faith. For example Jewish people are once again persecuted in many nations. She continued to explain to Giselle that because we are living in the last days, we will see great tribulation arising as never before in the history of mankind.

Then they will deliver you up to tribulation and kill you, and you will be hated by all nations for My name's sake. And then many will be offended, will betray one another, and will hate one

another. Then many false prophets will rise up and deceive many. And because lawlessness will abound, the love of many will grow cold. But he who endures to the end shall be saved. And this gospel of the kingdom will be preached in all the world as a witness to all the nations, and then the end will come. "Therefore when you see the 'abomination of desolation,' spoken of by Daniel the prophet, standing in the holy place" (whoever reads, let him understand), "Then let those who are in Judea flee to the mountains. Let him who is on the housetop not go down to take anything out of his house. And let him who is in the field not go back to get his clothes. But woe to those who are pregnant and to those who are nursing babies in those days! And pray that your flight may not be in winter or on the Sabbath. For then there will be great tribulation, such as has not been since the beginning of the world until this time, no, nor ever shall be. And unless those days were shortened, not flesh would be saved; but for the elect's sake those days will be shortened." **Mattithyahu / Matthew 24:9-22**

"You see Giselle, we are not at the time of the tribulation yet, however, we need to be alerted for it. We may be alive when this is going to take place. The enemy is working very hard to over through the government in order to be able to bring to power the man of sin." But Yehovah is not allowing him." "Who is the man of sin?" "The man of sin is the anti-Messiah, or the greatest dictator that ever lived, much worse than the Assyrians, Romans, Mussolini, and Hitler, or anyone else. Therefore you must love your neighbors and let them know you would do nothing to harm them. Show the love of the Father to them." Love is the key to solve all problems. When we are filled with the love of Yehovah, we will also demonstrate it, and they will want what we have."

Clemens shared with Giselle the radio message she had been preparing. Giselle loved any message she heard that was glorifying Yehovah. Today, if you are a Jew, a Muslim, Mason, or Illuminati, Baha'i, New Age, Jehovah Witness, Mormon, Satanist, Catholic, White or

Black, or any color in between, a Gentile of any nation, remember you have been created by one Elohim, and descend from one man, Adam, and all us have the same blood running in our veins. We are one in Mashiach. There is no difference of the color of your skin or mine. Each of us had the same great-great earthly grandfather Adam, and our real Father Yehovah!

The Prophet Isaiah spoke about the fact that we are the children of Yehovah.

"But now, Yehovah Avinu, we are the clay, and You our potter; and all we are the work of Your hand." **Yeshayahu / Isaiah 64:8**

Giselle was able to make it very clear to her neighbor that, Av is the Hebrew word for Father, and Avinu is the word for "Our Father." Let us today recognize our need for Yehovah Avinu, our heavenly Father in Heaven, and believe in His only Son, Yehoshua. Unity comes when we are under the same banner: Yehoshua's Banner!

As mentioned earlier as believers in Yehoshua we are the adopted children of Yehovah.

But when the fullness of time had come, Elohim sent forth His Son, born of a woman, born under the law, to redeem those who were under the law, that we might receive the adoption as sons. **Galatiyim / Galatians 4:5**

Blessed be the Elohim and Father of our Master Yehoshua haMashiach, who has blessed us with every spiritual blessing in the heavenly places in Mashiach, just as He chose us in Him before the foundation of the world, that we should be holy and without blame before Him in love Having predestined us to adoption as sons by Yehoshua HaMashiach to Himself, according to the good pleasure of His will to the praise of the glory of His grace, by which He has made us accepted in the Beloved. **Eph'siyim / Ephesians 1:3-6**

Behold what manner of love the Father has bestowed on us, that we should be called children of Elohim! Therefore the world does not know us, because it did not know Him. Beloved, now we are children of Elohim; and it has not yet been revealed what we shall be, but we know that when He is revealed, we shall be like Him, for we shall see him as He is. "And everyone who has this hope in Him purifies himself, just as He is pure. **Yochanan1 / 1 John 3:1-4**

Clemens continued to explain to Giselle that the reason people are so upset is because they have no hope. They fear their destruction is coming from the government. But they at the same time they are destroying themselves. If they would read the Scriptures they would have understanding of the earthly government. The government itself would be run by men and women who know their Creator and we would be at peace in the world. However, man wants to rule himself apart from Elohim, but falls miserably short and self-destruct. Man need to know Yehovah, and we must be His witnesses to share His love and His plan for all of us. We, as the disciples of Yehoshua, must be the light and salt on the earth, for this is our calling from Yehoshua.

CHAPTER 54

The Simple Message

Clemens continued to work on her radio message when the phone rang. She picked up the phone and to her surprise her old friend from Zurich was on the line. She had not yet given her life to Yehoshua, but she was searching. She grew up as a Buddhist, but she was very unhappy about her life. Many times she seemed aloof, distant, almost as she had Alzheimer! Clemens was concerned about her spiritual life, and she had spoken to her about Yehoshua. But she had unforgiveness against all Christians because as a child she went to a Catholic School, which was run by the Catholic nuns. Her rich Buddhist father had placed her and her sister there, thinking they would get a good education. He had already married about five wives, Theresa said to Clemens. He was a very busy man, and was not very holy, or very righteous indeed. He was not concerned about after life. He may have thought that he would come back as a cat or a dog, or any other species that would be attractive to men. The Buddhist religious people hope to better themselves in the course of many lives. They do not believe they only have one life to live, and after that the judgment. As long as they get another chance to better themselves they can mess up now, and hope for the best next time. The daughters were also taught Buddhism, and the nuns did not appreciate this fact, it seems. They would beat the girls regularly. They beat all the children who according to their discipline house rules did not submit to them. This is a true fact.

The girls who could have learned about our Savior and good Elohim, learned about a mean Elohim who loved to hurt them. Now as result of their past encounter with the nuns, as adults they do not want to listen to anything Christian. Theresa was one of them who opposed Yehoshua with all her heart for many years.

During the time that Clemens did many visitation in the Islands, she encountered many Buddhists who were not receptive to the gospel. Yet some of them who received some type of help from the Assemblies, did leave their ancestors religion. They found joy and were very faithful to Yehovah.

Clemens hoped for Theresa to be one of those who would one day voluntarily call her and ask question about Yehoshua. She would be ready to answer and welcome all the questions she may have. But for now she had to pray and wait upon her Father in Heaven to help her by giving her wisdom on how to minister to Theresa. She needed to know that she had a good and perfect Father in Heaven who loved her. Only the Ruach haQodesh would be able to convince her of this fact. Because of her negative experience with her own father it was difficult to her to understand that Elohim loved her. Buddha does not talk to her, but Yehovah can talk with her. Buddha does not listen to her, He is only and idol, but Yehovah listens to her heart and answers her prayer, if she will seek Him with all her heart. We have a Father in Heaven who loves us, even when we mess up. He is quick to forgive us when we repent, and He gives us His grace to stop sinning. We know our Father in Heaven is real. Each of us can have a relationship with Him. He is not distant and aloof, or not concerning about us. He cares for us, and has made provision for our salvation.

Yehovah, our Avinu, is our Father in Heaven. He is the One Being who created the universe and all that exists. He created us to have fellowship with Him, however, because of our sin; our connection to the Father has been blocked. Our sin separates us from Him. We must repent of our sins in order to be able to come before our Father Yehovah in Heaven. He waits on us to voluntarily come to Him, because He wants to forgive and love us.

"Come now, let us reason together." Says Yehovah, "Thought your sins are like scarlet, they shall be as white as snow; though they are red like crimson, they shall be as wool. **Yeshayahu/Isaiah 1:18**

"Repent and turn from all your transgressions, so that iniquity will not be your ruin. Cast away from you all the transgressions which you have committed, and get yourselves a new heart and a new spirit. For why should you die O house of Israel? For I have no pleasure in the death of one who dies." Says Adonai Yehovah. "Therefore turn and live." **Yechezqel/Ezekiel 18:30b-32**

He has made provision for us to be saved when He sent His only Ben/Son into this world to die for us.

But as many as received Him, to them He gave the right to become children of Elohim, to those who believe in His name; Who were born, not of blood, nor of the will of the flesh, nor of the will of man, but of Elohim. **Yochanan/John 1:12 -13**

Yehoshua said, as mentioned in other messages that He is the way, the truth, and the life. No one comes to the Father except through Him. This verse is very important, for there is no other way to the Father in Heaven, nor is there another way of salvation. Peter and Yochanan had been used by Yehovah to heal a cripple man who never walked before. He was born that way. Kepha/Peter commanded him to get up and walk in the name of Yehoshua of Nazareth. Peter took him by hand and lifted him up, and immediately his feet and ankle bones received strength. That poor man walking and leaping entered the Temple. Many came near and Kepha preached to them saying: *"Repent therefore and be converted that your sins bay be blotted out, so that times of refreshing may come from the presence of Yehoshua."* **Ma'aseh / Acts 3:19**

That day about five thousand people believed. The religious leaders arrested them, and asked them, *"By what power or by what name have you done this?"* Kepha explained that they did it in the name of Yehoshua of Nazareth.

"This is the stone which was rejected by you builders, which has become the chief cornerstone. "Nor is there salvation in any other, for there is no other name under heaven given among men by which we must be saved." **Ma'aseh / Acts 4:11- 12**

There is no other name in Heaven or on the earth who can save us but Him. We must believe in Him, and in the Resurrection in order to be saved. He is not dead, but alive.

The scriptures declare:

"That if you confess with your mouth the Lord Yeshua and believe in your heart that Elohim has raised Him from the dead, you will be saved. For with the heart one believes unto righteousness, and with the mouth confession is made unto salvation. For the Scriptures says, "Whoever believes on Him will not be put to shame." **Romiyim / Romans 10:9-11.**

Yehoshua died for our sins, and was buried, but on the third day He rose again. No one has risen from the dead and still lives. Buddha is dead. He cannot save anyone. He had to face the Creator of the Universe when he died. His teachings of reincarnation are purely fantasy. But many unlearned people believe those lies. He did not die for the sins of men. He died alone and faced judgment as all mankind. He did not came back in another form to better himself. His body is still in the grave somewhere. But Yehoshua's tomb is empty!

Our Savior is self Existing and is the Author of Life. He became Man in His Son Yehoshua who suffered and die, but rose again as He said, on the third day. Because He rose we also will rise again and live together with Him for all eternity.

The Tanakh, which is also called "Old Testament," declares,

Surely He has borne our griefs and carried our sorrows; Yet we esteemed Him stricken, smitten by Elohim, and afflicted. But He was wounded for our transgressions, He was bruised of or our iniquities; the chastisement for our peace was upon Him, and by His stripes we are healed. **Yeshayahu / Isaiah 53:4-5**

Yehoshua prophesied His own death and resurrection.

"For as Yonah was three days and three nights in the belly of the great fish, so will the Son of Man be three days and three nights in the heart of the earth." **Mattithyahu / Matthew 12:40**

Clemens continued to share the Word with Theresa. She was confident that one day Theresa will call upon the Name of Yehoshua and she will be saved from her idolatry. Yehovah loves her and will reveal Himself to her. Clemens duty is to simply continue to pray and believe.

Yehoshua said,

"And whatever you ask in My Name, that I will do, that the Father may be glorified in the Son. If you ask anything in My name, I will do it." **Yochanan / John 14:13-14**

The Word of Elohim is sure, and He will answer all our prayer. Our trust is in Him alone. And He alone will be glorified. All glory and praise be to Yehovah forever and ever. Amen!

CHAPTER 55

The Final Days

Clemens was at her desk writing when the phone rang. She would have preferred not to answer for she was involved on a special project. She felt the need to finish her manuscript in order to rest a while. However, she could not ignore the caller. Reluctantly she answered the telephone. The caller was her friend Miranda, a nominal Christian, who inquired of her health, since Clemens had been sick for a few weeks. They talked for a while, and then Miranda began to inform Clemens of someone who had received three dreams from Yehovah concerning the present situation in America. Miranda said, *"Clemens, Denis is an Assembly of God pastor, and has made a video telling about his dreams. He said that he had three dreams. The first dream came to pass. It concerned the Corona virus. Then he dreamed about the riots, and that there would be a people who do not want a government, but anarchy. He saw very angry mobs burning buildings and so forth. The last dream is about things that will happen in the months of September, October and November. He has said that Russia and China will be active in America and it seems that the end is coming."*

Clemens answered her, *"Miranda I told you in the past that Yehovah is allowing these things to happen to test us. However, He will judge the wicked. He is not doing this chaos, but allows it because of our sins. Satan has something against people, because they obey Yehovah and will reign with*

Him, and he will be lost and in the lake of fire. He wants the obedience of the children of Elohim to destroy, instead of building His Kingdom. Many Christians are obeying him, instead of Yehovah, therefore the accuser of the brethren, Satan, has legal right to attack and do havoc. Most people obey only what is convenient for them. There are going to be entire states that will burn with fire. Cataclysmic Events are going to take place all over America. There will be fire in several states and even some in Washington City and New York. Yehovah has spoken about these things. The Churches are not ready for His Coming because they are not obeying Him as we supposed to obey Him. Anarchy is prevalent even in the churches. He wants us to consecrate ourselves to Him, which means we love and serve Him with all our heart. He wants times of intimacy with us, in order to strengthens us. We must be ready for what is coming. We must be strong in faith, so that when the war begins we are prepared and will not fall away. He is the only one that can prepare us for the terrible times of tribulation when it comes." Miranda asked Clemens, "Do you suppose that the churches will go through the Tribulation?" "Of course Miranda. When was the last time you read the Gospel of Matthew?" "Oh, I do not remember, maybe last year." "Miranda, let me show you what are the signs of the end, which means the tribulation which precedes His second coming. The very first sign, is that the Gospel will be preached all over the World. And this is been done."

"The second huge sign is the return of the Yahudim or Jewish people to the land of Israel. Since 1948, against all odds Yisrael has become a Nation. In 1967 Yehovah gave them back Yerushalayim / Jerusalem. Presently there are over 30 thousands Jewish Believers in Yehovah and Yehoshua in Israel. And the revival is accelerating. This miracle only Yehovah could have done it. But it is necessary for His return. He had promised to them they would be back in their home land. And the Jews are back there now. The Hebrew language has been restored. These are big signs. Yerushalayim is Yehoshua's city, and He will return to that city and reign for a thousand years.

Miranda asked, *"OK, I can see this, but are there other signs that concern us, and the church?"* *"Well, yes, let me give you a list, although is not complete, but it will help you. But before I continue to give you the signs let me stress the fact that you have nothing to fear. No matter what will happen, you have to abide in Yehoshua day and night. His presence will protect you and be with you no matter what happens. You must read His Word, and obey Him. Love Him with all your heart, and keep being close to Him. To know and to receive His love is vital to you. Adhere yourself to Him and to His teaching all the time. Speak of Him with anyone who will listen. He is your Strength. And now let me give you some of the signs."*

Arise and shine; for you light has come! And the glory of Yehovah is risen upon you. For behold, the darkness shall cover the earth, and deep darkness the people; But Yehovah will arise over you, and His glory will be seen upon you. Yeshayahu/ Isaiah 60:1-2

You see the contrast? Deep darkness and the glory is happening at the same time. You cannot have the glory without the deep darkness. We read this again in the Sefer (Scroll of) Haggai.

"For thus says Yehovah of Hosts; 'Once more (it is a little while) I will shake Heaven and earth, the sea and dry land; and I will shake all nations, and they shall come to the Desire of All Nations, and I will fill this temple with glory,' says Yehovah of hosts. The silver is Mine, and the gold is Mine, 'says Yehovah of hosts. The glory of this latter temple shall be greater than the former,' says Yehovah of hosts." Chaggai/Haggai 2:6-8

Yehovah will shake the Heavens and earth. There will be cataclysmic events all over the world. He is the Creator and we have destroyed His creation with our inventions. We will not be able to rely on the weather or the produce of the earth. Here are signs in Mattithyahu/ Matthew 24

Deception (v. 4) is one of the signs. They call good what is evil, and evil what is good. Listen to the media who has indoctrinated the youth and all who would listen to them. They proclaim many false Christs. They also declare Yehoshua is coming at any moment before the Tribulation. (see vs. 29-30)

Nations will rise against nation, and kingdom against kingdom. **Famines, pestilences, and earthquakes in various places. (v. 7)**

These all beginning of sorrows. (v. 8) The real trouble has not yet arrived.

They will deliver you up to **Tribulation and kill you, and you will be hated by all nations for My name's sake. (v. 9)** This tribulation is for all who believe in Yehovah and Yehoshua. Jews and non Jews.

Offenses. I believe these offenses are believers who have not been told of the tribulation. They have been deceived to believe they would go up to Heaven before the Anti-Messiah or Anti-Christ, would come to power. The pastors did not prepare them.

Then I wished to know the truth about the fourth beast, which was different from all the others, exceedingly dreadful, with its teeth of iron and its nails of bronze, which devoured, broke in pieces, and trampled the residue with its feet; and the ten horns that were on its head, and the other horn which came up, before which three fell, namely, that horn which had eyes and a mouth which spoke pompous words, whose appearance was greater than his fellows. 21 I was watching; and the same horn was making war against the saints, and prevailing against them, 22 until the Ancient of Days came and a judgment was made in favor of the saints of the Most High, and the time of the saints to posses the kingdom.

25 He shall speak pompous words against the Most High, Shall persecute the saints of the Most High and shall intend to change times and law. Then the saints shall be given into his hand for a time and times and half a time. **Dani'el 7:19-21,22, 25**

After this things I looked, and behold, a great multitude which no one could number, of all nations, tribes, people, and tongues, standing before the throne and before the Lamb, clothed with white robes, with palm branches in their hands, 10 and crying out with a loud voice, saying, "Salvation belongs to our Elohim who sits on the throne, and to the Lamb!

11 All the angels stood around the throne and the elders and the four living creatures, and fell on their faces before the throne and worshiped Elohim,

12 saying: "Amen, Blessing and glory and wisdom, thanksgiving and honor and power and might, be to our Elohim forever and ever. Amen."

13 Then one of the elders answered, saying to me, "Who are these arrayed in white robes, and where did they come from?"

14 And I said to him "Sir, you know. So he said to me, "These are the ones who come out of the great tribulation, and washed their robes and made them white in the blood of the Lamb.

15 Therefore they are before the throne of Elohim, and serve Him day and night in His temple. And who sits on the throne will dwell among them. They shall neither hunger anymore nor thirst anymore. The sun shall not strike them, nor any heat;

17 for the Lamb who is in the midst of the throne will shepherd them and lead them to living fountains of waters. And Elohim will wipe away every tear from their eyes." **Chazon/ Revelation 7:9-17**

Miranda was perplexed! *"Clemens my pastor has not told me that if I am alive when Yehoshua return that I have to go through Tribulation and they will kill me. Why has he hidden this truth from me? What about the thousands of people that come to church and they will be in the middle of the tribulation and will be so hurt, and maybe stop serving Yehovah because they have been cheated of the truth. I read this before but I did not believe it applied to me, only to the Jews." "Miranda, sadly the churches have hidden many things from the disciples in these last days. Maybe I did not tell you before, but they took out the Commandment Yehovah has given us on Mt. Sinai, the Sabbath, and also the Feasts and dietary laws, and many more. When Constantine made Christianity legal, he took away and added to the Word, which is forbidden." He created a religion of syncretism, which is truth mixed with idolatry, because he was a Mithra sun god worshiper. After his death the church wrote canon 29, and made other changes along the way by which separated herself from basic Commandments Yehovah had given us.*

"You shall not add to the word which I command you, nor take from it, that you may keep the Commandments of Yehovah. Devarim/Deuteronomy 4:2

Whatever I Command you, be careful to observe it; you shall not add to it nor take away from it. **Devarim 12:32**

Almost all religious groups do this, but it began around 300 AD. The Churches have a lot to repent because they have continued the corruption of the Word from the original church; instead of going back to obey the Word as Yehovah gave it to us. Tribulation is a time of going back to basics: seek Yehovah. Hopefully the churches will respond to the challenge and repent so that they will be ready for His return. He wants to find His assembly, qahal, (Ekklesia), without spot or wrinkle.

Miranda added, *"I surely want to go with Him when He returns, don't you?" "Yes, Miranda, this is the reason I do what I am doing, for me to be ready to go with Yehoshua when He returns, and for the assemblies to also go with me." You know Minerva, that many preachers still prefer to talk about the miracles, but they do not touch the subject of taking the cross and follow Him. Sadly, this is truth." "Yes, I know,"* said Miranda. *"This is the reason the church goers fall into the same sins as the unbelievers. This is Satan's plan to destroy the kingdom of Yehovah."*

"You got it Miranda!" "Well do you still want me to continue to speak of the signs of His coming?" "Yes, Yes, I do. Please continue."

"Therefore when you see the abomination of desolation, spoken of by Daniel, then let those who are in Yahudah / Judea flee to the mountains. Mattithyahu 24:15.....

"The antiChrist will be seen in the temple and we will see him, if we are alive at that time. Miranda, remember that we do not know when all these things will happen. However we must know they will happen so that we can be ready."

Now, brethren, concerning the coming of our Adonai Yeshua haMashiach, and our gathering together to him, we ask you, not to be soon shaken in mind or troubled, either spirit or by word or by letter, as if from us, as though the day of Mashiach had come. Let no one deceive you by any means; for that Day will not come unless the falling away comes first, and the man of sin is revealed, the son of perdition, who opposes and exalts himself above all that is called Elohim or that is worshiped, so that he sits as Elohim in the temple of Elohim, showing himself that he is Elohim. Tas'loniqim 22 / 2 Thessalonians 2:1-4

Another **sign** is **the great falling away of believers.** Those are the believers who have been deceived by the false hope of a pre-tribulation rapture, but also the lukewarm believers who loved the world more than Him. Yehoshua continued to speak as we read in

Mattithyahu 24:

20 *Pray that your flight may not be in winter or on the Sabbath.*

21 *For there will be great tribulation*

24 *Many false christs.* His coming will be visible to all.

26 *For as the lightning comes from the east and flashes to the west, so also will the coming of the son of Man be.*

"When will the Son of Man come?"

"Immediately after the tribulation of those days the sun will be darkened, and the moon will not give its light; the stars will fall from heaven, shaken. Then the sign of the Son of man will appear in Heaven, and then all the tribes of the earth will mourn, and they will see the Son of Man coming in the clouds of Heaven with power and great glory. And He will send His angels with a great sound of a trumpet, and they will gather together His elect from the four winds, from one end of Heaven to the other." **Mattithyahu / Matthew 24:29-31**

The false teaching of an early secret rapture is revealed. Yehoshua spoke about his return and how it will happen. Everyone will see HIM. All tribes of the earth will mourn.

"And I will pour on the house of David and on the inhabitants of Yerushalayim the Spirit of grace and supplication; then they will look on Me whom they pierced. Yes , they will mourn for Him as one mourns for his only son, and grieve for Him as one grieves for a firstborn." **Zekharyah / Zechariah 12:10**

The Jewish people will recognize Yehoshua and there will be great mourning that day. At that time Yehoshua will destroy the nations that have come to attack Israel, and He will reign in Yerushalayim for one thousand years.

During His time on the earth, Satan will be bound.

Then I saw an angel coming down from Heaven, having the key to the bottomless pit and the great chain in his hand. He laid hold of the dragon, that serpent of old, who is the Devil and Satan, and bound him for a thousand years; and he cast him into the bottomless pit, and shut him up, an set a seal on him, so that he should deceive the nations no more till the thousand years were finished. But after these things he must be released for a little while. **Chazon/Revelation 20:1-3**

At this time the saints are going to reign with Yehoshua for one thousand years.

Then I saw the souls of those who had been beheaded for their witness to Yehoshua and for the word of Elohim, who had not worshiped the beast or his image, and had not received his mark on their foreheads or on their hands. And they lived and reigned with Mashiach for a thousand years. But the rest of the dead did not live again until the thousand years were finished. This is the first resurrection. Blessed and holy is he who has part in the first resurrection. Over such the second death has no power, but they shall be priests of Elohim and of Mashiach, and shall reign with Him a thousand years. **Chazon/Revelation 20:4-6**

The next few verses, 7-9 describe the last battle and then

"The devil who deceived them, was cast into the lake of fire and brimstone where the beast and the false prophet are. And they will be tormented day and night forever and ever. **Chazon/Revelation 20:10**

The White Throne of Judgment.

Then I saw a great white throne and Him who sat on it, from whose face the earth and the heaven fled away. And there was found no place for them. And I saw the dead, small and great, standing before Elohim, and books were opened. And another book was opened, which is the book of life. And the dead were judged according to their works, by the things which were written in the books. The sea gave up the dead who were in it, and Death and Hades delivered up the dead who were in them. And they were judged, each one according to his works. Then Death and Hades were cast into the lake of fire. This is the second death. Anyone not found written in the book of Life was cast into the lake of fire. **Chazon/Revelation 20:11-15**

We have to make sure our sins have been washed in the Blood of Yehoshua, and our name is found written in the Book of Life. There is only one way to salvation, and Yehoshua is the only Way.

Next Yehovah will create a **New Heaven and a New Earth.**

"For as the new Heavens and the new earth which I will make shall remain before Me, "says Yehovah, "So shall your descendants and your name remain." **Yeshayahu/Isaiah 66:22**

Now I saw a new Heaven and a new earth, for the first Heaven and the first earth had passed away. Also there was no more sea. Then I Yochanan (John), saw the holy city, New Jerusalem, coming down out of Heaven from Elohim, prepared as a bride adorned for her husband. And I heard a loud voice from Heaven saying, "Behold, the tabernacle of Elohim is with them, and they shall be His people. Elohim will be with them and be their Elohim. And Elohim will wipe away every tear from their eyes; there shall be no more death, nor sorrow, nor crying. There shall be no more pain, for the former things have passed away." Then He who

sat on the throne said, "Behold, I make all things new." And He said to me, "Write, for these words are true and faithful." Chazon/Revelation 21:1-5

Yochanan saw this in the Spirit. He did not yet die and go to Heaven, but He had been gifted with this gift as a sear. Imagine how he must have felt seeing and hearing all these things. First he saw the troubles that are coming upon the earth, then he saw the glory of the New Jerusalem, so adorned as the bride of Mashiach. Actually inside the city is the Bride of Mashiach. Those who have been faithful to Him, and have not submitted to the Anti-Messiah. Many of them have lost their lives for the sake of the witness of Yeshua. What a glorious day it will be. Yehovah Himself will wipe away the tears. You may ask the question, *"I thought there is not tears in Heaven."* I am sure you are right. But maybe there is something we do not understand. Maybe they cry is for those who did not make it to Heaven, those who failed the test when the trial come close to them, and denied Yehoshua. Could it be that some family member did not keep the faith, and many chose to obey the anti-Mashiach? Imagine if your spouse, son, or daughter, or mother or father or other relative chose to live instead of offering their life as a living sacrifice. Therefore, Yehovah will wipe away all their tears. They will cry no more.

Miranda realized that she needed to commit herself to preach the gospel with greater intensity. She needed to start doing blogs and connect with her family and friends. She had a job to do. She had to most of all intensely commit herself to pray and intercede for her family and friends to come to salvation. And when they would, she had to disciple them. She realized that she had to deny herself and take up the cross daily and follow Him. She had to share the gospel no matter if they were receptive or not. She was aware now that we do not have much time left. Sure Yehoshua is not telling us when He is coming back, for He Himself does not know it. Only the Father knows it. But we must be ready for His return that could be any time. Presently, we know that much, we are at the end of this age. Yehoshua is coming back to fight the enemies of Israel and to set His Kingdom in Yerusha-layim/Jerusalem, soon after the Anti-Messiah is coming to the end of his seven years rule.

Miranda's faith was strengthen that day. She had been in the kingdom of Yehovah a long time, but had not been as a very committed believer. Although she was part of the Bride of Mashiach, she did not know much about the end times. But now she felt as though she was a true warrior, ready to go to battle and bring souls to Mashiach. What a miracle! That morning Yehovah placed His zeal in her soul. She would no longer rely on cigarettes or alcohol to make her happy. She was done with those surrogates. She was free to serve her Savior and to make His name known. What a change! Truth always produces good fruit. Pastors need to learn the lesson and should never hide the truth in order to make converts, for they may be lost for eternity if they are not informed of the future. However, believers in Mashiach have the responsibility to search the scriptures and pray for the Ruach haQodesh to help them understand the Word. Yehoshua has given Him to us to be our Helper, and our Teacher.

"And I will pray the Father, and He will give you another Helper, that He may abide with you forever-the Spirit of truth, whom the world cannot receive, because it neither sees Him nor knows Him; but you know Him, for He dwells with you and will be in you. I will not leave your orphans; I will come to you." **Yochanan/John 14:16-18**

He is the One we need to rely on to help us during our pilgrimage to eternity. He is the very Spirit of Yehoshua, the Spirit of Yehovah.

The Spirit of Yehovah taught her many things from that moment on. He began to give her a desire to know more of Him. And she bought a study bible that she read for the very first time in her life. Her husband had his grandmother's bible, but although she tried to read it, she could not grasp what she read. However, now the Spirit of Elohim in her taught her, and the Word made sense. Miranda began to change little by little. One of the great changes in her life was that she began to love and forgive her family. She knew that they also needed to know the truth and she wanted to teach them what she has learned. She began to pray and fast for the salvation of the whole family. She cut off television and spent her time interceding for the lost. Yehovah would answer her prayers in His time. Her faith was in Him alone.

LAST WORDS

Yehoshua is indeed our Good Shepherd, and each of us need Him to give us eternal life. Our bodies will rot once we our soul leaves this body, but our soul and Spirit live forever. Trusting our lives in Him will assure that our name is written in His Book, and we will be with Him forever and ever. I hope that you, beloved reader, have surrendered your life to Him, and if you have not yet done it, please do it now. Simply believe that Yehoshua is your Messiah, and your Savior. You must believe that He rose from the dead. (Romiyim / Romans 10:9) Because He rose from the dead, you will also rise again from the dead. The resurrection proves that He is Elohim. Next, you need to repent of Your sin and ask Him to live His life in you. He is here now to listen to your decision. Never forget that He, Yehoshua is your only Shepherd, and the One who gives you life. Serve Him, by obeying His Commandments, and be a witness of His grace to you.

I am the good shepherd. The good shepherd gives His life for the sheep. My sheep hear My voice, and I know them, and they follow Me. And I give them eternal life, and they shall never perish; neither shall anyone snatch them out of My hand. My Father, who has given them to Me, is greater than all; and no one is able to snatch them out of My Father's hand. I and My Father are one." Yochanan/John 10:11, 27-30

Shema' Yisrael Yehovah Eloheinu, Yehovah Echad- Hear O Israel, Yehovah our Elohim, Yehovah is One.

www.ingramcontent.com/pod-product-compliance
Lightning Source LLC
Chambersburg PA
CBHW071923150726

47999CB00001B/85